D0876354

THE

SYMBOLIC

ROSE

THE

SYMBOLIC

ROSE

BARBARA SEWARD

COLUMBIA UNIVERSITY PRESS   NEW YORK   1960

809.93
Se 8s

Translations signed J.P.S. were provided
by John P. Seward.

48375

December, 1964

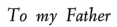

To my Father

BARBARA SEWARD

1928–1958

1948   B.A. Barnard College, *magna cum laude,* Phi Beta Kappa
1950   M.A. University of California, Los Angeles
1950–51   Lizette Andrews Fisher Fellowship, Columbia University
1953   Ph.D. Columbia University
1953–58   Lecturer and instructor in English, Columbia University

Member

Modern Language Association
National Council of Teachers of English
Dante Society of America

Publications

Articles in *Current Biography,* 1952–53
"Dante's Mystic Rose," *Studies in Philology,* October, 1955
"Elizabeth Bowen's World of Impoverished Love," *College English,* October, 1956
"The Artist and the Rose," *University of Toronto Quarterly,* January, 1957
"Graham Greene: A Hint of an Explanation," *The Western Review,* Winter, 1958

PREFACE

Much in the past half century has been written under the threat of war. In fact, the wasteland has been so prevailing a symbol of our era that it is surprising as well as encouraging to find it rivaled by the rose. In the following pages I have sought to reveal the extent of that rivalry and the importance of the rose symbol as a central expression of current times. I have sought to explain its special appeal to almost every modern writer who uses symbolism, and to analyze in detail its dominance in the works of Yeats, Eliot, and Joyce, the three leading British writers of our century. This attempt has required a study of the symbolic technic itself, which is supreme among modern technics, as is the rose among modern symbols. And since neither symbols nor roses are fresh-born phenomena of our age, it has also required a study of the long Western tradition of roses which has formed today's symbolic use of the multiple flower as surely as the past has formed today.

But the history of roses, even in the Western world alone, is too vast in its totality for a single study. Nor is historical exhaustiveness essential to an understanding of the contemporary symbol. I have limited my focus to modern British roses, and have accordingly not treated the parallel symbolic flowers of such Continental writers as Valéry and Rilke, or the unquestionably abundant though generally less suggestive roses of America. With British literature as focus, I have limited my background to those roses that have helped to form the current British symbol.

Western literary roses began in ancient Greece and Rome,

but the pagan heritage was sharply modified by Christianity. Romantic roses, of which our roses are a part, began in the early Renaissance but their significance was altered in the nineteenth century. Contemporary roses draw their life first from the roses of the Catholic Middle Ages and next from the roses of the romantic nineteenth century. Thus I have given proportionately less emphasis to classical and Renaissance flowers than to medieval and romantic symbols. The bulk of the study treats the modern British rose.

My aim is not to be exhaustive but to be embracing. Explanations of the rose's basic appeal to mankind, past and present, correlations between our writers and their predecessors, and particular analyses of particular authors' works are given partly for their own sake but primarily for the sake of throwing light on our modern art. Certainly the unique importance of today's symbolic rose, the reasons for its dominance and the qualities of its manifestation are intimately bound up with the contemporary mood. I have sought to understand the links between our time and past times as revealed in the continuous abundance of the rose symbol. The importance of this flower in the classics and in the Middle Ages has gained some recognition and inspired some interest. Yet the roses of our own era's literature have surpassed all earlier roses in number and symbolic scope.

In tracing the symbol through the centuries I have received some help from friends and colleagues. I wish to thank Roger Sherman Loomis for suggestions on medieval roses, Joseph E. Mazzeo for suggestions on Dante, and William York Tindall for suggestions on some of the modern writers. I particularly wish to thank Mark Van Doren for invaluable encouragement as well as advice on the work as a whole. And last but far from least, I wish to thank my husband, Walter W. Price, for his patience, understanding, and continual interest in criticizing the manuscript at all stages of its growth.

Barbara Seward

CONTENTS

THE
SYMBOLIC
ROSE

I

QUEST

FOR

ORIGINS

Gertrude Stein, considering the queen of the flowers, declared that "a rose is a rose is a rose." Later she put that statement into a ring to indicate by a typographical trick that it could be repeated time without end and yet gain added meaning from each repetition. Her theory was that the same word repeated is each time altered slightly in emphasis, and therefore that her ring around a rose expressed the rich expressiveness of nouns. It may be held to Gertrude Stein's credit that, whether the theory is profound or silly, it is at any rate nothing in between. It may be even more to her credit that the manner in which she illustrated her theory was as perspicacious as it was unfair. For surely she herself must have been the first to realize that the noun she had chosen was no ordinary noun, and that the circle she had made of it would be a magic circle not because it clasped a noun but because it clasped a rose.

It is, in fact, almost impossible to imagine an entity more evocative than the rose. Not only do its roots extend at least to the beginnings of recorded time, but its petals embrace the deepest positive values ever held by man. Although the flower is equaled in age and profundity by such fundamental symbols as sea, sun, bird, star, and cross, it would be difficult to prove that it has been surpassed by any. Moreover, to the twentieth century Gertrude Stein's or any rose must have particular appeal. For in our age, as in no other age since Dante's, the queen of flowers, rivaled only by the wasteland, remains ascendant in imaginative writing. British literature specifically, the focus of this study, is as prolific of writers who are partial to the rose as it is chary of writers who repeatedly ignore it. And of the former, the three greatest in our era—T. S. Eliot, James Joyce, and William Butler Yeats—reveal such an abundance of important roses as to place beyond all question the flower's present sovereignty.

Because it plays so important a role, an understanding of the rose adds much to an understanding of modern literature. Of course, as a simple token of love or beauty, the twentieth-century flower is neither unique nor especially interesting. But the roses are generally not simple tokens in a literature whose keynote is complexity. And it is in their role as multifoliate symbols of intricate attitudes, values, or beliefs that they cast their indispensable light on major aspects of contemporary method and outlook. At the same time they reveal the full extent of the present-day reliance on tradition. For modern writers, seeking escape or salvation, have attempted to relate their era to the whole past, and so have reflected in symbols and roses not only their own but their ancestors' values. The roses of Joyce and Eliot, for example, acquire a good part of their meaning from associations with the rose of Dante, while Yeats's rose receives much of its coloring from a cluster of nineteenth-century blossoms. In fact, a study of the modern rose, so important in understanding modern literature, itself necessitates no less than a study of the heritage of Western roses.

Since the flower has flourished wherever symbolism flourished, a history of the rose becomes a history of symbolism. Even the nonsymbolic roses blossoming throughout the literature of all ages become a part of the history of the symbol from which they have derived and to which they have returned their values. The distinction between symbolic and nonsymbolic roses is itself not indisputable, since definitions of the symbol cover a wide range and vary from one field of study to another. But for literary purposes it is most accurate to define it as the concrete embodiment of a conception too intricate, vast, or mysterious to be adequately expressed in any other way. A literary symbol contains within itself a multiplicity of meanings and can therefore be employed to suggest either a complex of concordant ideas or a fundamental harmony beneath apparent discords. Beyond this, the whole is greater than the sum of its parts. The several meanings expressed by the symbol, when these meanings are analyzed in ordinary language, cannot equal the total significance of the symbol. For an essential aspect of symbolism is the interaction between elements of form and content to convey a particular emotional effect that no other combination of sounds and meanings can fully encompass.

For example, the rose that culminates Dante's *Comedy* embraces Mary, Paradise, grace, and Divine Love, and at the same time reconciles these spiritual concepts with the hitherto opposing concept of terrestrial courtly love. Moreover, in the context of the work as a whole and in the particular language of its poetry, these meanings gain associations and emotions impossible to communicate in our usual words. Such a symbol can clearly be distinguished from its cousins—the metaphor, simile, image, or allegorical device—by its exceptional level of complexity. For though the symbol, like the rest, is in some sense a form of imagery, the difference in degree if not in kind is marked. A simile presents an explicit comparison between one thing or concept and another, a metaphor presents a like comparison implicitly, an image substitutes identification for comparison, and an allegorical device is most commonly employed as the vehicle of a single abstract idea. Various as they are, all four resemble each other and differ from the symbol in expressing little more than simple, definite correspondences between two analogous conceptions. Thus when Dante at the outset of the *Comedy* compares his soul bent down by sin to flowers bent down by nightly chill, he is expressing a far more limited and definable idea than that encompassed by his ultimate flower of God.

Because of its ability to imply indefinite levels of significance, the symbol has always held special appeal for religious or romantic writers seeking to express the inexpressible. Religious writers in general and mystics in particular have employed it in an attempt to convey some fraction of the manifold wonder that ordinary words cannot even approach. Romantic writers, pursuing a more personal but equally intangible vision, have employed it as the only possible means of suggesting their transcendent ecstasy or longing. The religious writer tends to draw his symbols from the traditional stores provided by the world's religions, while the romantic writer may create his own symbols or give his own interpretation to those of tradition. But in either case there is generally overlapping. The traditional symbol derives freshness and vitality from the undertones of an author's private sensibility; the personal symbol derives universality from its relation to the accumulated meanings of the ages. And whether traditional or personal in outlook, religious and romantic symbolists alike share the fundamental impulse to communicate ideals that transcend the material limits of life and the denotative limits of language.

Accordingly, the eras most favorable to symbolism have been the Catholic Middle Ages and the romantic nineteenth and twentieth centuries. Although symbolism can occasionally be found in the humanistic Renaissance and rationalistic neoclassical periods, it has been a dominant mode of literary expression only in medieval and romantic times. Just as its prevalence before the Renaissance can be traced to an otherworldly habit of mind, so its decline in the centuries following can be traced to an emphasis, religious and secular, on the human, immediate world. Moreover, the great resurgence of symbolism during the romantic era has been in large part the complicated result of a diminishing faith in measurable values, a reaction against rational and positivist attitudes, and a need to find transcendental outlets for man's baffled emotional and spiritual desires. If in the present century the symbol has developed on a scale surpassing even that of the nineteenth, it is chiefly because trends apparent in Blake's day have assumed still greater proportions in ours. Among the motives that underlie the modern symbol are the quest for order despite apparent chaos, the quest for clarity despite increasing complexity, and the quest for inner values or spiritual goals despite a barren, mechanistic world. These motives can all be traced to roots in the early days of the romantic era, while their flowers bear the particular coloring of a war- and nightmare-ridden age.

The ubiquitous rose reflects this progression. For the nineteenth century it became the symbol of a multiplicity of subjective values that might redeem the sensitive individual in a presumably insensate world; for the twentieth century it has become the symbol of any and all affirmative values that might redeem the insensate world itself. The progress of mechanism and materialism, threatening to the lofty idealism of romantics, has been deepened by the havoc of total war, threatening to the very existence of humanity. Recognizing that to preserve the individual they must also preserve the desperate planet, writers of our time have attempted to bridge the widening gulf between man and society. In doing so, they have at once assimilated the private flower of the romantics and at the same time looked to the more objective values expressed by the flower of public traditions. The quest for a rose that could, like Isaiah's, redeem a wasteland has led some contemporaries back through literature to the Middle Ages and even beyond them to pre-Christian times. In addition, with the help of anthropologists and psychologists, many writers have discovered in the fertile rose the well-springs of the life instinct itself.

Certainly no other symbol than the rose could have better filled the complex modern need for affirmation, integration, and universality. Capable of bearing a vast range of meanings, the flower has symbolized man's happiest dreams for countless centuries. As a creation of beauty appearing in spring, it has been associated with love and woman, concepts which have in turn been transposed to their religious equivalents, divine love and female fertility deities or Christ and the Virgin. The associations with woman and female deities, reinforced by the flower's annual appearance after the barren winter season, have led to further associations of the rose with the ideas of motherhood and mother nature. From the concept of mother it is not a great step to the concept of the flower as symbol of the mother country, as it was used in ancient Gaul and is still used today in England and Ireland. But even more closely allied to mother are the ideas of birth and of rebirth, both of which have been symbolized by the rose, together with the joys of time or eternity to which the awakening soul has been born. Considered together, these associations with love, beauty, life, joy, creation, and eternity have made the rose relevant to all human ideals, whether the ideals be worldly or religious, personal or universal.

The flower of joy has also symbolized sorrow. Fading quickly, it has been identified with death and with the evanescence of earthly beauties. Surrounded by thorns, it has been identified with pain and with the ambivalence involved in mortal love and in most mortal values. Even as a religious symbol of eternal promise, it has often been related to the thorns of anguish that surround its glory and the blood of martyrs shed for its sake. Yet, whenever the flower has bled most profusely, it has been most affirmative by implication. Its early death has given grief because life matters; its thorns have pierced because love and ideals mean much. In fact, as symbol of life's darker hours, it has remained a warning not to waste our brighter times. That the rose of life should be enjoyed before it withers, and that the rose of love or paradise is worth the price of thorns, are themes perhaps as old as poetry and as enduring as the rose itself. If the flower of joy has also been the flower of sorrow, it has belonged to sorrow only because it first belonged to joy.

Why the rose, above all other flowers, should comprise within itself so vast a range of meanings is a question that cannot be finally answered. However, certain modern theories in combination with each other may go some distance towards explaining this intriguing circumstance. In Freudian belief the explanation is sexual. Blossoms and flowers in general are said to represent the female sexual organs, while the particular shape of the rose associates it most directly with the shape of the vulva. In other words, to Freud the rose of spring is first and foremost the rose of sexual love. And his theory receives ample reinforcement from primitive folk and fairy lore. For roses in early times served as potent ingredients in love philters, and folk superstitions to this day abound in roses signifying love or marriage. Songs and ballads of indeterminate antiquity are likewise filled with roses as flowers of love, while fairy tales of all nations and ages use the rose as the name or the magic flower of beautiful girls. "Briar Rose, or The Sleeping Beauty," wherein a virgin princess sleeps surrounded by roses and protected by thorns until the right prince comes along, is only the best known of countless rosy tales.

But sex and women are not the only contexts in which the rose is prominent in the primitive mind. Sir James G. Frazer discusses its role as a symbol of fecundity in seasonal ceremonies. Here it seems to be not the rose's shape but its early appearance in many parts of the world that determines its predominance over other flowers. For in Frazer's view the spirit of vegetation, often believed to be embodied in a tree, has also been thought to manifest itself in the flower of early spring. On May Day in Alsace a girl called Little May Rose carries a small May tree and sings a song about May roses. In a number of Silesian villages the fourth Sunday of Lent is celebrated by a festival wherein a barren effigy of Death is replaced by a Summer Tree decked with roses. And in the celebrated rites of Adonis, symbolic of the yearly decay and renewal of vegetable life, roses make their appearance in accord with the legend that the red rose sprang from the dead youth's blood.[1] To Frazer, perceiving primitive customs as attempts to propitiate nature deities, the rose in these and similar rituals is employed primarily as an emblem of fertility, an embodiment of the spirit of vegetation thriving beneath the life-giving sun of spring.

Jung, who shares Frazer's concern with rebirth and Freud's concern with the personal psyche, also perceives in ancient uses of the rose relationships to fundamental life processes. For him man's central emotional experience is the integration of the personality or the attainment of a harmonious balance between the conscious and unconscious minds. In fact, he believes that this psychic process, involving death to an old self and rebirth to a new, is the universal motive and goal underlying the myths and religions of the world. Accordingly we find continuous parallels among the legends and symbols of all peoples, while the rose in particular turns out to be a part of the symbol, perhaps most significant of all. In Jung's view it is both the rose's circular shape (suggesting the sun, wholeness, and perfection) and its relation to nature's fertility (suggesting birth or rebirth in beauty) that accounts for its repeated preeminence. For the rose is a part of what Jung calls the mandala, a symbolic design recurrent in myths and dreams, which has among its basic constituents a circle

[1] James G. Frazer, *The Golden Bough*, 3rd ed. (London, 1922), II, 74; IV, 246; V, 225–26, 233–35.

and a center. In its conscious religious art forms in Occident and Orient the rose or lotus often forms the circle, while the created God—Christ, Buddha, or Siva—comprises the center. In dream images produced by the secular unconscious the rose is one of a few basic natural images that may occupy the center itself. Since the mandala is to Jung the principal symbol of the completion or end of the integrative process, the rose in his theory symbolizes rebirth, psychic harmony, and the fulfillment of man's being.

The views of Freud, Frazer, and Jung, together with those of their numerous followers, have intensified awareness and approached explanation of the rose's basic appeal to man throughout the centuries. These views have also helped to account for the flower's abundance in modern literature, since our writers have been repeatedly concerned with the depths of the human psyche and with myth, folklore, or pagan literature as manifestations of those depths. Even writers not directly concerned have been indirectly influenced by the widespread attempt to discover symbols that would express our basic qualities and values. The current probing of man's unconscious, an outgrowth of the nineteenth-century probing of man's inner emotional life, is a part of the whole contemporary attempt to develop the symbolic method itself; for the unconscious manifests itself in symbols, and the expression of unconscious processes, which exist simultaneously with conscious ones, involves a medium that can embrace more than one layer of meaning at a time. The current probing of myth, lore, and pagan letters is a part of the whole contemporary attempt to integrate the artist's deepest impulses with those of humanity at large; for such integration offers relief from a tendency to be overly subjective and from a prevalent sense of aloneness in the modern mechanistic world. Beyond this, an effort to find a human or spiritual common denominator to integrate our time with all time is often at the root of a simultaneous probing both of the private unconscious expressed in sleeping or waking dreams and of the public unconscious expressed in myths and the consequent literature of pre-Christian times.

Freud, Frazer, and Jung offer different but compatible explanations of the rose's extraordinary supremacy. For sexual, natural, and spiritual birth or rebirth are certainly related interpretations of man's fundamental attempts to encompass the mystery at the core of created life. Whichever of their concepts may be the most basic in the human psyche, a relationship between the life-giving processes in man and nature has been perceived and expressed in myth and literature since earliest times. The symbol of a rose or rose-shaped flower vitalized by an omnipotent sun, which was later to culminate in Dante's Catholic *Comedy,* was central among the earliest organized attempts of man to comprehend the universe around him. This ancient integration of sun and flower was intended to symbolize simultaneously the sexual union of male and female creative forces, the physical fertility of all natural things, and the spiritual attainment of ultimate harmony. For example, the religions of India and Egypt alike employed the sun-flower relationship to express the complex mystery of life. In India Brahma, the ultimate creator and hence a power affiliated with the sun, was believed to have been born from the rose-like lotus and then to have in turn created from its petals the entire living universe. Furthermore, the lotus to the Hindus was a symbol of the solar matrix, the maternal womb from which the sun itself each morning rose to renew the world.[2]

In ancient Egypt similar concepts were symbolized by the rose of Isis, a flower that replaced the original lotus when the cultivation of roses spread to Egypt. Lotus or rose, the plant sacred to Isis was again maternal and solar in significance. For

[2] Goblet D'Alviella, *The Migration of Symbols* (New York, 1956), pp. 28–31; William H. Goodyear, *The Grammar of the Lotus* (London, 1891), *passim.*

Isis was wife to Osiris, a sun god, and mother to Horus, a new sun god born shortly after Osiris' murder. As such, she was the personification of universal nature, mother of all living things, so that her flower represented the female generative principle in the world at large. Beyond this, the goddess and her symbol developed certain moral connotations in keeping with their generative role. The rose came to symbolize the power of love as it operated in the human heart, and it is in this role that roses appear in *The Golden Ass* of Lucius Apuleius. A student of the mysteries of Isis as practiced in second-century Corinth, Apuleius tells the allegorical story of a man transformed by lust into a beast. The roses of Isis eaten by the ass, which finally return him to his human form, symbolize the pure devotion that is able to redeem the heart of man as it redeemed the golden ass.

The flower of Egypt surpassed even that of India in suggesting the source not only of all natural life but also of the spiritual passion through which men's noblest ideals are born. Since the highly developed religion of Isis spread beyond Egypt to the Greek and Roman world, it is sometimes held that the rose of the Virgin was adopted directly from her great Eastern rival. But Isis was not the only deity flourishing in the early years of Christianity who had a rose for her particular flower. Aphrodite or Venus, also to be reckoned with, was also associated with the rose. It is true that in the Greek and Roman religions she was not by any means the leading goddess. It is also true that she was frequently regarded as the goddess primarily of mortal love. However, mortal love was not unimportant, nor was it the whole of Aphrodite's story. For she had also been in origin a great earth mother somewhat on the order of Isis. And if her roles both as primitive goddess of nature and as classical goddess of human passion retain a special interest for us, it is because Aphrodite of all pagan goddesses bore the rose which has most directly affected the history of Western literary blossoms.

Aphrodite's home was the island of Cyprus, where she had been the chief deity in a matriarchal land. Lacking the spiritual attributes of Isis, she had nonetheless possessed the full natural powers of the typical primitive earth mother and as such had represented all fertility and growth in animal and vegetable domains. Her adoption by the Greeks brought her into competition with such well-established goddesses as Hera and Demeter, and consequently tended to limit her activities to the procreative passion in human creatures.[3] But traces of her former powers still clung to her and were in particular reflected in her flower. Anacreon in an ode to the rose alludes to the legend that it first came into bloom at the moment Aphrodite was born from the sea. And Bion among others refers to its birth from the blood of Adonis when Aphrodite mourned his death.[4] These associations between Aphrodite's flower and ideas of birth from the watery maternal element or from the blood of a dying nature god reveal underlying concepts of fertility which are vaster than the human sexual impulse. Moreover, as late as the second century A.D. one finds an anonymous Latin poet attributing to Venus the fertility of the earth and making use of the unfolding rose to symbolize her generative powers: "A glossy freshness hence the rose receives, / And blushes sweet through all her silken leaves." [5]

But even in her more limited role as goddess of love Aphrodite had great influence. Her rose pervaded the life of the people, appearing repeatedly in customs celebrating love. Newlyweds and lovers slept on beds strewn with roses, pillows too were often filled with roses, bridal wreaths were com-

[3] Paul Carus, *The Venus of Milo* (London, 1916), *passim;* Jane E. Harrison, *Mythology* (Boston, 1924), pp. 102–6.
[4] Charles Joret, *La Rose dans l'Antiquité et au Moyen Age* (Paris, 1892), pp. 45–47. Joret cites Cyprian, Ovid, and Servius, as well as Bion's "Lament for Adonis."
[5] *The Latin Poets*, ed. R. B. Godolphin (New York, 1949), p. 600. The poem, which uses the rose extensively, was probably written in connection with Hadrian's revival of the spring festival of Venus Genetrix.

prised of roses, and lovers hung rose wreaths on the doors of their beloveds.[6] More important, it is as a simple token of human love that Aphrodite's rose has most deeply impressed literature. For although the limited goddess held a limited flower, it was one so extravagantly popular with poets that few later roses have been unaffected by it. The flower of love pervaded Greek and Latin poetry from at least the days of Sappho's "rosy-fingered morn" throughout the many centuries before the fall of Rome. Anacreon, for instance, overflows with roses, Meleager writes continually of his favorite flower of love, and the famous *Greek Anthology* is a garden of rose blossoms. In fact, by the time of the great Roman poets the still abundant flower had become a veritable cliché for the physical attributes of the beloved or the physical setting of love encounters. When Martial describes a youth whose breath is sweeter than Paestan roses or Horace speaks of making love on roses in a cave, each is simply echoing an association ever present in the customs and lyrics of his day.

Inevitably this recurrent association spread to whatever areas the queen of love might touch. Aphrodite's son Eros adopted her roses, as did her companions, the three lovely Graces. As early as the sixth century B.C., Anacreon had written of an Eros crowned with roses and sleeping in rose beds, while he and Sappho both had identified the flower with the attendant Graces. Associations with the Muses, also to be found in Anacreon and Sappho, may again have been the indirect result of the rose's relation to Aphrodite, inasmuch as love was often said to be the inspiration of song. But this derivation is a good deal less certain than that of her kinfolk, Eros and the Graces. For although Aphrodite ruled a multitude of roses, she did not by any means enjoy a monopoly. Eos or Aurora, the goddess of dawn, had since the time

---

[6] References to classical customs here and throughout this chapter are based on E. C. Lovatelli, "Die Rose im Alterthum," in *Römische Essays,* tr. E. Petersen (Leipzig, 1891), pp. 89–118.

of Homer been allied with roses. Persephone, the harbinger of spring, had gathered roses among other early flowers in the ancient Homeric *Hymn to Demeter*. And Dionysus, the god of wine—and therefore, like love, an inspiration to song— had come close to rivaling Aphrodite as possessor of a widely popular rose.

Dionysus too was a nature god whose province was vaster than the vine he is noted for. But this god of the tree and all blossoming things represented in man the natural passions unbounded by rational controls. Consequently the essence of his worship was drunkenness, thought of as literal possession by the god, and his rose of natural fecundity was most frequently limited specifically to wine. Therefore the flower decorated tables at banquets, was worn in wreaths around the heads of guests, and was shredded to petals and tossed in wine bowls. It blossomed in classical lyrics from the time of Anacreon, whose flower exhales "Sweet incense to mortals from Bacchanal wreaths," through and beyond exhortations like Martial's: "In thy dark wine-cup mingle summer snows, / And wreathe thy temples with the blushing rose." [7] Most important of all, because wine betokened ecstasy, Dionysus' rose could be linked with Aphrodite's as the flower of a compound joy that encompassed wine, love, beauty, song, spring, and youth. Once again we find lines as far back as Anacreon that establish the tenor for the ages to follow: "The rose of the Loves who forever entice us / O let us mix for divine Dionysus!" [8]

Of course, in classical times as in all times an excess of joy could spill over into sorrow. When Propertius speaks sadly of withering garlands and Horace speaks of roses that are fading fast, they echo the recurrent human lament for the brevity of joy and of life itself. But perhaps because the

---

[7] *Odes of Anacreon*, tr. Erastus Richardson (New Haven, 1928), p. 63; *The Latin Poets*, ed. R. B. Godolphin, p. 593.

[8] *Odes of Anacreon*, tr. Richardson, p. 51.

flower's principal flaw was the fact that it could not endure forever, it early acquired an immortal counterpart blossoming in the realm of ideals. In Rome, for example, it became a custom to place roses on graves and on the foreheads of the dead as tokens of enduring love. And the flower of life had been the flower of the afterlife from at least the time of Pindar's description of Elysium, "reddening with the rose, their paradise," through Propertius' vision of "Elysian roses" or Tibullus' Elysian garden bursting with "the blossoms of the fragrant rose." [9] The rose of life might be watered with tears as well as wine, but its bloom was all the richer for this interfusion. In fact, had the flower not encompassed death and heaven, it could not have been the symbol it was destined to become.

For although the roses of classical literature did not themselves attain symbolic complexity, they helped to prepare the particular soil in which their multifoliate successors would be planted. In their varied roles as metaphors for life's essential joys, as well as for its one incontrovertible sorrow, the roses of Greek and Roman lyrics covered most of the meanings to be granted to the flower on the plane of earthly life. As such, these roses would continue in our literature in an unbroken although modified stream through the secular lyrics of the Middle Ages to those of the classics-loving Renaissance. And the simple roses of early modern times would themselves contribute their aggregate of meanings to the intricate, romantic symbols of the nineteenth and twentieth centuries. Moreover, the decorative flowers of Elysium were to reappear in early Christian writings as ornaments of Eden and of the heavenly Paradise, concepts that in turn would gain symbolic qualities in the religious writings of succeeding centuries. For however far the symbol roses of the

[9] *The Oxford Book of Greek Verse in Translation,* ed. T. F. Higham and C. M. Bowra (Oxford, 1953), p. 329 (Pindar); *The Latin Poets,* ed. Godolphin, pp. 381 (Propertius), 330 (Tibullus).

Christian era might travel from the metaphors of classical times, they would never quite escape their distant pagan roots in beauty, love, spring, joy, festivity, and the afterlife.

All of which is not to say that the classical poets originated anything new to the rose. It is clear that their flower itself was derived from a plant rooted deep in the primitive mind, and that in fact in their lyrical art it had lost a great part of its original meaning. For the rose's cosmic origins in fundamental, primitive explanations of the universe had been greatly diminished in the customs and lyrics of an entirely civilized people. Even its specific alliance with Aphrodite, Dionysus, the Graces, and the Muses had become increasingly subordinate to its general identification with love, beauty, wine, and all related delights irrespective of their origins. Nevertheless, the classical writers did happen to be the ones to give the first Western literary form to the blossom of still more ancient times. They were, therefore, the first to provide a poetic tradition in which were established certain roles for the flower of the future. As such they were also the first to provide a definite literary point of departure from which later writers, like Lawrence or Joyce, might follow the classical metaphor to its deep, embracing source.

For modern writers who return to the classics generally differ in motive from those of the Renaissance or of the neoclassical period. They are not, like Renaissance writers, discovering for the first time a new and many-splendored thing from which to learn new approaches to art and experience: the thing has long since been discovered and made part of our heritage. Nor are they, like the Augustans, seeking a formal discipline and a controlled perfection within ordered terrestrial bonds: their quest for order takes them more often to the supraterrestrial Middle Ages. Rather, contemporary writers are attempting to trace human nature to its universal, timeless source in an effort to understand the world or even to reassure themselves that it is not a grotesque, disjointed world.

But with little in the qualities of their particular age to praise, they are compelled, to a greater extent than writers in most ages, to find their affirmations in those values which transcend the particular limits of any age. Consequently, they plumb the depths of the individual psyche, seeking in turn to give it broader validity through placing it in relation to the fundamental human psyche. In doing so they are aided by pagan myths and letters as well as by social scientists who help them to uncover the universal in pagan thought.

They are also vastly aided by their own more immediate heritage. For modern writers who wish to discover primitive, unconscious, or historical origins must inevitably return to those origins from the perspective of a Christian era. The classics provided a literary tradition that in turn derived much from primitive beliefs. But both primitive roots and classical blossoms have come down to us filtered through the Christian centuries. In seeking the wellsprings of Western society or even of the universal human psyche, modern symbolists have often returned to pagan origins through the media of psychology, anthropology, or literature. They have still more often sought for fundamentals through the media of traditions established within Christianity or through a combination of the Christian with the pagan. Consequently, more important to modern literature than the pagan flower as such has been that flower's great indirect effect upon the flower of the Christian world. For the pagan rose had achieved such popularity that it had to be taken account of and adapted to Christian purposes by the early Church. Certainly most of its meanings on the planes of earth and heaven had already existed long before the Christian era. But Christianity offered a new spiritual vision and a new method of expressing that vision that permanently altered the quality of the rose. In fact, so important has this alteration been that the early Catholic uses of the pagan flower can most properly be said to blossom at the literary fountainhead of Western roses.

2

THE

MEDIEVAL

HERITAGE

The Middle Ages saw the development of the particular quality of love that characterizes Christianity. For in the Catholic scheme of things the God who is the final power in the cosmos is a God of love. And since human beings are believed to be created in the image and likeness of their Creator, it follows that men are akin to God in their ability to love. Furthermore, in the person of Christ man had been granted an immediate vision of the ultimate mystery in the universe: the incarnation of eternal spirit in mortal flesh achieved through love. Accordingly, the conscientious Christian sought to pattern his life on the precepts of Christ and hence to cultivate within himself the disinterested, heaven-directed love that Christ had taught. Within this framework the queen of flowers, long a symbol of love in the natural universe, was to become an important Catholic symbol of the spiritual love incarnated in Christ. As such it was gradually to acquire a complex of interrelated meanings involved in the basic conception of love as a manifestation of God in the world.

At the same time the associations already acquired by the flower of pre-Christian days were to undergo much modification. Indeed, when the meaning of material things was found to lie in their expression of their spiritual Creator, a reversal of pagan values was inevitable. If God, who was the one ultimate reality, was identifiable with the power of love, then in the last analysis all facets of creation were explainable in terms of that transcendent power. All goodness became a reflection of God and all evil a misuse of his gift in a vision that presented the entire universe swinging on the hinges of good and evil love. Temporal glories, once in high repute, were now at best but passing shadows of divine realities and were at worst a delusion and a snare. For the sin of self-love had brought death into the world, and only through love redirected to its source with the aid of Christ's grace could spiritual redemption be attained. Pagan delight in earthly beauties for their own sake was vanity of vanities and worse than vanity, being a perversion of the power of love and hence resulting in its own destruction.

At first the medieval shift from joy in created things for themselves to joy in them only for the sake of their Creator resulted in a disparagement of the rose that had long been a token of pagan sensuality. Tertullian and Clement of Alexandria, early doctors of the Church writing in the second century, proscribed the crowns of roses worn on festal occasions.[1] As an emblem of Venus related to sex, the flower was for a time the compulsory badge worn by prostitutes as a mark of disgrace. But the rose's persistent popularity among the people was not to be stifled. The Church was gradually obliged to adopt the indefatigable plant, and in the process to redirect its meanings in accordance with the whole redirection of values involved in Catholicism. Queen of the flowers in classical Elysium, it became the chief flower of the garden of Paradise. Token of death and the sadness of mortality, it came to represent the deaths of Christ and the martyrs and the joys of eternal life achieved thereby. Sign of Venus and the earthly love of woman, it grew to be a symbol of the Virgin and the spiritual love expressed through her.

[1] J. P. Migne, ed., *Patrologia Latina*, 221 vols. (Paris, 1844–64), II, 101–2; J. P. Migne, ed., *Patrologia Graeca*, VIII, 166 vols. (Paris, 1857–66), 466–90.

In short, the pagan festal rose wreath, cruelly parodied in Christ's crown of thorns, became a flowering Christian halo signifying charity, holiness, and peace.

In acquiring supernatural meanings, the metaphor of classical lyrics emerged as an allegorical expression of interrelated spiritual ideas. The rose is of course but one example of the medieval allegorical habit of mind as shaped by Christianity and expressed in religious literature. At its simplest this allegorical habit involved the perception of single spiritual correspondences in and behind the words of Scripture and the phenomena of nature. But medieval allegory was not an exact science, and in its more elaborate forms apparently disparate meanings were sometimes attached to the same object. An allegorical rose might signify either the Virgin or Christ or Paradise or martyrdom. At another time the same flower might signify two or more of these meanings. And in such a work as the *Divine Comedy* it seems to comprehend all four in a pattern of considerable intricacy. When, as in Dante, an allegorical object is given meanings too indefinite, complex, or mysterious to be adequately expressed in any other way, the object can legitimately be termed a symbol.

In fact, the symbol in Western literature appears to have evolved from religious allegory. One might almost maintain that in our society the symbolic method in general can claim specific origin in the allegorical rose. For Dante's multifoliate rose of heaven, emerging towards the close of the Middle Ages, represented the West's first major formulation in literature of a truly elaborate symbolic technic. And Dante's important flower itself was the heir of countless less complicated roses preceding it in the works of the period. To begin with, the rose had been related to the earthly paradise of Eden and by analogy to the Paradise of the blessed from the early days of the Church. Saints Basil and Ambrose of the fourth century set the tradition that before man's fall it grew in Eden without thorns.[2] The fifth-century poet, Dracontius, in his

---

[2] Migne, *PG,* XXXII, 1211; Migne, *PL,* XIV, 188.

De Laudibus Dei, describes Adam and Eve rejoicing among flower beds and roses. And medieval religious art offers plentiful illustration of the heavenly as well as earthly Paradise depicted as a garden of roses and lilies in accordance with the scriptural description of heaven given in II Esdras 2:19: "fountains flowing with milk and honey, and seven mighty mountains, whereupon there grow roses and lilies, whereby I will fill thy children with joy."

The red rose was still more commonly conceived of as the flower of martyrdom. In this respect it was appropriate both because its color suggested blood and because it carried a long Roman tradition as the reward of noble action. The writings of such important ecclesiastics as St. Augustine, St. Cyprian, Hrabanus Maurus, Walafrid Strabo, and Albertus Magnus refer to the conventional alliance of roses with the temporal sufferings and eternal triumphs of martyred saints. More dramatic illustration of this alliance is to be found in *The Golden Legend,* Jacobus de Voragine's thirteenth-century collection of the saints' lives popular in his day. The life of martyred St. Cecelia, for instance, stresses the crown of roses from Paradise brought her by an angel as tribute to her virtue. The life of St. Dorothy, executed for her faith, reaches its climax in the basket of heavenly roses she sent after her death to her earthly persecutor. And the tale of the Assumption of the Virgin describes the miracle occurring when Mary was laid in the sepulchre: "And anon she was environed with flowers of roses, that was the company of the martyrs." [3]

The flower of martyrs was the flower as well of the supreme martyr of Christianity. As a sign of Christ's Passion, the redness of the rose was again associated with blood, while the surrounding thorns signified his crown of thorns. At the same time, the Resurrection that followed the Passion was figured in the splendor of the rose in bloom. St. Ambrose and Walafrid Strabo, for instance, associate the rose with the

[3] *The Golden Legend,* ed. F. S. Ellis (London, 1900), VI, 247–53.

blood of Christ, while Albertus Magnus and Bernard of Clairvaux both subordinate this aspect to that of the spiritual redemption achieved for all mankind through Christ's great agony. St. Bernard describes Christ as the flower of the Resurrection blossoming after the rain of unbelief, and Albertus Magnus describes him as the rose of Jericho blossoming in the Resurrection of the flesh that had been poured forth in the red blood of the Passion.[4] Nor were Christ's roses those of martyrdom alone. As Son of God and Redeemer of man, Christ had pointed the way to eternal salvation. He was therefore further identified with the Rose of Sharon, allegorical lover of the Church in the *Song of Solomon,* and with the flower of Isaiah's "Messianic" prophecy that "the wilderness shall blossom like a rose."

But the Catholic rose is perhaps most frequently a symbol of the Virgin. Identified with woman from earliest times and the classical attribute of the goddess of earthly love, the pagan queen of flowers reappears quite naturally as the chief symbol of the Christian queen of heaven. Surprising only is the fact that the rose was granted its most popular religious meaning comparatively late in the Catholic era. Perhaps this was because it had long been the flower of Venus and so of sexual license; perhaps it was because before the twelfth century the Virgin had not yet attained her high position in Catholic ritual and devotion. But whatever the reasons, the fact remains that Mary, who had long been identified with Isaiah's rod of Jesse blossoming in the holy flower of Christ, did not herself become a rose until the advent of her twelfth-century devotee, St. Bernard of Clairvaux. Then, as if to make up for lost time and lost analogies, both Bernard and the Catholic writers who followed him established Mary as the most elaborate of ecclesiastical roses to date.

[4] Migne, *PL,* CLXXXIII, 1059 (Bernard); Albertus Magnus, *Opera Omnia* (Paris, 1898), XXXVI, 670. (Cf. St. Ambrose and Walafrid Strabo, in Migne, *PL,* XV, 1566; CXIV, 1130, respectively.)

In a sermon Bernard begins with a contrast between two fundamental women, Eve and Mary, setting the thorn of sin that brought death into the world against the radiant flower that brings spiritual health. He goes on to develop extensive comparisons between Mary and the white rose of virtue, virginity, and love of God, Mary and the red rose of charity, spirituality, and annihilation of vice.[5] Following Bernard in the next century, both Bonaventura and Albertus Magnus wrote of Mary as a perfect, thornless rose.[6] And in the same context Albertus Magnus worked out a comparison between Mary and her flower that rivaled St. Bernard's in its elaboration. Such evident likenesses as beauty, modesty, and queenliness were only an introduction. The red rose was further akin to Mary in charity and grief indicated by its color (that of fire and blood), complexity of spirit indicated by its many petals, and virgin birth indicated by the bud that opens only to the sun.

Moreover, the ingenuities of theological writers were no more than a beginning, for the popularity of the Virgin's rose was developed in countless medieval lyrics. Simple, conventional associations between Mary and her roses recur throughout the period. Typical are such obvious comparisons as the simile in "A Song of Love to the Blessed Virgin"—"Heo is of colour and beate / As fresch as is the Rose in May"—or the metaphor in "Enixa Est Puerpa"—"Lady, flor of all thing, / rosa sine spina." Occasionally too one finds a more elaborate treatment of the Mary-rose analogy. In the well-known carol, "Of a rose, a lovely rose," Mary, the rose that bore the flower of Christ, receives tribute for Christ's various deeds conceived of as the "branchis of that rose." And finally in the fifteenth-century carol, "There is no rose of swich vertu," the formation of genuine symbolic conception is clearly discernible:

[5] Migne, *PL*, CLXXXIV, 1020.
[6] St. Bonaventura, "Ad beatam Mariam virginem deiparam," in *Das Deutsche Kirchenlied*, ed. P. Wackernagel (Leipzig, 1864), I, 142; Albertus Magnus, *Opera Omnia*, XXXVI, 670–71.

> For in this rose conteined was
> Hevene and erthe in litel space.
> *Res miranda.*
>
> Be that rose we may weel see
> There be o God in persones three,
> *Pares forma.*

Mary's rose is here perceived as containing within itself the Son of God, who in turn was the embodiment of God and hence of heaven, earth, and the Trinity. As such, the flower has assumed a vast significance as the manifestation to all mankind of the ultimate mysteries in and under heaven.

Of course, such conceptions as these received their fullest development in Dante's *Comedy*. There the Virgin's rose expands to become a multi-leveled symbol of spiritual perfection, grace, Paradise, Christ's triumph, and the eternal love in which all temporal things find their fulfillment and their end. Moreover, in his final symbol Dante not only brought to culmination the varied religious attributes of the rose but also managed for the first time in literature to express them in an all-encompassing symbolic form. But Dante was led to the rose of heaven by the well-traveled way of earthly love, so that in his *Comedy*'s ultimate symbol the heritage of Catholic roses is blended with the heritage of the rose of mortal passion. Although before Dante there had been no real harmony between worldly and otherworldly love, the rose in secular lyrics to women played a role parallel to and at least as important as that in religious lyrics to Mary. And since mortal roses in the medieval era were tokens of a love that rivaled in power that of the Catholic Church itself, one must examine their varied blossoms before going on to consider Dante's all-embracing plant.

Roses pervaded the love songs of medieval Europe, retaining the popularity they had had in pagan times as flowers of earthly love, especially in spring. Except in such a special instance as Froissart's "Debate Between the Rose and the Violet" (where the lily is proclaimed supreme because of its French political background), the rose continues as queen of the flowers and hence as attribute of the poet's beloved. Goliardic poems are fragrant with romance's roses. "Flower of all maidens, / My love, / Rose o'er all roses / Above," sings one now anonymous wandering scholar; and another presents the queen flower itself to that flower's human counterpart:

> Take thou this Rose, O Rose,
> Since Love's own flower it is
> And by that rose
> Thy lover captive is.[7]

Troubadours and minnesingers were equally enthralled by roses. Peire Vidal, for example, claims his beloved to be "as fresh as is a rose in spring." Der Wilde Alexander compares his inaccessible sweetheart to a rose in a dense thicket: "A rose there is—I weep her yet! / Within so dense a thicket set, / No joys may come anear." And in the late twelfth-century song, "Rosa fressca aulentissima," probably the earliest Italian lyric extant, the poet grants to his beloved the standard rosy eulogy: "Thou sweetly smelling fresh red rose / That near thy summer art." [8]

Although perhaps less abundant in England than on the Continent, the rose here too was a popular tribute to beauty, love, or spring. Briefly mentioned in the well-known song, "Lenten is come with love to town," it receives more attention in certain ballads. "Rose the Red and White Lily" or "Jennifer gentle and Rosemaree" grace beautiful maidens with flower names; "Fair Margaret and Sweet William" concludes with the age-old fantasy of a wedlock between the

---

[7] *Medieval Latin Lyrics*, tr. Helen Waddell, 4th ed. (London, 1951), p. 253.

[8] *Anthology of the Provençal Troubadours*, ed. R. T. Hill and T. G. Bergin (New Haven, 1941), p. 100; *Old German Love Songs*, tr. Frank Nicholson (Chicago, 1907), p. 163; *Italian Poets Chiefly Before Dante*, tr. D. G. Rossetti (Stratford, 1908), pp. 1–2.

roses that grow atop two lovers' graves. Chaucer, who translated a sizable portion of the *Roman de la Rose,* uses an occasional rose in his own original work: "For with the rose colour
stroof hire hewe," or "she was fayr as is the rose in May." And
the anonymous thirteenth-century lyric, "Lady Have Ruth on
Me," employs a century before Chaucer the same popular
simile: "Lylie-whyt hue is / hire rode so rose on rys, / that
reveth me mi rest."

It is true that the rose in most of these instances has become little more than a cliché. Yet even the cliché is important, for the very fact that so worn a coin could retain its
ancient value for poets testifies to the flower's continued as-
cendance in the universe of love. It was because of this ascend-
ance that a handful of poets could go on to develop beyond
convention an intricate secular rose. In fact, at a time when
sexual love was largely at odds with religious devotion, one
finds allegorical secular roses at once competing with and
resembling religious roses that expressed the Virgin's likeness
to a flower. For example, "Li Contes de la Rose," a thirteenth-
century French poem by Baudouin de Condé, concludes with
an extensive though straightforward comparison between the
beloved and the rose in respect to beauty, color, fragrance,
queenliness, and like qualities. And two poems of the late
twelfth or early thirteenth century, which may have influenced
the subsequent *Roman de la Rose,* are even more significant.
Not only do they offer detailed development of the rose-woman
kinship, but they go beyond this to reveal an incipient shift
from simple, explicit analogy to the implicit analogy of allegory.

The anonymous French "Dit de la Rose," although explicitly
a comparison between the beloved and the most beautiful
flower, has in it the germs of allegory. For the poet is not content with conventional, surface likenesses. He therefore dips
into imagination at least far enough to procure a moderately
resourceful likeness (later developed in the *Roman*) between

the rose's thorns and the many slanderers hindering his love:

> Just as the unblemished rose
> Exists among sharp thorns,
> So the mistress of my heart
> Exists among sharp tongues.[9]

The Latin "Carmen de Rosa," also anonymous, shows a little more developed if uneven allegorical character. Although the poet sometimes forgets he is speaking of a flower, and so mars his allegory with disturbing praises of golden hair, ivory teeth, and starlike eyes, nevertheless the dominant figure in his poem is a rose. And the important difference between this and the usual secular rose poem is that here the comparison is no longer in any way explicit. The beloved is not described as "resembling" a rose; in fact, the beloved as such is not described at all. Rather, the flower itself stands alone as an allegorical cloak for a human counterpart who can now be only understood:

> See the flower of all flowers,
> See the flower of flowers,
> Look upon the rose of May,
> Loveliest in creation.[10]

But it was of course the *Roman de la Rose* that brought to secular literature an allegorical method as fully developed as that current in religious literature since Prudentius' *Psychomachia* of the fourth century. Although largely lacking the multiple meanings sustained throughout Dantesque allegory, the *Roman* displays an elaboration of single-leveled correspondences on a par with the moral personifications of the average religious allegorical poem. Furthermore, in one highly

[9] Author's translation. For complete French text, see K. Bartsch, *La Langue et la Littérature Françaises* (Paris, 1887), pp. 603–10.
[10] Author's translation. For complete Latin text, see *Carmina Burana*, ed. J. A. Schmeller (Stuttgart, 1847), pp. 141–45. For full discussion of the last two poems in relation to the *Roman de la Rose*, see Ernest Langlois, *Origines et Sources du Roman de la Rose* (Paris, 1891), pp. 36–39, 42–46.

significant feature the *Roman* does attain symbolic suggestiveness. While the bulk of the poem is little more than extended personification allegory, the rose and the garden in which it grows have the force of genuine symbols. For although whatever is analyzable in the poets' views on life and love is dramatically enacted by a series of allegorical persons, whatever remains at the emotional, untranslatable core of the work has been embodied in the complex, suggestive figures of rose and garden. Perhaps because they were treating a subject that by the mid-thirteenth century had been fully developed in art and society, Guillaume de Lorris and his continuator, Jean de Meun, were able to handle the theme of earthly love in a poetic form at least as intricate as that long current in the treatment of spiritual beliefs.

For during the twelfth century the conception of love between man and woman had been elaborated and codified into the system of rules and attitudes we refer to as courtly love. Whereas in classical times love had generally been regarded as frank sensuality, tragic madness, or resistless passion, it emerged in the Middle Ages in the new and softer guise it would with modifications continue to wear to the present day. The courtly love system, which grew up in eleventh-century Provence and became formalized during the following century in the courts of Eleanor of Aquitaine and Marie of Champagne, presented love as a highly romantic, almost transcendent power. In addition, the new devotion displayed certain characteristics paralleling and rivaling those of the era's ruling religion. The fact that adultery and secrecy were deemed essential to its existence did not prevent romantic love from being considered the most ennobling influence in secular life, attribute of those alone who possessed potential moral excellence. And the source of this ennobling influence, the beloved woman who was seen as superior, often worshiped from afar, and served in hardship and peril, played a role in the secular world not altogether dissimilar to that played by the Virgin in the world of the devout.

Of course the essential opposition between religious and courtly love was as evident as their likeness. The adoration of a woman, particularly another man's wife, could hardly be viewed as consistent with the adoration of Mary. Yet during the twelfth century both adorations were becoming entrenched in European society. The worship of the Virgin was being promoted by the Church and celebrated in hymns and lyrics at the very same time that the worship of her various earthly rivals was being established in the courts of Europe and immortalized by courtly poets. The situation created a conflict for those who worshiped both Virgin and woman, and this conflict is important to the history of roses. It was after all to a great extent as a result of attempts at resolution that the rose became one of the earliest and richest of literary symbols. For although precise degrees and directions of influence are obscure, it is clear that the striking literary parallels between certain courtly love devotions and religious devotions to Mary were more than coincidence. Nor could the writers, courtly or churchly, who used the rose so often, have been unaware of its equal abundance in the realms of flesh and spirit. Whether as the defiant result of an uneasy conscience or as the earnest result of a longing to reconcile earth and heaven, courtly love poets throughout the period frequently chose to describe their beloveds in similar terms and through similar roses to those found in tales and hymns of Mary.

Analogous forms alone were not enough to resolve the discords between divine and earthly love. But the use, for instance, of the same flower and a like development of its various meanings for the realms of both time and eternity paved the way to the ultimate harmony achieved in Dante's rose of heaven. A major step in this progression and a major symbol in its own right is the dominant figure in the *Roman de la Rose.* For the flower here, though reflecting a discord between courtly and Catholic ideals, nonetheless brings to culmination the whole secular side of love. Here, as in no other poem, the courtly love system and outlook, implicit in the lyrics of minnesinger and troubadour, is given thorough, explicit literary expression. To begin with, Guillaume de Lorris, author of the first portion of the poem, brings to his subject a full measure of courtly idealism. To him we owe the central symbol of a rose in a spring garden, watered by preceding centuries of traditional analogy and cultivated once again in part to convey the surpassing excellence of the woman beloved:

> Worthy of love is she, and fit,
> Before all other maids I swear,
> The fragrant name of Rose to bear.[11]

One feels that even had the courtly code not required that the woman's name be secret, Guillaume would still have chosen the ancient flower of female perfection for the name as well as symbol of his idealized beloved.

However, the rose is not the embodiment of the woman as such, for her various characteristics—Modesty, Chastity, Pity, Fair Welcome—are expressed by personifications. Rather the rose, more important than these, acts as symbol of the whole complex of qualities that inspire and hence comprise the poet's singular devotion. Its first appearance to him, reflected in the two crystals at the bottom of the Fountain of Narcissus, provides an initial clue to its symbolic purport. Since the crystals are intended to represent the lover's eyes, the reflection in them of the rose is undoubtedly meant to suggest that the lover perceives in his flower the embodiment of his private ideal. This ideal itself appears from the outset to be heavily sexual, making valid a Freudian view of rose and garden:

[11] *The Romance of the Rose,* tr. F. S. Ellis, 3 vols. (London, 1900), I, 2. Citations from the *Roman* in this chapter are to this edition.

My longing drew
Me towards the rose-bush and then flew
Through all my soul its savour sweet,
Which set my heart and pulse abeat
Like fire. And were it not for fear
That I the scot might pay too dear,
I surely should have dared to seize
A rosebud, seen nought else could please
My senses equally. (ll. 1695–1703)

Clearly, sexual longing, which provides the initial motive for all that will come after, is a principal ingredient in the poet's rosy love.

But sexuality, though essential to the kindling and persistence of love, was at the same time only one aspect of the courtly lover's ideal and therefore only one among many meanings expressed by Guillaume's rose. Since the flower is the central symbol of his entire poem, it acquires much of its special significance from the allegorical context in which it blooms. The surrounding garden, for instance, is the garden of courtly love, presided over by such figures as Idleness, Gladness, Courtesy, Wealth, Generosity, and Youth, and excluding such as Hate, Villainy, Avarice, Poverty, Sorrow, and Age. Thriving in an atmosphere of privilege and happiness, the flower nevertheless is not devoid of thorns. Pride, Evil-Tongue, Modesty, Fear, among others, make its acquisition difficult and so create the lover's woes. His goal remains within the realm of the attainable only if he is careful to shun all baseness of character and to cultivate the virtues of courtesy, generosity, cheerfulness, and absolute devotion. The rose of earthly love, that demands such qualities of its pursuers and requires so luxuriant a garden in which to bloom, thus becomes a symbol of a highly developed courtly ideal. Although it is certainly engendered by sexual desire, the love in question expands to embrace what the poet claims are his highest conceptions of beauty, goodness, and a joy whose very "memory will suffice / To hold my soul in paradise" (ll. 3643–44). In fact, C. S. Lewis has pointed out that on a more fundamental level the rose's garden suggests the mythical garden of perfect bliss shared alike by many peoples.[12] Although for the courtly poet this garden is aristocratic, it resembles such universal Arcadias as Tirna nOg, the Hesperides, Eden, or Heaven itself. Moreover, an anology between love's garden and its Christian counterparts, Eden or the heavenly Paradise, is deliberately created near the outset of Guillaume's poem:

> Then burst on my astonished eyes
> A dream—an Earthly Paradise:
> And suddenly my soul seemed riven
> From earth to dwell in highest heaven.
>
> (ll. 649–52)

This analogy is important because it serves to exalt earthly love through comparison with the divine and at the same time to take account of their essential antagonism. Making no attempt to reconcile temporal with eternal, Guillaume explicitly seeks instead to set the former above the latter. To this end he goes on to embody in his secular rose garden all of the beauty, sweetness, and charm that have made it the object of such rapture as he feels must transcend that which heaven might hold: "Yet doubt I much if heaven can give / A place where I so soon would live" (ll. 653–54). And since the rapture of the garden is epitomized in the rose, it is inevitable that the poet should make her transcendent glory manifest at the moment of his kiss, the climax of his poem:

> God save and bless
> Her everywise, whose tenderness
> To me were far more rich reward
> Than earth and heaven beside afford.
>
> (ll. 3661–64)

---

[12] *The Allegory of Love* (Oxford, 1951), pp. 119–20.

Guillaume de Lorris was an idealist who sought to exalt earthly love by placing it on a level with religious rapture. But he did not live to complete his poem, and when Jean de Meun undertook to do so, he approached the matter from a new angle. Where Guillaume had set up an earthly garden as a rival to Paradise, Jean de Meun attempted to reconcile the realms of earth and heaven. Approaching the subject of secular love with more realism than Guillaume, he began by attacking courtly romanticism in matter-of-fact terms:

> The burning love which overcame
> Thy heart was carnal, purer flame
> Burnt not within thee; thou the Rose
> Thereof didst wish to pluck, God knows!
>
> (ll. 4885–88)

His attack was nevertheless not motivated by negativity or cynicism. Rather, Jean de Meun's intent was to replace sugar-coated courtly sentiments with philosophical conceptions that he believed truer and more constructive. For Jean de Meun, a disciple of the naturalistic thinkers of Chartres, saw in Guillaume's rose and garden suitable vehicles for expressing certain naturalistic doctrines of generation and replenishment.

It was principally from Bernard Sylvester and Alanus de Insulis, twelfth-century poets of the school of Chartres, that Jean de Meun drew his belief in the importance of the reproductive function for replenishing the natural world and thereby carrying on the plan of its Creator. Raising this doctrine from its secondary place in the works of his predecessors, he made of it a central theme in his allegorical rose quest.[13] Accordingly, in Jean de Meun's portion of the *Roman de la Rose*, we find that heterosexual love is valued not for romantic reasons but because it is Nature's means of perpetuating the race:

[13] For full discussion of Jean de Meun's doctrines and their sources, see Alan M. F. Gunn, *The Mirror of Love* (Lubbock, Texas, 1952), pp. 218 ff., 255.

> Behold the end for which should mate
> Man with a woman; to create
> One who may follow him when he
> Through God's goodwill hath ceased to be.
> For when the parents pass away,
> Nature hath ordered it that they
> Shall children leave, who following still
> Their forbears, shall the world refill.   (ll. 4687–94)

Love then is good not because it is beautiful but because it fulfills an essential function that is in fact divine. For Nature turns out to be God's "queenly deputy," and man must obey her commands in the garden of this world if he would attain eternity in the garden of Paradise:

> Honour ye Nature, be your aim
> To do her work, unlet by blame
>
> .   .   .
>
> And then shall you that marvellous
> And beauteous park at last attain
>
> .   .   .
>
> The while your footsteps follow near
> Those of the Lamb, and ye shall be
> His friends through all eternity.   (ll. 21511–30)

In the light of these controlling ideas, Jean de Meun's symbols of rose and garden express chiefly various levels of fertility. At once sexual and philosophical, rose and garden are reinforced by surrounding symbols in the romance. The hammer and anvil of Nature, the staff and purse of the lover, and the golden arrows of Cupid are, like the rose, at once sexual symbols and symbols of the natural plenitude provided by the Creator.[14] As the poem's chief sexual symbol, the rose is the poet's supreme expression of humanity's highest duty, the replenishment of the earth. As the poem's chief philosophical symbol, the rose in its ultimate union with the lover expresses man's fulfillment of the goal of his being:

[14] *Ibid.*, p. 301.

O'er all is LOVE supreme, and we
Are bound his servitors to be.
What Virgil saith of that great word
Is true, for it through time hath stirred
Men's spirits, till they have defied
The world for it, and lightly died.
Fair son, I now beseech thee, give
Consent that with the Rose may live
This Lover till their hands death part.
(ll. 21805–13)

Love is supreme in the human world because it alone ensures the existence of the human world. Moreover, beyond and because of this, the rose garden of temporal love is itself but the mortal image of its immortal counterpart. Through fulfillment of himself man has fulfilled God's aims on earth and can therefore await his eternal reward in the garden of the spirit:

In peace led everlastingly
Through fair green pastures sprinkled o'er
With violets, daisies, and rich store
Of fragrant blossoms, while on high
Hang roses which nor fade nor die.   (ll. 21132–36)

Guillaume de Lorris, in idealizing the rose of courtly love, had set it up as a rival to the love of heaven, while Jean de Meun attempted to reconcile the two loves in terms of a particular naturalistic philosophy. As a result partly of their divergent approaches, the *Roman de la Rose* is the most comprehensive of medieval poems on earthly love and its rose is the culmination of countless secular predecessors. At the same time, the authors' dissimilar viewpoints created a real disparity between the attitudes towards love and consequent meanings of the rose expressed in the two portions of the single poem. Moreover, neither poet was able to bring about a truly adequate harmony between the realms of sense and soul. Guillaume de Lorris' attempts to attribute to heterosexual love the transcendent emotions of mystic rapture served largely to stress the distance between the two ideals. Nor could Jean de Meun's attempts to reconcile earth and heaven on a naturalistic basis hope to satisfy his era's hunger for God. Although the rose of their poem unquestionably surpasses all other medieval secular blossoms, it remained for the poets of Italy to further the task of uniting mortal and immortal love and for the supreme Italian poet to complete this needful union in his rose of eternity.

Certainly as the culminating expression of both earthly and heavenly love the rose of Dante's *Comedy* was the culmination of dominant strains in the medieval period. While courtly love embraced much of the spirit of courtly life, Divine Love as interpreted in Catholic theology embraced the entire social as well as religious order. The union of courtly and churchly attitudes towards love, with all that they implied of social and spiritual significance, was no meager poetic achievement. The union of all this in a single sunlit rose produced a symbol that would remain among the most complex in literature. For Dante had attempted to concentrate in a flower no less than his solution to the riddle of the universe, and had developed for this purpose a symbolic vehicle that far surpassed in richness the richest of ordinary words. Of course, in the last analysis the significance of God transcends man's limited powers of communication. Nonetheless Dante's intricate symbol goes as far perhaps as language can towards a suggestion of the glory at the heart of the Catholic idea of love.

The sunlit rose that dominates the final cantos of the *Paradiso* proclaims the complete fulfillment of the poet's long spiritual quest. Purged of sin and perfected in holiness, he is granted a mystic vision of eternal glory. In this vision, which is twofold, he first perceives a gigantic white rose on whose petals are enthroned the entire company of saints. He then lifts his eyes to the sun, symbol of the Trinity, shining down upon the rose. It has been noted that the dual nature of this vision corresponds to the two stages of mystic contemplation defined by St. Bernard, the first stage revealing the saints in glory and the second revealing God himself.[15] The rose, symbolizing the lower of these stages, serves as necessary precursor of the higher. Moreover, the symbols of sun and rose are interdependent and inseparable. It is the sun that gives life to the rose and the rose that makes manifest the sun's power and glory. A full comprehension of the mystic relation between the Creator and his creation marks the end of Dante's journey and the highest attainment of spiritual vision.

As an essential aspect of the final vision towards which the entire *Comedy* moves, the rose embodies the chief spiritual implications of the poem as a whole. Blossoming beneath the sun of God, it is an intricate expression of the fulfillment in eternity of all temporal things. In selecting a symbol that could bear so great a burden, Dante was undoubtedly influenced by the roles already established for the rose in medieval religious and literary traditions. For although the depiction of all Paradise as a single rose appears to be original with Dante, the various conceptions expressed by this rose have analogues in secular and religious tradition. Choosing for his culminating symbol the established flower of Paradise, saints, Christ, Mary, and earthly woman, Dante was aided by traditional associations in evoking simultaneously these meanings, which are all important in his *Comedy*.

The rose of the *Comedy* is, of course, far more than a borrowed symbol. No earlier writer had attempted to express through a single rose the diversity of meanings associated with that flower. None had demonstrated the poetic genius needed for such an achievement, nor had any yet succeeded in fully reconciling such seemingly disparate qualities as carnal and spiritual love. Further, Dante expressed the traditional meanings in an individual way by merging them with per-

[15] Bernard, Abbot of Clairvaux, *The Steps of Humility,* tr. George Bosworth Burch (Cambridge, Mass., 1940), pp. 77–81, 245–46.

sonal meanings derived from his particular experience. Dante's love for Beatrice, like man's love for woman, finds its ultimate goal in God, and Dante's soul, like Everyman's, is led by grace from the dark wood of sense to the sunlit rose of spirit. Through this reconciliation of traditional with personal meanings Dante has given religious teaching immediate relevance to the individual life and at the same time has given personal experience transcendent significance in eternity.

Comprehension of the personal transfigured in the universal was not attained easily. The rose is, in one sense, the flower of Beatrice, but of Beatrice exalted in eternal glory beyond the mortal woman Dante had known. Dante's love for Beatrice led him to his love for God, but it was many years before he fully understood the religious implications of his early love. Moreover, this understanding was prepared for not only by private experience but also by the intellectual climate in which he lived. For during the late thirteenth century the forms and motifs of secular love songs were becoming stale and standardized, and were in addition being applied with increasing frequency to religious celebrations of the Virgin. The combination of triteness with a growing awareness of conflict between courtly love and religion made essential a renewal of feeling along altered lines. In Italy Guido Guinizelli, founder of the *dolce stil nuovo*, set out to achieve this renewal through effecting an adequate harmony between mortal and immortal love. He introduced the idea that a beloved woman could symbolize an angelic intelligence,[16] and in his "Al cor gentil ripara sempre Amore" maintained that earthly love is an attribute of the noble heart, an exalted emotion akin to the adoration of God.

In the *Purgatorio* Dante would hail Guinizelli as his father in poetry. In the *Vita Nuova* he paid tribute to Guinizelli's ode: "Amore e cor gentil sono una cosa / Siccom 'il Saggio in suo dittato pone" (*VN* XX, *Son.* X: "Love and the gentle

[16] Karl Vossler, *Die philosophischen Grundlagen zum "Süssen neun Stil"* (Heidelberg, 1904), p. 63.

heart are one same thing, / Even as the wise man in his ditty saith."—Dante Gabriel Rossetti). More important, the *Vita Nuova* added new levels of meaning to the doctrines it adopted. While the poem's principal theme is Dante's rebirth through love to a noble conception of earthly life, the envisioned transfiguration of Beatrice after her death forecasts the role she was later to play as guide to his ultimate vision of God:

> Oltre la spera, che più larga gira,
> Passa il sospiro ch' esce del mio core:
> Intelligenza nuova, che l'Amore
> Piangendo mette in lui, pur su lo tira.
>
> (*VN* XLI, *Son.* XXV)

> Beyond the sphere which spreads to widest space
>   Now soars the sigh that my heart sends above;
>   A new perception born of grieving Love
> Guideth it upward the untrodden ways.
>
> —Dante Gabriel Rossetti

Guinizelli had united the courtly love pattern of devotion to an exalted woman with his own conception of earthly love as the product of a noble heart aspiring to a still nobler object. And Dante has carried this synthesis yet another step towards the final reconciliation between man's love and God. No longer perceived even in her life as an attainable object of desire, the beloved woman has in her death become a transcendent object of worship. Moreover, it is his quest for a wholly spiritual Beatrice that will in the end lead Dante to the rose whose petals enfold alike the immediate object of his love and the ultimate object of all love.

For the *Divine Comedy* is at once the fulfillment of the *Vita Nuova* and of the exaltation of woman that characterizes courtly love. Behind the apotheosis of Beatrice, seated in glory on the heavenly rose, lie generations of courtly poets praising their beloveds in the highest terms they know. Behind it also in the life of Dante lie years of trial and error expended in the search for the true meaning of his love. Other loves for Dante have temporarily darkened her image: the Lady Philosophy has appealed to his intellectual faculties and Pietra has entrammeled him in hopeless bondage to a lower passion. But these ladies themselves turn out to have been indispensable precursors of his return to Beatrice with a full understanding of her worth. The Lady Philosophy has shown him the place of reason as handmaiden to the revelation Beatrice is to be. Pietra, whose image in the *Canzoniere* is related to stone and winter cold, has marked the contrast between irrational bondage and the fructifying love that ultimately blossoms in a sunlit rose.

Straying from the true way shortly after Beatrice's death, Dante has followed his false images deep into the dismal wood of the *Comedy*'s opening cantos. From this error and confusion it is his former love for Beatrice that makes him worthy of salvation and the guidance of Beatrice that becomes the immediate means to that salvation. It is Beatrice who entreats Vergil to lead Dante through Hell and Purgatory and who herself leads him through Heaven once he had been made fit to meet her. Her first appearance to him in the Earthly Paradise after the purging of his soul from sin serves at once as counterpart and fulfillment of the *Vita Nuova*:

> questi fu tal nella sua vita nuova
> virtualmente, ch' ogni abito destro
> fatto averebbe in lui mirabil prova.
>
> . . . .
>
> Sì tosto come in su la soglia fui
> di mia seconda etade, e mutai vita,
> questi si tolse a me. . .
>
> . . . .
>
> Tanto giù cadde, che tutti argomenti
> alla salute sua eran già corti,
> fuor che mostrargli le perdute genti.
>
> Per questo visitai l' uscio dei morti.
>
> (*Purg.* XXX, 115–39)

this man was such, potentially, in his young life
   that every good disposition
   might have come to marvelous fruition;

      .   .   .   .

As soon as I was on the threshold
   of my second age, and changed life,
   he abandoned me, . . .

      .   .   .   .

He fell so low that all means
   for his salvation would have been unavailing
   except to show him the lost people.

Therefore, I visited the portal of the dead.   —H. R. Huse

In the *Vita Nuova* Dante had been reborn through love in earthly life and here through the same power is to be born again in spirit. From him unworthy, Beatrice's image had been taken and he had gone astray; to him now worthy, Beatrice is returned and he is to be led by love to a true vision of her essence embodied in the rose of ultimate Love.

Beatrice's guidance ceases only at the foot of the rose. Leaving a regenerated Dante to the care of St. Bernard, she returns to her true place in heavenly glory and hence enters the mystic vision she herself has made possible. The rose of heaven is far more than the symbol of a glorified Beatrice; she occupies one petal of the multifoliate flower that transcends her. But of this flower she is a part and the part that has most immediately affected Dante. For it is through comprehension of his love for her that he has come to comprehend that heavenly love of which she was a temporal manifestation:

     . . . gli occhi su levai,
       e vidi lei che si facea corona,
       riflettendo da sè gli eterni rai.

         .   .   .   .

   "O donna, in cui la mia speranza vige,
      e che soffristi per la mia salute
      in Inferno lasciar le tue vestige;

di tante cose, quante io ho vedute,
　　dal tuo potere e dalla tua bontate
　　riconosco la grazia e la virtute."

(*Par.* XXXI, 70–72, 79–84)

. . . I lifted up my eyes
　　and saw her, making herself a crown
　　and reflecting from herself the eternal rays.

.　　.　　.　　.

"O lady in whom my hope is strong,
　　you who for my salvation endured
　　to leave your footprints in Hell,
In all the things that I have seen
　　I recognize the grace and the virtue
　　of your power and goodness."　　　—H. R. Huse

In this important sense the rose is Beatrice's flower and, in effect, the flower of mortal love revealed as symbol and agent of the immortal. The apotheosis of Beatrice, finally perceived in her true glory in the Empyrean, is the supreme apotheosis of medieval woman:

La bellezza ch' io vidi si trasmoda
　　non pur di là da noi, ma certo io credo
　　che solo il suo fattor tutta la goda

.　　.　　.　　.

ma or convien che mio seguir desista
　　più retro a sua bellezza, poetando,
　　come all' ultimo suo ciascuno artista.

(*Par.* XXX, 19–21, 31–33)

The beauty that I saw transcends not only
　　all measure of ours, but I believe
　　that only its Maker enjoys it wholly.

.　　.　　.　　.

but now my pursuit which has followed
　　her beauty in my poetry must stop
　　as every artist at his utmost.　　　—H. R. Huse

The love of woman, that had begun as a secular rival to the love of God, has become the most immediate means for the transmission of that love to man. The rose of carnal and adulterous courtly love has finally been identified with the mystic symbol of the soul's marriage to its God and with the flower of the saints, the Virgin, Paradise, and Christ.

As flower of Divine Love, the rose is more complicated. In order to express as much of spiritual truth as possible, Dante adopted for his *Comedy* the allegorical method of scriptural interpretation standard in his day. Theologians had long believed that behind the words of Scripture lay complex spiritual truths, and by the time of Aquinas four levels of meaning were elaborated: literal, allegorical, moral, and anagogical. On the literal level things or events were delineated, on the allegorical level those things or events represented aspects of Christ's mission to humanity, on the moral level they were expressions of the meaning of Christianity for the inner life of man, and on the anagogical, symbolic of God's eternal glory. That Dante transformed this method of interpretation into a new method of literary creation is evident from his *Epistle to Can Grande*. In it he explicitly states that the whole *Comedy* is to be understood in terms of the four theological levels of meaning.[17] And in her comprehensive study, *Symbolism in Medieval Thought* (Yale, 1927), Helen Flanders Dunbar has shown with what remarkable intricacy the various parts of the *Comedy* have been so integrated as to bear out the fourfold pattern in its relation to Dante, Christ, man's salvation, and God. There is no reason to believe that at the very end and climax of his poem Dante suddenly abandoned this carefully developed method. On the contrary, an interpretation of the rose in terms of the four theological meanings turns out to be both consistent and illuminating.

[17] *Dantis Alagherii Epistolae,* ed. Paget Toynbee (Oxford, 1920), pp. 173–74. Dante's definitions of the four levels are essentially those to be found in St. Thomas Aquinas, *Summa Theologica,* Pars. I, qu. 1, art. 10.

Literally the flower is an image of Paradise. It appears in the Empyrean as a gigantic white rose illumined by the sun. On the separate petals are the saints and on the highest petal nearest to the sun is the Virgin, queen of this realm. The actual substance of Dante's vision, then, is the whole company of the Church Triumphant in its eternal abode:

> In forma dunque di candida rosa
> mi si mostrava la milizia santa,
> che nel suo sangue Cristo fece sposa.
>
> *(Par.* XXXI, 1–3)

> In the form then of a white rose
> the holy company which Christ with his blood
> made his spouse showed itself to me.   —H. R. Huse

And this vision is appropriately crowned by the Virgin in her position as type of the Church, Christ's spouse: "la Regina, / cui questo regno è suddito e devoto" *(Par.* XXXI, 116–17: ". . . the Queen, / to whom this realm is loyal and devoted." —H. R. Huse).

On the allegorical level the rose is symbolic of Christ's mission to humanity. It represents the spiritual transfiguration not only of Church but of Empire, and both of these in Dante's view were sanctioned by Christ to guide mankind along the road he designated. The temporal Church as the mystical union of all mankind in the Body of Christ, and the ultimate transfiguration of the blessed followers of Christ in the eternal Church Triumphant were good Catholic doctrines. But in symbolizing the eternal triumph of Empire as well as Church, Dante was departing from orthodoxy. Since politics was of major importance to him, it is not surprising to find the entire *Comedy* suffused with his political opinions and the rose of heaven tinged with his political theory.[18]

---

[18] Cf. Edmund Gardner, *Dante's Ten Heavens* (Westminster, 1900), pp. 273–75. Gardner points out that the rose symbolizes the triumph of Empire as well as Church, but he associates both triumphs with Mary rather than Christ.

The *De Monarchia* (Bk. II, chs. 12–13) had expressed Dante's particular belief that the medieval Empire was a continuation of the Roman Empire, and that Christ gave divine sanction to both through his birth and death under Roman authority. There was a hint in the *Purgatorio* of the political meaning to be expressed by the rose:

> Qui sarai tu poco tempo silvano,
> e sarai meco, senza fine, cive
> di quella Roma onde Cristo è Romano.
>
> (*Purg.* XXXII, 100–2)

> You will be for a while a forest dweller
> and then you will be with me forever a citizen
> of that Rome in which Christ is a Roman.
>
> —H. R. Huse

In the vision of the rose itself analogies make apparent the symbol's significance as the culmination in eternity of a true political leadership on earth. Dante has passed "di Fiorenza in popol giusto e sano" (XXXI, 39: "from Florence / to a people just and sane"—H. R. Huse), for he felt that Florence had gone astray for want of true civil guidance by the emperor, whose powers the pope had usurped. Further, the saints in glory are "i gran patrici di questo imperio giustissimo e pio" (XXXII, 116–17: "the great patricians / of this most just and devout empire"—H. R. Huse), and the Virgin is "Augusta" (XXXII, 119). By uniting the apotheosis of Empire with that of Church, Dante's rose suggests his belief, also expressed in the *De Monarchia* (Bk. III, chs. 1–16), that the two should function as coequal guides to man in their respective temporal and spiritual spheres. Beyond this the flower expresses the divine triumph of Christ's mission through the triumph of the media he authorized to carry on his work.

In some ways the mother of Christ was a more immediate force than Church or Empire in the salvation of the individual soul. On the moral level the rose is primarily Mary's flower. Here it symbolizes the spiritual love that brings about salvation in the human heart. Mary's importance in imparting this love to man had been heavily stressed during the thirteenth century, especially by St. Bernard, whom Dante admired. First, as Christ's mother she had been quite literally the means of God's manifestation to humanity, as Dante's rose suggests:

> Nel ventre tuo si raccese l' amore
>   per lo cui caldo nell' eterna pace
>   così è germinato questo fiore.
>
> (*Par.* XXXIII, 7–9)

> Within thy womb was rekindled the love
>   through whose warmth this flower
>   has blossomed in eternal peace.   —H. R. Huse

Second, she was regarded as a great figure of mercy, intercessor in heaven between man and God. As such, Mary was man's chief source of grace and hence salvation, a conception Dante follows in making her the ultimate principle in his quest for redemption.

It is Mary who in the beginning procures the grace Beatrice bears to Dante and who in the end makes possible his vision of God. Since she is the moving spirit behind his entire journey, it is not surprising that her rose should serve as the fulfillment of certain symbolic presagings encountered on his way. Fertility images in the *Comedy* are contrasted with those of sterility; sunlight and flowers characterize Divine Love, just as their antitheses—ice, rock, and a dark wood—express the perversion or absence of love. On first reception of the grace that will redeem him from sin, Dante makes this comparison:

> Quali i fioretti dal notturno gelo
>   chinati e chiusi, poi che il sol gl' imbianca,
>   si drizzan tutti aperti in loro stelo:
>
> tal mi fec' io, di mia virtute stanca.   (*Inf.* II, 127–30)

As little flowers, bent down and closed by the frost of night,
    stand up, all open on their stems,
    when the sun comes back to warm and brighten them,

so I revived my failing strength.   —H. R. Huse

But he can enter no gardens until he has passed through Hell
and Purgatory.

The Garden of Eden, crowning the purgatorial mount, is
the realm wherein mankind has reattained primal innocence
or natural perfection and is ready for the ascent to God.
Christ's garden in the Stellar Heaven, crowning the paradisal
spheres, serves as celestial counterpart to Eden. Here the soul
has attained spiritual perfection, and the promise of redemption after the fall from Eden is fulfilled.[19] The Earthly Paradise and Stellar Heaven are the most evident precursors of
the Empyrean. Each is presented in the form of a sunlit
garden, and each marks an important stage in the soul's journey towards salvation. Just as Eden was a forerunner of
Christ's garden, Christ's garden in turn is an adumbration of
the Empyrean, for here the company of saints appears in
symbolic triumph and the Virgin blossoms as a rose beneath
Christ's sun. The Empyrean itself is tempered to Dante's
vision by first emerging as a river of light with saints as
flowers blooming on its banks. But the rivers and flowers, like
the visions hitherto, are "di lor vero ombriferi prefazii" (*Par.*
XXX, 78: ". . . the shadowy prefaces of the reality"—H. R.
Huse). The scene, changing shape, becomes the final flower
of Paradise, where the souls of the blessed, who appeared symbolically in lesser heavenly spheres, have their eternal abode:

> così mi si cambiaro in maggior feste
> li fiori e le faville, sì ch' io vidi
> ambo le corti del ciel manifeste.
>
> (*Par.* XXX, 94–96)

[19] *Ibid.,* p. 189.

>   thus the flowers and the sparks changed
>   into a greater festival, so that I saw,
>   made manifest, both courts of Heaven.
>   —H. R. Huse

The heavenly rose is the reality of which all else has been imperfect shadow. It is the culmination not only of its most apparent precursors, Eden and Christ's garden, but of all Paradise as well. The references throughout the *Paradiso* to the saints as flowers, Paradise as a garden, and God as the eternal Gardener bear out metaphorically the explicit meaning of the poem.[20] Since Paradise is itself the culmination and goal of the created universe, Mary, as the highest of created beings, is fitly throned in glory at the summit of the rose illumined by the immediate light of God:

>   Io vidi sopra lei tanta allegrezza
>   piover . . .
>
>   .   .   .   .
>
>   che quantunque io avea visto davante,
>   di tanta ammirazion non mi sospese,
>   nè mi mostrò di Dio tanto sembiante.
>   (*Par.* XXXII, 88–89, 91–93)
>
>   I saw such joy rain upon her
>
>   .   .   .   .
>
>   that nothing I had seen before
>   had kept me suspended in such wonder
>   or revealed to me such likeness to God.
>   —H. R. Huse

Since she is the dispenser to man of the divine grace that brings about salvation, the rose on the moral level, expressing the redemption of Dante's soul from sin, is unquestionably Mary's flower.

Above the Virgin there is only God. The rose on the ana-

[20] See esp. *Par.* X, 91–93; XII, 19–20; XIX, 22–24; XXII, 46–57; XXVI, 64–66; XXVIII, 115–17.

gogical level is the flower of God. In its relationship with the divine sun, it is intended as a symbolic expression of the mystery of the created universe. In the *Primum Mobile* Dante had had a vision of the nine concentric planetary spheres circling a still center of intensest light that represented the Unmoved Mover of the universe:

> La natura del mondo, che quieta
> il mezzo, e tutto l' altro intorno move,
> quinci comincia come da sua meta.
>
> . . . .
>
> Luce ed amor d' un cerchio lui comprende.
>
> . . . .
>
> E come il tempo tenga in cotal testo
> le sue radici e negli altri le fronde,
> omai a te puot' esser manifesto.
>   (*Par.* XXVII, 106–8, 112, 118–20)
>
> The order of the universe, which holds its center
> motionless and moves all the rest around,
> begins here as from its starting point,
>
> . . . .
>
> Light and love enclose it in a sphere
>
> . . . .
>
> and how Time has its roots in such a vessel
> and in the others its leaves,
> now can be manifest to you.   —H. R. Huse

This seems an anticipation of his vision in the Empyrean of a white rose whose petals form concentric circles, illumined from the center outwards by the sun:

> Lume è lassù, che visible face
> lo Creatore a quella creatura,
>
> . . . .
>
> e si distende in circular figura
> in tanto che la sua circonferenza
> sarebbe al sol troppo larga cintura.
>
> . . . .

E se l' infimo grado in se raccoglie
   sì grande lume, quant' è la larghezza
   di questa rosa nell' estreme foglie?

(*Par.* XXX, 100–5, 115–17)

There is a light up there which makes the Creator
   visible to that creature,

.   .   .   .

And it extends in the form of a circle,
   the circumference of which
   would be too large a belt for the sun.

.   .   .   .

and if the lowest row gathers to itself
   so much light, how great is the width
   of this rose in its outermost petals!   —H. R. Huse

As the created universe is the material expression in time of the love of its Creator, so the rose is the spiritual expression in eternity of that Divine Love. The flower that could not exist without the sun is the supreme manifestation of the highest power in the cosmos.

With the vision of the eternal rose deriving life from the divine sun Dante has approached the end of his journey. He has experienced the first stage of mystic contemplation as defined by St. Bernard. Beyond this there remains the immediate vision of the Trinity, greater but less expressible than the vision of the rose. Raising his eyes to the sun itself, Dante sees God:

Nel suo profondo vidi che s' interna,
   legato con amore in un volume,
   ciò che per l' universo si squaderna;

sustanzia ed accidenti, e lor costume,
   quasi conflati insieme per tal modo,
   che ciò ch' io dico è un semplice lume.

(*Par.* XXXIII, 85–90)

In its depths I saw contained, bound with love
   in one volume, what is scattered
   on leaves throughout the world—

substances and accidents and their modes
   as if fused together in such a way
   that what I speak of is a single light.   —H. R. Huse

Within this simple flame lies the solution to life's mystery. Love is the end as it was the beginning of Dante's journey and of all that is. Although the nature of Divine Love is ineffable, Dante's integration of sun and rose approaches as nearly as symbolism can the final expression of God's glory.

The sunlit rose that achieves so much marks at once the peak and the end of an era. A culmination of all earlier roses, Dante's flower had at last attained a symbolic harmony between the seeming dualities of sense and soul. But it had attained this harmony within a Catholic religious and social framework that was about to lose its all-embracing sway. The rose had derived its life from a universal, authoritarian tradition and had derived its form from the established method of interpreting that tradition. It was the last great literary bloom of the Middle Ages. Never was there again to be a method at once so systematic yet so indefinitely suggestive. Nor was there again to be a comprehensive symbol that relied so heavily on tradition in the synthesis of even private emotion. For with the Renaissance a new outlook arose with a new individualism that would permanently alter the future of symbols and roses. Although later writers—William Blake, James Joyce, or William Butler Yeats—would develop symbolic systems equal to Dante's in intricacy, their systems would be products of a humanistic orientation sufficiently distinct from Dante's to set their roses apart from his.

Nonetheless, the final flower of the *Comedy* was to be a major influence not only on subsequent Catholic symbolists but also on symbolists whose values and insights were re-mote from Dante's. Although this influence would be little felt in the Renaissance, or in the eighteenth or nineteenth centuries, it would reemerge as a factor of consequence in the symbolist writings of our time. For Dante's traditional symbolic method had given order, detachment, and universality to his private emotions of love and faith. And in contemporary society the need for bridging the gulf between private emotions and a now frequently alien world has been deeply felt. Modern symbolists, with their roots in the nineteenth century but attempting to broaden their romantic base, have taken from Dante as much of tradition as has been compatible with their more subjective creeds. In doing so, they have learned from his method a good deal about ways and means of uniting personal with public values in a single, multi-leveled symbol. Accordingly, when seeking to express a comprehensive vision of their complicated age, they have often returned to the medieval poet who was able to encompass all time and eternity in a sunlit rose.

3

THE

ROMANTIC

HERITAGE

When modern writers return to their medieval inheritance, they must do so from the perspective of romantic times. Dante had perfected a symbolic method that relies on tradition for the validity of its matter and manner. But the writers who followed him often lacked a stable, external orientation and so tended to rely on private perception or belief in organizing experience. From this new subjectivity a new type of symbolism developed, one which was ultimately to blend itself with that of Dante in the creation of contemporary symbols. It is true that the new symbolism developed only gradually. In the centuries immediately following Dante's, symbolic complexity was not prevalent in prose or poetry. Although literary roses blossomed throughout the Renaissance, those approaching the subtlety of genuine symbols were the exception, not the rule. However, the limited Renaissance flower cannot lightly be dismissed, for it is the most immediate ancestor of the romantic symbol. Largely lacking the objective background of Dante's rose, the rose of the sixteenth and seventeenth centuries was primarily a vehicle for subjective attitudes. And it is to the subjectivity of simple Renaissance metaphors that nineteenth- and twentieth-century symbols can trace their origins.

For symbolism is as much a matter of outlook as of method. While Dante's rose evolved from traditional Catholicism, the symbolist movement that developed in the nineteenth century evolved from an idealistic romanticism stemming in part from forces working in the Renaissance. Although these forces in themselves were not provocative of symbols, they helped to pave the way to romantic symbolism. For instance, hand in hand with the gradual decline of the medieval Catholic orientation came an emphasis on man's temporal life which altered the tone of both religious and secular literature. The religious outlook shifted from contempt of the world and acceptance of authority to pursuit of Christian virtues for the betterment of mortal life and to encouragement of personal approaches to God. The secular outlook shifted from uneasy awareness of religion to unhesitant delight in earthly beauties for their own sake freed of the necessity for subordinating them to spiritual values or for elevating them to spiritual heights. As a result, poets of the Renaissance were able to celebrate a world or a flower in terms of their own emotions without benefit or hindrance of external creeds.

The forces promoting the new individualism were of course manifold and are well known. Not only the rise of Protestant religious attitudes but also the growth of classical knowledge, commerce, and, most basically, the middle class contributed strongly to Renaissance humanism. Since these forces, later carried to far greater lengths, were also in large part to mold romantic idealism, it is small wonder that the simple Renaissance flower bears in itself the seeds of the complex romantic rose. This does not mean at all that literature began anew after the conclusion of the Middle Ages. The religious rose, for instance, while becoming often Protestant, continued to express those fundamental meanings which are shared alike by all the Christian faiths. The secular rose, while becoming almost wholly a-religious, retained its old associations with beauty, love, and spring. But the Renaissance, indebted to its own forerunners, did contribute to the flower of a past tradition the distinctive color that, with modifications, it has retained throughout the centuries down to the present day.

Specifically, the rose in English Renaissance poetry carried over from the Middle Ages its secular role as metaphor of love. But an increased knowledge of classical literature brought about some alteration even on this level. Familiar with the whole range of Latin erotic poetry and less distrustful of natural feelings than before, Renaissance poets often sang of love in terms more frankly sensual than was common in the Middle Ages. The inevitable rose of cheeks, lips, breath, or over-all physical beauty of the women beloved began to appear in poems of undisguised sexual content. Although the sexual rose reached its height in the lyrics of the Cavalier poets, it was already much in vogue in the age of Elizabeth. Generally a cliché, it sometimes received more notable treatment, as for example in Spenser's Bower of Bliss. Here Spenser's allegory recalls the *Roman de la Rose* in setting and method, but significantly indicts the sensuality Lorris exalted. In fact, the traditional love garden presided over by Genius appears in Spenser not as a setting for idealized love but rather as a warning against the lures of lust.

While Spenser's moralistic attitude was not the norm for the age, his use of the rose as a sexual metaphor was. The song of the rose heard in his Bower expresses a recurrent Renaissance motif:[1]

> Gather therefore the Rose, whilest yet is prime,
> For soone comes age, that will her pride deflowre,
> Gather the Rose of love, whilest yet is time,
> Whilest loving thou mayst loved be with equal crime.
> (*Faerie Queene*, Bk. II, Canto 75)

In its role as reminder that time flies and should therefore be

---

[1] H. J. C. Grierson, in *Cross Currents in English Literature of the Seventeenth Century* (London, 1929), p. 53, points out that Spenser's song is a translation from Tasso. Ronsard's well-known ode "A Cassandre" is of course in the same tradition.

quickly made the most of, the flower traces its lineage back through the ages at least as far as the apocryphal Wisdom of Solomon, 2:8: "Let us crown ourselves with rosebuds before they be withered." But during its Renaissance vogue, the *carpe diem* rose was, more directly than ever before, related to seduction. Repeatedly making its appearance in the lyrics of major and minor poets, the rose of sexual seduction embraced alike Spenser's moralistic song, Herrick's cheerful "Gather ye rosebuds," and Waller's wistful "Go Lovely Rose." The well-known lines from Shakespeare's *A Midsummer Night's Dream* are only typical of their day:

> But earthlier happy is the rose distill'd
> Than that which withering on the virgin thorn
> Grows, lives, and dies in single blessedness.

Nor is sexual love the only secular context in which the popular rose is found. By way of heraldry it had become the flower of Tudor England when Henry VII united the red rose of Lancaster with the white rose of York.[2] As such it appears in Renaissance lyrics as the flower of Elizabeth, doubly appropriate to her who was both a woman and England's queen. Spenser's *Daphnaida* refers to Elizabeth as "the rose, the glorie of the day," and Sir John Davies's "To the Rose" (from *Hymns of Astraea*) concludes with an encomium:

> R ose of the Queene of Love belov'd;
> E ngland's great Kings, divinely mov'd,
> G ave Roses in their banner;
> I t shewed that Beautie's Rose indeed

---

[2] The use of the rose as a royal device or badge appears to have been first introduced by Eleanor of Provence, wife of Henry III, in the twelfth century; see J. L. André, "Antiquarian Notes on the Rose," *The Archaeological Journal*, LII (1895), 217. The origin of the red rose on the arms of the house of Lancaster is traceable to the Count of Egmont, head of the family of Lancaster, who discovered the device during a campaign in Provence around 1277. The house of York chose a white rose out of contrariety when York and Lancaster became opposing factions in the mid-fifteenth century; see J. L. A. Loiseleur-Deslongchamps, *La Rose, Son Histoire, Sa Culture, Sa Poésie* (Paris, 1844), pp. 67–68.

N ow in this age them should succeed,
A nd raigne in more sweet manner.

Then Herrick, who was partial to roses, derived further roles for them from the classics. In "Mr. Robert Herrick, his farewell unto poetry," he relates his favorite flower to wine: "Thus crowned with rosebuds, sack, thou mad'st me fly / Like fire-drakes, yet didst me no harm thereby." And in "To His Muse" he bestows upon his poetic inspiration the notable title, "Muse of Roses."

Further, the beauty of the flower itself, implicit in its frequent appearance as metaphor of earthly values, was sometimes enlarged upon directly. Old as the classics and abundant throughout the Middle Ages, the rose as queen of the flowers reappears in such typical Renaissance lyrics as Thomas Howell's "The Rose" (from *The Arbor of Amity*): "In time of pleasant year / Of all the pleasant flowers in June / The red rose hath no peer." More extensive and original treatment of the flower's sensuous beauty is found in the conclusion to Sir Thomas Browne's *Garden of Cyrus*. Here the dullness of the senses in sleep is pointed up by their insensibility even to the roses traditionally strewn on Cleopatra's bed: "Nor will the sweetest delight of gardens afford much comfort in sleep; wherein the dulness of that sense shakes hands with delectable odours; and though in the Bed of Cleopatra, can hardly with any delight raise up the ghost of a Rose." And Shakespeare's frequent roses, whether they appear as similes or genuine flowers, express the poet's very real awareness of their natural qualities: "Nor did I wonder at the lily's white / Nor praise the deep vermilion in the rose. . . ."

All of these happy associations—love, wine, poetry, natural beauty—were in the Renaissance as in the past the secular rose's chief attributes. At the same time, the versatile Renaissance flower, like its classical predecessor, served now and then as a sober image of inevitable decay. Christopher Marlowe had cheerfully written, "Come live with me and be my love . . . / And I will make thee beds of roses." But this offer Sir Walter Raleigh declined in "The Nymph's Reply to the Passionate Shepherd": "Thy gowns, thy shoes, thy beds of roses . . . / Soon break, soon wither, soon forgotten." And Edmund Waller's "Go Lovely Rose," although a seduction poem, shows greater concern with time than with love in its somber tone and final lines:

> Then die, that she
> The common fate of all things rare
> May read in thee;
> How small a part of time they share
> That are so wondrous sweet and faire!

This note of pessimism, more prevalent in Waller's century than in Raleigh's, produces in the religious roses of the later Renaissance a haunting melancholy not to be found in simpler lyrics of secular joys.

For devotional poetry reached a high level in the troubled seventeenth century, as it had not in Elizabeth's time. And religious poets, being aware of the rose's secular roles, often evoked the temporal flower to express the vanity of temporal joys. William Drummond of Hawthornden, for example, in the opening sonnet of his *Urania,* employs a secular rose to disparage the values that rose represents:

> Ah! when I had what most I did admire,
> And seen of life's delights the last extremes,
> I found all but a rose hedged with a briar,
> A nought, a thought, a show of mocking dreams.

Henry Vaughan in "The Garland" repudiates the traditional festal crown of roses for eternity's unfading garland: "who spares them here shall find / A garland, where comes neither rain nor wind." And George Herbert, treating a similar theme in "Virtue," chooses the rose to point up the evanescence of moral beauty:

> Sweet rose, whose hue angrie and brave
> Bids the rash gazer wipe his eye;
> Thy root is ever in its grave,
>   And thou must die.

The rose was also the traditional symbol of Mary, Christ, Paradise, and Divine Love. But devotional poets of the seventeenth century made far less use of its Christian meanings than had their medieval predecessors. This is perhaps because it had been a predominantly secular flower in the early Renaissance and therefore lay ready to hand as a natural image of secular follies. It is perhaps because the widespread classical revival had reinforced the rose's position as an emblem of temporal values. It is not because the medieval religious meanings had vanished. For throughout the Renaissance occasional Christian roses blossomed, showing that the old associations with Christ, Heaven, and the Virgin were still alive. William Dunbar, Robert Herrick, Richard Crashaw, and Giles Fletcher, to mention only a few, reveal a sporadic interest in simple spiritual roses.[3] And in one or two late Renaissance poems a religious flower even attains the now almost forgotten complexity of a symbol.

Henry Vaughan's "Peace," describing Paradise, contains one such symbolic rose:

> There above noise and danger
> Sweet peace sits crowned with smiles,
> And one born in a manger
> Commands the beauteous files;
>
>   .   .   .   .
>
> If thou canst get but thither,
> There grows the flower of peace,
> The rose that cannot wither,
> Thy fortress and thy ease.

[3] The rose in Giles Fletcher's "Christ's Triumph and Victory," though nonsymbolic, is notable. Throughout the poem roses appear either as similes for Christ's spiritual beauties, as floral adornments of his earthly or heavenly paths, or as worldly temptations.

In context this rose suggests not only refuge from sorrow in the peace of eternity but also Christ's love, which procured that peace for man, and the absolute beauty of all holiness as it appeared to Vaughan. In Andrew Marvell's poem, "The Nymph Complaining for the Death of Her Fawn," still more intriguing hints occur. For while it is a secular poem, the roses and lilies in which the fawn lived before he was shot by wanton troopers seem to carry Christian associations with love, purity, and martyrdom, as well as earthly associations with innocence, beauty, and joy:

> Upon the roses it would feed,
> Until its lips e'en seemed to bleed;
> And then to me 'twould boldly trip,
> And print those roses on my lip.
> But all its chief delight was still
> On roses thus itself to fill;
> And its pure virgin limbs to fold
> In whitest sheets of lilies cold.
> Had it lived long, it would have been
> Roses without, lilies within.

The flowers' traditional meanings, both secular and Christian, add much to the poem's richness. Not only do the nymph's love and grief for her fawn gain in significance thereby, but the fawn becomes a suggestive symbol of all finite and infinite goodness needlessly destroyed by an insensate world.

It is true that symbols such as Vaughan's and Marvell's were unusual for an age in which the extended metaphor or conceit was the more prevalent mode of poetic expression. Perhaps for this very reason they gain in importance as indications of a universal tendency to use symbols to express ideas too vast for ordinary words. But be that as it may, the content of the two poems is typical of the age and illustrates both the fact that the rose's religious meanings had not been submerged in the Renaissance and that these meanings in a Protestant country had gained elasticity. In other words, the religious poets, like their secular contemporaries, bequeathed to posterity not a new, complex symbolic form but a new outlook and new subject matter that would in its development help to create the climate in which the new form would later grow. For during the Renaissance the heritage of classical roses with their frankly sensual meanings was introduced into English literature, while the religious rose in becoming Protestant became relevant to aspects of personal, spiritual experience other than those established in medieval Catholic tradition. The simple but versatile Renaissance flower, blossoming beyond the pale of the Church, had become the vehicle for private experience that it has chiefly continued to be.

Roses as well as symbolic expression were out of fashion in the rationalistic stream of eighteenth-century literature. What few there were seldom even metaphoric and then were usually the hackneyed flowers of cheeks or lips. But side by side with eighteenth-century rationalism persisted a minor literary stream maintaining the importance of emotion and imaginative creation. Gathering force, this stream burst forth towards the end of the century in the romantic reaction against neoclassicism. And with the reassertion of emotional intensity, the Renaissance heritage made itself felt. Similar to their Renaissance predecessors in proclaiming the importance of human experience for its own sake, romantic poets similarly stressed the lyrical effusion of personal feelings. The feelings were different because the times were different, but the differences were in degree more often than in kind. For it was essentially on the Renaissance faith in the validity of the individual's private emotions that the romantics built their more uneasy, more intense and anxious world.

The differences in degree created symbols where metaphors had once prevailed. In many ways the nineteenth century was more disturbing to the artist than preceding times and so demanded a method of expression equal to the task of coping with an intricate distress. Industry, for instance, was rapidly expanding, and with it cities, factories, poverty, and wealth. The middle class was therefore prospering and spreading the contagion of commercial goals. In addition conformity, which thrives in middle-class societies, was threatening to bestow upon the masses of humanity a single set of moral as well as material values. Such an atmosphere was hardly the most likely to encourage either the intangible qualities of art or the liberty of conscience essential to the artist. Released from the rationalism of the eighteenth century, the artist found himself engulfed by the commercialism of his own. Appalled by the insensitivity of his era, he followed a dissenting course that took him first away from cities where the industrial class held power and then away from concourse with society at large. Inevitably he had to develop private values to fill the emptiness created by the failure of his world. And as the outer failure became more and more inclusive, the values he created became more and more complex.

The early romantics, fleeing social excesses, often looked first to the unspoiled countryside for the fundamental values they could not find in urban centers. Nature, as the enduring background of human life and the inspiration of various emotions, tended to dominate their quest for values that would be in accord with human sentiment. Creating or confirming the poet's mood, nature itself was a repeated subject for poetry, and with the emphasis on natural glories came a revival of the poetic rose. Sometimes its own beauty was sufficient subject for comment, as in Wordsworth's "Lovely is the rose" or Keats's "coming musk-rose full of dewy wine." More often its loveliness made it the appropriate metaphor for one of its traditional meanings—love, beauty, joy, or mutability. Burns's "My love is like a red, red rose" expresses his beloved's beauty through evoking the flower's; Keats's "glut thy sorrow on a morning rose" employs the flower to convey the theme of beauty's evanescence. Such roses as these, and there were many like them, are simple and not particularly original. Nevertheless, they are important indications of a state of mind that led directly to the growth of symbols.

For in the natural universe romantic poets often sought more than metaphorical enhancement of subjective moods. The same quest for basic, nonmaterial values that motivated their return to nature in the first place, motivated their pursuit of spiritual visions that would at once include and transcend natural glories. Since the progress of science, which had aided industry, had at the same time undermined the Christian faith, some poets searched the beauties of nature for a faith that they could reconcile with current knowledge. The rose, long the focus of earthly emotions or of traditional Christian beliefs, came more and more to be the focus of unorthodox transcendental longings. In the process it assumed new personal meanings often overshadowing its natural beauties and sometimes transplanting it entirely from the soil of actual gardens to the soil of symbolic dreams. Spontaneous emotional responses to a rose, begun in the Renaissance and revived with romanticism, became increasingly intricate responses to natural or supernatural realms in which that rose was only incidentally a flower.

The gradual development of flower into symbol began early in the romantic era. Feeling in nature transcendent powers akin to those which animated their own hearts, and therefore adopting or creating a semimystical view of the cosmos, some romantics perceived in a flower the ultimate ordering of all things. Wordsworth, for instance, saw the primrose as a "lasting link in nature's chain / From highest heaven let down"; he derived from this vision an insight into the wondrous pattern of a pantheistic universe. And more important for the history of symbols, William Blake saw "a heaven in a wild flower"; he developed for the first time in English literature an intricate symbolic system in which a rose could become the expression of a personal mysticism. For Blake, who believed he "must create [his] own system or be enslaved by another man's," turned his back on all established tradition and fashioned of his private perceptions an elaborate semireligious outlook expressed through a private symbolic mythology.

Although not a recurrent symbol in Blake, the rose is central in one of his best and best-known poems. Since flower and poem are at least as complex as Blake's work in general tends to be, his becomes the first rose in English literature to embody an intricate system of thought. Deceptively simple in form and language, "The Sick Rose" is actually weighted with meaning and embraces some of the most basic convictions to be found in Blake's entire personal creed. It is, first and foremost, a sexual poem and has therefore inspired Freudian critics:

> O rose, thou art sick!
> The invisible worm
> That flies in the night
> In the howling storm,
>
> Has found out thy bed
> Of crimson joy,
> And his dark secret love
> Does thy life destroy.

Interpreted in Freudian terms, the destruction of rose by worm in a night storm clearly suggests the violation of virginity. But while this interpretation is valid and approaches some portion of Blake's meaning, it is by no means the whole of the story and by itself can be misleading. For Blake's concern with the sexual act is inseparable from his outlook on society and morals. To him the rose is sick not because of sex as such but because of the world's warped sexual views.

The poem then must be understood in terms of Blake's larger vision of things. Believing in the basic goodness of man and in the basic harmony between man and the universe,

Blake believed that humanity's misery stemmed from a distorted conception of reality. The Church, for example, missing Christ's point, had promoted the notion of original sin and had followed this up with a system of ethics often corrupting to man's true original innocence. Based on reason and not imagination, the Christian moral values guiding Western society had fostered repression, sublimation, and self-doubt, all of which in turn had fostered human ills and human anguish. Clearly, in order to return to innocence and to the eternal harmony that is his birthright, man would have to achieve a liberation from "morality," including misguided sexual mores. Placed against this background, "The Sick Rose" suggests the contamination of natural love by the rational Christian moral view that regards unfettered love as evil. As such, the poem takes appropriate place among the *Songs of Experience* as an expression of the suffering awaiting a child who grows to awareness of the ways of the world. Because the symbols of rose and worm are suggestive of innocence drowned by experience, goodness distorted by social corruption, imagination stifled by reason, and eternity obscured by time, they become indefinitely suggestive of the manifold destructions of love by death in the realms of both sense and soul.

It happens that Blake's multifoliate rose was an isolated entity in his England, finding neither cousins nor heirs before the complex roses of Yeats and Joyce. Nevertheless, it was an expression of the same romantic impulse that was leading on the Continent to a widespread symbolist movement. More extreme in some ways than Blake, French symbolists in particular were soon to develop a symbolic method that would later be carried to England and unite with the method of Blake as a primary influence on modern symbols. For romantics on the Continent were, like the English, revolting from social and rational bonds in proclaiming the validity of private emotion, imagination, and art. German idealist philosophy, loosely interpreted in terms of a pervasive spiritual level of being, was gradually infiltrating literary circles throughout Europe. It gained artistic expression in the symbolic blue flower of the German Novalis,[4] it influenced Coleridge's doctrine of the shaping imagination,[5] and it provided for the French an alternative system to the positivist doctrines promulgated by Comte. The mystical writings of Boehme and Swedenborg were also being read. Blended with the works of German philosophy, they helped to provide intellectual backing for the poet's belief that the world he created in imaginative art was truer than the one apparent to his senses.

There was, then, evolving within romanticism a tendency to attribute a semimystical value to imaginative ideals. As the nineteenth century wore on, this tendency was intensified by the increasing recoil of the artist from the increasing entrenchment of the middle class. Going beyond Blake and his contemporaries, French writers of later decades led the way in a growing attempt to remove their art almost entirely from external social contexts and to direct it instead to the expression of a private religious idealism revealed to the inward gaze alone. Given these ends, it seems inevitable that they developed symbolism. The most adequate medium for suggesting the ineffable visions of religious mystics was after all

[4] Novalis's *Heinrich Von Ofterdingen* is dominated by a symbolic blue flower that reconciles the novel's themes on a basis of mystical idealism. The flower as symbol of the poet's dead beloved becomes symbolic of the inspiration of his work and hence of the spirit of poetry. Moreover, the poet's conception of poetry as an expression of ultimate reality associates his blue flower with the eternal mysteries of a pervasive divinity. In fact, on a smaller scale Novalis's blue flower does for romantic idealism what the white rose of Dante does for Catholic theology.

[5] In the *Biographia Literaria* (1817; London and New York, 1947), Coleridge discusses the relationship between his conception of imagination and the metaphysical conceptions of reality expressed by such idealist philosophers as Kant or Schelling. And the transcendental basis of Coleridge's doctrine of imagination is not unlike the theoretical basis of much French symbolist practice: "The primary Imagination I hold to be the living power and prime agent of all human perception, and as a repetition in the finite mind of the eternal act of creation in the infinite I AM" (pp. 145–46, 1947 ed.).

the most adequate medium for suggesting the personal visions of unorthodox but equally transported writers. Consequently French poets, like their medieval forebears, created a multi-leveled technic which could express many meanings and yet remain in the end indefinable. Of course, the Renaissance had driven an enduring wedge between the medieval era and all subsequent days, so that the second great symbolist movement in Western literature had to form new channels for its new subjective flow. Resembling the medieval symbolists in intricacy and indefiniteness, romantic symbolists differed in largely replacing outer traditions with a reliance on inner visions for their values and ideals. In doing so, they made symbolist methods applicable to private experience and thereby enriched for later writers the fading symbols of tradition with the fresh life of personal meaning.

Spiritual vision for the French poets often became inseparable from esthetic experience. Baudelaire, for example, had read Swedenborg. Deriving from him the doctrine of correspondences whereby all entities in the natural world have their supernatural counterparts, Baudelaire believed that the entities in his poems symbolized transcendent realities. Beyond this, he believed that these entities or symbols also corresponded to states of his own soul. Mallarmé, not content with mere correspondences, wished to communicate through symbols the pure ideal itself. He therefore became obsessed with the paradoxical attempt to express what was by its nature inexpressible. To Baudelaire, Mallarmé, and their successors the only realm of consequence became that of the semimystical ideal and the only activity of any importance that of discovering esthetic means for expressing insights that transcend ordinary words. Since the insights in question were private, the symbols tended to be obscure, but symbolists were not trying to enlighten the bourgeois world at large. For them, highly personal symbols gained sufficient validity from their presumed relation to an ideal level of being perceived by the perceptive through the visionary powers of their own souls.

Symbolism involved more than the use of symbols. For the expression of transcendent qualities in a poem the entire organization of sounds, moods, rhythms, ideas, and images was also significant. To Baudelaire a Paris scene, to Verlaine an evocative landscape, to Mallarmé the typographical pattern of words on a page could become symbolic of ideals. Most commonly, however, indefinitely suggestive concrete entities or symbols, supported by the surrounding context of the work, formed the foci of symbolist writings. Of course, a concrete image, in becoming the symbol of an ideality perceived in the writer's visionary soul, tended to lose touch with the sensuous qualities of its appearance to ordinary physical vision. Flowers that had grown in the gardens of cruder romantics as beautiful products of harmonious nature became for the symbolists mysterious indications of a superior, supersensuous ideal. As Mallarmé expressed it in his essay, *Variations sur un Sujet,* "Je dis: une fleur! et, hors de l'oubli où ma voix relègue aucun contour, en tant que quelque chose d'autre que les calices sus, musicalement se lève idée même et sauve, l'absente de tous bouquets" ("That is to say: the mere word *flower* creates an ideal flower obviously absent from all real bouquets, different from all known chalices, which rises up precisely because I forget, in its favor, every distinct outline"—Charles Mauron).[6]

Typical of symbols in general, the transcendental rose that is no kin to earthly blossoms was to become queen of the symbols as its earthly cousin was queen of flowers. And although it did not gain this stature overnight, its failings were distinctly important in determining its later strengths. To begin with, the rose was not notably popular among the early French symbolists. In Baudelaire's *Fleurs du Mal,*

[6] Translated by Mauron in a footnote to his introduction to Roger Fry's translation of Mallarmé's poems. —J. P. S.

despite the title, few flowers appear and almost no roses save for scattered metaphors of lust: "Le succube verdâtre et le rose lutin / T'ont-ils versé la peur et l'amour de leurs urnes" ("La Muse Malade": "Have the green lemure and the goblin red / Poured on thee love and terror from their urn?"—F. P. Sturm). Rimbaud employs no roses to speak of beyond that in the prose poem, "Fleurs," wherein a rose appears as one among many alchemical images: "des bouquets de satin blanc et de fines verges de rubis entourent la rose d'eau" ("bouquets of white satin and delicate stalks of rubies surround the water rose"—Wallace Fowlie). Verlaine uses occasional roses in his lyrics. Sometimes they suggest the beauty of life: "Chante dants le vent / Et cueille la rose!" ("Conseil Falot": "Sing back at the breeze / and go pick the rose!"—C. F. MacIntyre.); sometimes they enhance a mood: "Les roses étaient toutes rouges / Et les lierres étaient tout noirs" ("Spleen": "The roses they were all so red, / and the ivy was all black"—C. F. MacIntyre). But even in these instances the flower itself is little more than a rose, however suggestive the atmosphere it helps to create may be. Conspicuous by its neglect, the rose was most probably unpopular among the early symbolists because of the initial difficulty involved in divorcing it from its alliance with earthly beauties or with traditional Christian religious beliefs.

Mallarmé does attempt to make of the rose an ethereal symbol, but even this most abstract of symbolists generally fails to uproot the flower wholly from earthly soil. Instead it becomes in his work a symbol of conflicting attitudes towards the sensual and of his artistic inability to transform actuality into the ideality of his dreams. "La faute idéale de roses" ("The ideal lack of roses"—C. F. MacIntyre) of "L'Aprésmidi d'un Faune" symbolizes the sensual love that shares the shortcomings of all things earthly; and yet it is with sadness that the faun turns from imperfect longing to seek a loftier dream. On the other hand, sadness equally colors the sonnet, "Victorieusement fui le suicide beau," where the opposite situation occurs: the roses of imperfect love are accepted in place of an unattained ideal. Again, in the "Hérodiade" the sensual perfume of roses, like sensual love, is renounced for an ideal, while in "Surgi de la croupe et du bond" the impossibility of perfect love in the actual world is symbolized by the failure to blossom of "une rose dans les ténèbres" ("a rose in the dark"—J. P. S.).

The conflict expressed through these various roses was Mallarmé's own. "Las de l'amer repos" relates the rose directly to his personal self-doubts:

> Las de l'amer repos où ma paresse offense
> Une gloire pour qui jadis j'ai fui l'enfance
> Adorable des bois de roses sous l'azur
> Naturel, et plus las sept fois du pacte dur
> De creuser par veillée une fosse nouvelle
> Dans le terrain avare et froid de ma cervelle,
> Fossoyeur sans pitié pour la stérilité,
> —Que dire à cette Aurore, ô Rêves, visité
> Par les roses, quand, peur de ses roses livides,
> Le vaste cimitière unira les trous vides?

> Tired of the bitter repose where my idleness hurts
> A glory for which I once fled the adorable
> Childhood of roses and woods beneath nature's
> Azure, and seven times more tired of the harsh
> Pact to scoop out every night a fresh grave
> In the cold and niggard soil of my brain,
> Pitiless sexton of sterility,
> —What, my Dreams, can I, rose visited, say
> To that Dawn when fearful of its livid roses
> The vast cemetery joins its hollow graves?   —Roger Fry

Here the rose symbolizes both sides of Mallarmé's conflict at the same time. It is linked with the natural joys of childhood, which he had fled to pursue an ideal, and also with the sick roses of his failure to express that ideal in art. When the dawn of actuality mocks his sterile efforts, what can he say to justify himself who had abandoned the childhood promise of things possible for an ideal that he never attained? It is true that he was able to praise a writer he felt had achieved the desired goal. "Toast Funèbre" pays high tribute to Théophile Gautier, who through his art had transmuted the actual into the ideal. And Gautier's achievement is significantly expressed by the transfiguration of rose and lily into transcendental flowers.

> Le Maître, par un oeil profond, a, sur ses pas,
> Apaisé de l'éden l'inquiète merveille
> Dont le frisson final, dans sa voix seule, éveille
> Pour la Rose et le Lys le mystère d'un nom.
>
> . . . .
>
> A qui s'évanouit, hier, dans le devoir
> Idéal que nous font les jardins de cet astre,
> Survivre pour l'honneur du tranquille désastre
> Une agitation solennelle par l'air
> De paroles, pourpre ivre et grand calice clair.

> The Master, by his deep eye, has, as he went,
> Appeased the disquieting marvel of Eden
> Of which the last quiver, in his voice, awakes
> For the Rose and the Lily the mystery of a name.
>
> . . . .
>
> Him who, yesterday, vanished in the ideal
> Duty imposed by the gardens of this star,
> Survived for the honor of the calm disaster
> By a solemn agitation in the air of words,
> Ebrious purple and great clear chalice.   —Roger Fry

Nevertheless, it was not in his own work but only in that of another that Mallarmé was able to see the natural rose transmuted into the desired "idée . . . l'absente de tous bouquets."

Because throughout his life he was tormented by his inability to realize his dream in art, Mallarmé displayed the limitations of symbolism and the weaknesses inherent in the French doctrine. Failing to express what words could not express, he fell back on repeated expressions of his failure. Attempting to transform a private idealism into an objective reality, he became obsessed with ever more rarified subjective imaginings. He and the rest had done something important. They had created a new symbolic theory to fit a new emotional outlook, with the result that future writers would be able to use symbols to suggest simultaneous levels of feeling discovered in intricate inner worlds. But the early symbolists had carried too far their own major innovation. Not content to express their subtle reactions to the usual world, they had attempted to ignore the very existence of that world and to create in its stead an unusual world in which indefinable heights of emotion retained sole and eternal sway. Up to a point this was healthy, but human emotions are limited and inner springs run dry if cut off from the larger stream of life. Symbolists of the twentieth century would be able to resolve the conflict of subject and object, real and ideal, in Mallarmé's rose. But in so doing they would be forced to acknowledge its roots in Western tradition and its life in the external as well as inner world.

Meanwhile in France those symbolists seeking a personally satisfying ideal were to grow weary and decadent. Paradoxically, in their decline their rose would begin to flourish. For as they exhausted more and more of their initial stores of energy, they were driven almost in spite of themselves to seek new areas of strength. Mallarmé felt that he had failed to express in poetry the ideal values he perceived in inner vision; symbolists of the next generation felt that they had failed to discover any real values in life at all. The quest for transcendent meanings in an entirely inner world had gradually declined into an overrefinement of sensibility that was inevitably becoming jaded. The social world of bourgeois materialism offered even less comfort. But the traditional sources of spiritual comfort for those whom the inner and outer life has failed were also closed to many. To such the

Catholic Church sometimes seemed the only adequate refuge and, because no longer acceptable, the epitome of lost illusions. Illusion or no, the Catholic outlook returned to poetry and with it the Catholic rose, a rose now greatly altered by introversion and disbelief but one in the end also destined to alter the forces that altered it.

Jules Laforgue, who was brought up a Catholic, lost his faith but retained his wish to believe. In his lyrics the rose is often evoked in contexts affirming his longing and loss. The flower itself generally appears not as a Catholic but rather as an anti-Catholic symbol. It is the flower of all sensual lusts, an impoverished substitute for the joys of the soul. "Roses ouvertes/Divines pertes" ("Roses in full bloom/Divine loss" —J. P. S.), laments Laforgue who can find nothing in mortal life to compensate for the loss of the immortal. More poignantly still, his "Complainte du Roi de Thulé" contrasts the lily of God with the sensual rose to point up the tragedy of a king who had exchanged divine for earthly love:

> Il était un roi de Thulé
> Immaculé
> Qui loin des jupes et des choses
> Pleurait sur la métempsychose
> De lys en roses.

> There once was a king of Thulé
>   Without stain,
> From skirts and things far away,
> Who wept for the metempsychosis
>   Of lilies to roses.   —Patricia Terry

And in the poem that particularly impressed T. S. Eliot,[7] "Complainte de cette bonne Lune," Laforgue expresses di-

---

[7] It is known that in "Rhapsody on a Windy Night" Eliot adapts a quotation from this poem: "La lune ne garde aucune rancune." But it is also distinctly possible that the closing lines of "The Hollow Men" ("Here we go round the prickly pear . . .") echo Laforgue's closing lines: "Sous l'plafond/Sans fond,/On y danse, on y danse,/Sous l'plafond/ Sans fond,/On y danse tous en rond."

rectly his own desperation through presenting the fickle moon as a rose queen, an inadequate Virgin for inadequate souls:

> Va donc, rosière enfarinée!
> Hé! Notre-Dame des gens saouls!
> Des filous et des loups-garous!
> Metteuse en rut des vieux matous!
>   Coucou!

> Go, then, rose-awarded maiden with floured face!
> Hé! Our Lady of drunks!
> Of pickpockets and cutthroats!
> Inciter of old tomcats!
>   Cuckoo!   —J. P. S.

But Laforgue did not admire all aspects of Catholicism. Although he lamented the loss of the Catholic dream, which might have given meaning to a meaningless world, he remained disturbed by Church corruptions and hypocrisies. In the prose tale, *Les Miracles des Roses,* he emphasizes the cruelty hypocritically veiled by Catholic holiness. The heroine, seemingly too blessed for this world but actually a sadist who drives countless men to suicide, exemplifies the true bloodiness concealed at the core of hypocritical piety. Used ironically, the symbolism of roses becomes the chief means for making the point. While the tale itself parodies the saints' lives, the climactic miracle whereby the blood of the heroine's numerous victims is transformed into roses parodies the tendency of saints' lives to exalt the agonies of the faithful by confounding their pain with roses. An example of the literary sacrilege popular in the late nineteenth century, Laforgue's story uses Catholic devices for purposes of exposing the centuries of blood that have watered the Catholic flower and the long history of cruelty behind the Catholic creed of love.

Laforgue, then, admired the Catholic ideals but not their usual manifestations in the Church of this world. Remy de

Gourmont, also disappointed by Catholicism, had lost his admiration even for the ideals themselves. More extreme than Laforgue, he carried sacrilege farther. His "Litanies de la Rose" makes of the Church's mystical flower a symbol again of hypocrisy, but of a hypocrisy that cuts beneath false surface appearances to a falsity at the heart of human life itself. Gourmont, believing like Blake in the supreme importance of sex, likewise opposed the religion he felt had distorted and stifled it. But Gourmont, unlike Blake, had no transcendental faith to support his sensual views and therefore was forced to confront the hard core of disillusion in mortal as well as religious values. His point is subtle and is conveyed almost entirely through his symbol: the spiritual ecstasy of the Church is a false substitute for sex, while sexual ecstasy is true but a poor substitute for God. The rose in its variety of color and type throughout the litany becomes the culminating symbol of a variety of lost illusions related to each other by the same refrain, "Fleur hypocrite/Fleur du silence."

As a female sexual symbol, the flower in its loveliness is revealed as the guise beneath which lie the deceit, vice, and cruelty of woman from prostitute to virgin: "rose au coeur prostitué . . . o vierge des futures. trahisons" ("rose with the prostitute heart . . . O virgin of future betrayals"— Richard Aldington). The deception is initially sexual, and the female rose is at the outset a symbol of the unsatisfying nature of sex. Promising much and leaving behind little, the flower of sexual ecstasy and its disappointment expands to become a symbol of disappointed human idealism and of the deception that life is: "rose couleur d'aurore, couleur du temps, couleur de rien . . . sourire ouvert sur le néant" ("Dawn-coloured rose, colour of the sky, colour of nothing . . . smile opening upon nothingness"—Richard Aldington). Finally, in the litany's culminating stanzas, it becomes the hypocritical flower of the Catholic Church, whose otherworldly idealism

is not only a delusion but also a betrayal of the humanity its
founder preached: "Rose papale, rose arrosée des mains qui
bénissent le monde, rose papale, ton coeur d'or est en cuivre,
et les larmes qui perlent sur ta vaine corolle, ce sont les pleurs
du Christ, fleur hypocrite, fleur du silence" ("Papal rose,
rose watered by the hands that bless the world, papal rose,
your golden heart is of copper, and the tears empearled upon
your vain corolla are the tears of Christ, hypocritical flower,
flower of silence"—Richard Aldington). Gourmont here
makes explicit his dissatisfaction with the Church, a dissatisfaction implicit in his inverted use of the rose and the
litany. He shows himself negative, bitter, and defiant towards
a Church that deludes us with empty hopes. Yet deeper than
sacrilege or indictment runs a strong current of regret for the
Catholic dream whose loss no other dream has quite made
good.

The important thing about the roses of Laforgue and
Gourmont is that they apply objective tradition to subjective
vision and so point the way of the future. They do not by
any means go far enough. The roses are narrow and negative,
and their beauty is that of decay. More exhausted even than
Mallarmé's, they blossom in the absence of ideals. Yet these
roses reveal in their own disillusion a very real need for some
sort of belief transcending not merely the limits of time but
the limits of the poet's particular mind. They are typical of
the late nineteenth century, a time when poets were despairing, yearning, and dissident, but seeking a spiritual dream
to fill a spiritual void. There were ways of approaching the
problem other than lamenting or desecrating a lost faith. Some
who could not accept a church but were unwilling or unable
to accept despair threw themselves into the creation of creeds
that would be in accord with their desires. In fact, Paris
towards the close of the century was the center of sundry
unusual cults, a few of which inspired writing on as high
a level as Laforgue's. But like Laforgue's and Gourmont's,

despite the presence of faith, the writings of the occultists were sad, quite often world-denying, and in the end influential as much by their failings as by their strengths. The Rosicrucian from a literary standpoint was the most important of the Paris cults. In 1888 Stanislas de Guaita and the Sâr Péladan founded the Kabbalistic Order of the Rosy Cross. A mystical society believing in an all-pervasive soul of the world, the order gave to some symbolists the support of an external belief that embodied their private spiritual leanings. Moreover, the founders of the society were themselves engaged in literary as well as occultist activities and therefore promoted the idea that symbolist art held transcendent significance as a kind of revelation of supersensual truths. "La mysticisme! toute la poésie est là . . . c'est l'amour de nos coeurs pour les songes de nos cervaux" ("Mysticism! all poetry is there . . . it is the love of our hearts for the dreams of our brains"—J. P. S.), proclaimed Stanislas de Guaita. And the Sâr Péladan was still more explicit: "Artiste, tu es prêtre: l'art est le grand mystère" ("Artist, you are priest: art is the great mystery"—J. P. S.).[8] As expression of the great mystery, art in fact became magic. Baudelaire, following Swedenborg, had believed that the symbols in his poems corresponded to immaterial qualities; the Rosicrucians, following magic, systematized much the same sort of thing. Just as the material symbols of magic evoked spiritual correspondences, so also the symbols of a poem evoked like correspondences in the soul of the reader.

The Rosicrucian doctrine of a spiritual realm accessible through the magic power of symbols gave to susceptible poets a temporary stimulus. Beyond this, the Rosicrucians had an advantage over the nonelect in being able to build on symbols already rich in ancient meanings. Most important, of course, were the symbols of rose and cross, and even the cross re-

---

[8] Stanislas de Guaita, *Rosa Mystica* (Paris, 1885), pp. 2–3; Josephin Péladan, *L'Art Idéaliste et Mystique* (Paris, 1894), p. 17.

mained subsidiary to the rose. For the rose of eternity was to
be gained through suffering renunciation on the cross of
time. The rose itself was the glorious goal. Essentially it
symbolized a mystical condition in which the human values
of love, beauty, goodness, and joy would be marvelously
transfigured and the apparent divisions of mortal life would
be seen in their eternal, ineffable union. Sufficiently vague,
the Rosicrucian flower had certain advantages over its Catholic
counterpart. It was free of the more specific doctrinal associations of the Catholic symbol, yet at the same time could give
supernatural validity to the poet's highest imaginings. Believing in the truth of poetry, Rosicrucian writers could evoke
through an esoteric rose the spiritual correspondences of their
personal ideals. Accordingly, in the preface to his volume of
spiritual poems, significantly entitled *Rosa Mystica*, Stanislas
de Guaita offered his creed to the sensitive: "La Rose que je
vous invite à cueillir . . . ne fleurit pas aux rives des con-
trées lointaines. . . . Etes-vous susceptible d'une émotion
vive de l'intellect? et vos pensers favoris vous hantent-ils
jusqu'à vous donner parfois l'illusion du réel?—Vous êtes
donc magicien, et la Rose mystique ira d'elle-même, pour peu
que vous le vouliez, fleurir en votre jardin" ("The Rose that
I invite you to pick . . . does not grow on the shores of far
countries . . . Are you subject to keen intellectual emotion?
and do your favorite thoughts haunt you to the point of giving
you at times the illusion of reality? Then you are a magician,
and the mystic Rose will go of itself, however little you wish
it, to bloom in your garden"—J. P. S.).

   Villiers de l'Isle-Adam accepted the offer and in his symbolic drama, *Axël,* gave literary expression to Rosicrucian
doctrines. His hero and heroine, Axël and Sara, are both
exiles from the usual life of the world. Beyond this, they have
both renounced the spiritual vocations open to them: Catholicism for her, the Rosy Cross for him. Setting forth on
separate quests for a treasure whose true nature is at the time

unknown, they simultaneously discover material riches and each other. For a moment they are tempted by the heights of earthly happiness now available to them in the forms of wealth and love. But Sara, who has become a devotee of matters Rosicrucian, reminds Axël of his neglected faith. Thereupon they resolve on suicide in order to bring about the crucifixion of the temporal and the attainment of the eternal rose. Comprehending the rose's import—"symbole de mon destin, *correspondance* familiale et divine"—Sara points it out to Axël as symbolic indication of the way they are to take: "Regarde, comme si nous étions seuls sur la terre, perdus entre la rève et la vie, cette mystérieuse fleur. . . . Vois l'inconsolable rose" ("Look, as if we were alone on the earth, lost between dream and life, look at that mysterious flower. . . . See the inconsolable rose"—J. P. S.).

The inconsolable rose of human longing for what cannot be attained in time made a deep mark on symbolic writing; its promise of eternity was to become the consolation of English as well as French poets lost between life and the dream. Where earlier symbolists had floundered in the mists of subjective ideals, Rosicrucians seemed to have found a haven in the mists of occult beliefs. Using esoteric doctrine, Villiers' play had presented not only a dissatisfaction all too common to his age, but also a vision that might look hopeful to those who had no other hope. For the occult after all provided a framework to accommodate private religious needs and a mystico-magical doctrine to justify private symbols. More significant than esthetics, art could become a kind of gospel and the poet a kind of priest. Indeed, for those who could accept it the occult seemed to offer a solution to the *fin-de-siècle* dilemma. Finding nothing desirable in the temporal world and nothing believable in the Church, wishful writers could find value, art, and heaven too in Rosicrucian realms.

But the problem was more complex than it at first appeared, and the solution provided by the occult was to prove in large part unsatisfactory. In the hands of despairing poets the denial of time for eternity's sake too often served only to reinforce negative attitudes towards the world. What began as a hopeful quest for affirmative beliefs frequently ended as a rejection of every human value. Villiers' well-known remark—"Vivre? les serviteurs feront cela pour nous" ("Live? Servants will do that for us"—J. P. S.)—is well known because it expresses a typical attitude. Actually more jaded than Baudelaire or Mallarmé, Rosicrucian writers carried their quest for personal ideals into realms of absolute negation. It is only in William Butler Yeats, who followed the same rose, that we find a writer of sufficient stature to transform that rose's lethal magic into vital creative art. And even Yeats's rose, despite its genuine importance, is also planted deep within the late romantic gloom. Following the English who were following the French, the Irish writer went beyond them to achieve great poetry. But before the inner tensions of English, French, or Irish could come into adequate focus and the art of Yeats itself emerge from decadence to health, the subjective distresses of the century had to exhaust themselves.

For the decline from private dreams grown stale in the early years of symbolism, to despair, sacrilege, or occult escapism in the decadent *fin de siècle,* was not limited to France but had its parallels throughout Europe. In England, by the end of the century, poets were beginning to discover their affinities with the French, and French ideas only half understood were beginning to create the literary atmosphere out of which British symbolism would grow. Differences in background were also important in determining the nature of the French influence. In place of a symbolist movement, there had at first been in England an esthetic movement created chiefly by Walter Pater, William Morris, and Dante Gabriel Rossetti. All three were striving to reassert the significance of beauty in a society that was growing steadily more materialistic. Like the French, they depended largely on the world of subjective impressions for their values and their art; like the French, they were spiritual exiles from middle-class attitudes. But unlike the French, they found in beauty their sufficient religion and in the esthetic experience their sufficient goal. Art, which was worshiped in France for its expression of ideal truths, was worshiped in England for itself.

Lacking the transcendentalizing tendencies of the French, the British lacked the motive that gives rise to symbolism. It was not necessary that beauty be truth on any plane; it was enough that it be beauty. A poem or a rose was sufficient in itself provided it gave rise to an esthetic experience. The roses in the poems of Morris and Rossetti are a far cry from Mallarmé's complicated blossoms. Simple and limited, they exist for esthetic purposes alone. For instance, although Rossetti sometimes employs a Catholic rose, he employs it not to convey a spiritual message or lack of message but solely to enhance the poetic effectiveness of his work. The "white rose of Mary's gift" worn on the blessed damozel's robe is decorative, poetic, well known, and little else. And although Morris employs numerous roses in his poems, he generally does so to enhance his medieval settings by evoking equally simple and decorative associations with courtly love. The knight's refrain in "Two Red Roses across the Moon" is atmospheric, while the rose garlands worn by the knights and ladies in "Golden Wings" are picturesque.

But the pursuit of beauty for the sake of sensation or sensation for the sake of beauty wore itself out in England at about the same time that the symbolist quest for private spiritual values was wearing itself out in France. As esthetic sensibilities became increasingly jaded, new areas of sensation were tested, drawing writers ever farther beyond the social pale and resulting in their defensive delight in shocking the middle class. The romantic association of beauty with melancholy was developed, becoming in some a recurrent lament over the vanities of life and in others a masochistic cultivation of perversion, sacrilege, or pain. It was during these decadent years at the close of the century that certain French symbolist poets held particular appeal. Baudelaire's sacrilegious sadism, Mallarmé's esthetic refinement, Verlaine's despair over himself, Laforgue's despair over human life now began to affect the English. But since they were lacking a background of symbolic conception and had come at too spent a time to create one, English poets of the decadence misunderstood the deeper elements in French idealism and its consequences for artistic expression. Concerned with their own sensations and with their place as shocking exiles in or from the social setup, they overemphasized the morbid in their ignorance of the mystic.

In keeping with their morbidity was their partiality to roses. For the flower of all positive values was singularly appropriate to the expression of the loss or desecration of values. It was easy enough to express disillusion through plucking a rose and watching it die, nor was it hard to express desecration through defiling the flower of virtue with sin. Deriving from France themes of sacrilege, sadism, and lament for life's vanity, *fin-de-siècle* English poets sprinkled these themes with roses. Swinburne, for example, as early as the 1860s was introducing Baudelaire to England through criticism and poetry. In "Dolores" he related the rose to the sacrilegious-sadistic theme, setting up his "mystical rose of the mire" as an anti-Virgin and finding the "raptures and roses of vice" the more alluring for their contrast with the traditional rose of grace. George Moore was likewise intrigued fairly early by Baudelairean depravity. In *Flowers of Passion,* attempting to capture the spirit of *Fleurs du Mal,* he used the rose Baudelaire rarely mentioned to create watered-down Swinburnian effects. Erroneously styled "symbol flowers," Moore's roses are actually no more than simple similes of lust under foolishly morbid circumstances. That in "The Corpse," describing the decaying body of a dead love, is typical: "The bosom rent/Is opening rose-like 'neath the sun's warm ray."

Poets of the eighteen nineties continued this sort of thing with modifications. Aware of the Baudelairean element infiltrating English literature, they tended to suffuse it with a plaintive melancholy. Arthur Symons, who through his critical writings did much to introduce French poets to England, shows some French influence in his own rather anemic poems. In "Rosa Flammae" the "rose that is rooted in hell" appears as a typical decadent metaphor of sacrilegious lust. In "Rosa Mundi" it faintly approaches at least the theory of symbolism. Earthly love in the course of the poem is treated as sexual desire, infinite longing, pain, and joy. In the final stanza it is intended to comprise all this and more. For it becomes man's unattainable ideal through an identification, more sorrowful than sacrilegious, with the mystical rose of a lost faith:

> Then I saw that the rose was fair,
> And the mystical rose afar
> A glimmering shadow of light,
> Paled to a star in the night;
> And the angel whispered, "Beware,
> Love is a wandering star."

Though hardly very successful either as symbolism or poetry, "Rosa Mundi" well illustrates the melancholy, disenchanted, and weakly imitative condition of the waning poetry of the nineties.

Equally wistful and better in quality but even less symbolic are the poems of Ernest Dowson and Lionel Johnson. Dowson lamented mutability and his own misery. Although he "flung roses, roses riotously with the throng" (Cynara"), he could not forget that "the days of wine and roses" are vanishing and therefore sad. Like some of his French contemporaries, he looked to the Catholic Church as a refuge from the sorrow of mortality. But he was never truly able to substitute for the roses of mortal joys the everlasting beauties of Christ, "whose thorns are sweet as never roses are" ("Quid Non Speremus, Amantes"). Lionel Johnson, also saddened by life, sought with rather more success a similar refuge in Catholicism and applied to spiritual values in traditional fashion the rose that Dowson associated with fading earthly loves. For instance, his reference to the Virgin as "Rose of the Paradise: Mystical Rose" ("Flos Florum") is wholly in keeping with Catholic tradition. Yet although it is clearly religious, Johnson's flower is no more symbolic than Dowson's, being simply a revival of a traditional metaphor. Typical of their place and decade in weariness, disillusion, and sorrow, Johnson and Dowson were also typical in their failure to comprehend and achieve the esthetic complexity of the French poets whose mood they partly emulated.

But there was a writer very much of the nineties who possessed sufficient stature to bring to the decadent English rose the symbolic quality of the French. Oscar Wilde, among the foremost of British *fin-de-siècle* writers, learned with more success than his compeers the lessons of the Continent. It is true that his fairy tale, "The Nightingale and the Rose," is neither French nor symbolic, being rather a simple allegory of the destruction of love and beauty by a materialistic civilization.[9] But *The Picture of Dorian Gray* opens with portentous roses in the very first sentence: "The studio was filled with the rich odor of roses"; and these roses are again referred to just as the portrait itself is completed: "The heavy scent of the roses seemed to brood over everything." Suggestive of an indefinite doom lurking in the studio's sur-

---

[9] "The Nightingale and the Rose" employs for modern allegory a popular theme of ancient Persia. In Persian legend the nightingale fell in love with the white rose and sang to it until he collapsed exhausted on its thorns, thereby staining it red with his life's blood. From this legend was derived the theme of the red rose as inspiration for all poets of love, a theme that appears repeatedly in Persian poetry (Lovatelli, "Die Rose im Alterthum," in *Römische Essays*, tr. E. Petersen [Leipzig, 1891], pp. 90–92).

charged air, the roses of this opening scene help to create a sense of corruption. And although despite the roses *Dorian Gray* is not on the whole symbolic, the intangible flowers of its outset reappear in Wilde's unmistakably symbolic drama, *Salomé*.

Written under the influence of Mallarmé, Flaubert, and Laforgue, and with the aid of several symbolists of the Théatre d'Art, *Salomé* approaches the effects of the French and its roses approach the symbol flowers of Mallarmé. The drama, which is decadent in theme and tone, is pervaded by an atmosphere of horror, sharpened by sadism and deepened by sacrilege. The roses, like the moon, change in color and quality, reflecting the steady progress of evil throughout the play. At the beginning Salomé, who has been compared to the dead white moon, is compared in similar terms to a dead white rose: "How pale the Princess is! Never have I seen her so pale. She is like the shadow of a white rose in a mirror of silver." Through such comparisons is suggested the coldness of a virginity that in its narcissism is akin to cruelty and in its cruelty is the agent of death. Later Salomé likens John the Baptist's flesh to white roses: "The roses in the garden of the Queen of Arabia are not so white as thy body. . . . Suffer me to touch thy body." In context it is clear that beneath her cruel virginity lies a still more cruel lust, a lust that will cause the red blood of martyrdom to stain the whiteness of the saint's purity and of her own fierce virginity.

Finally Herod, the third and last major character, is also given his roses. Just before the murder of John the Baptist, he becomes aware of the rose garland he wears: "It is my garland that hurts me, my garland of roses. The flowers are like fire. . . . They are like stains of blood." An omen suggesting Christ's crown of thorns, Herod's garland suggests the anti-Christian act that Herod, like another Pilate, is about to sanction. His roses reinforce those of Salomé and John the Baptist, which have already acquired implications of cruelty, lust, blood, death, virgin purity, martyrdom, and anti-Christ. Moreover, like theirs, Herod's roses enhance moods of indefinable terror or horror. The sound of the beating wings of death or madness, the sharp contrasts of significant colors, and the moon changing hue and aspect throughout until it becomes blood red as the roses, interact in the play's context with the ominous flowers. From all of this Wilde's roses derive a symbolic mysteriousness and complexity that carry them well beyond the more usual decadent roses of simple sacrilege, lust, or self-conscious depravity assumed by admirers of Baudelaire.

Of course, in its intricacy of form, *Salomé* at the close of an era, like the work of Blake at its outset, is not typical of nineteenth-century literature in England. Although the rose had been present throughout the century, gradually changing from the healthy flower of natural beauties into the morbid product of cultivated sins, it had seldom assumed the proportions of a symbol in a country in which the symbolic method had not yet received widespread attention. Nonetheless, the romantic outlook in its intricacy of content had unquestionably paved the road that would lead to the predominance of symbolism over every other literary method in contemporary British writing. The subjective, individualistic viewpoints inherited from the Renaissance had been developed and applied to new, intangible areas of psychic or spiritual exploration. And the subjective methods of the French symbolists, though not yet fully understood, were by the end of the century arousing both interest and imitation. Since symbolism inevitably is the result of a state of mind working out its most adequate mode of expression, the nineteenth-century attitudes towards nature, man, and art, whether or not they found actual outlet in symbolic form, were the immediate soil and substance from which British symbols were to grow.

It is true that the twentieth century would bring about changes and new developments. An increased awareness of emotional complexity and an increased understanding of the French were not the only factors that contributed to the modern symbol. The discoveries of psychoanalysts were to open up the unconscious for systematic study, and the discoveries of anthropologists were to stimulate new interest in the roles and properties of myth. Furthermore, enhanced distress in a materialistic, war-torn world was to lead to a revival of traditional religion that would bring back the manner and matter of Dante as a powerful influence on modern writing. But these developments and others would stem from the immediate past. The concern with the unconscious, furthered by Freud and the rest, had been prepared for by the concern with the subtleties of man's emotions reflected in nineteenth-century art. And the return to religious tradition, even specifically to Dante, had often appeared in inverted form both in early and decadent symbolist writers. New factors would be vital in transforming the faded flower of the nineteenth century into the flexible symbol of the twentieth. Nonetheless, the major changes to be brought about would exist within a romantic framework and would give new voice and compass to a romantic point of view.

4

YEATS

AND

TRANSITION

While English writers of the 1890s were reducing French symbolism to romantic decadence, an Irish writer of remarkable stature was independently developing a symbolic method that would resuscitate the dwindling romantic movement. In fact, William Butler Yeats more than any other single writer can be said to have created the modern British symbol. He was perhaps the greatest and certainly the first to build a new and powerful symbolic art upon the ruins of romantic hyper-subjectivity. Moreover, he himself in the first years of his career was grappling with the forces that were devitalizing art. Because his own achievement was the result of struggle, it is possible to trace in the pattern of his work the evolution of the mystical, too personal romantic symbol into the firmer, more objective, more adaptable symbol of our time. And in his rose, symbolic flower of his early, overly subjective writing, it is possible to see the causes and initial stages of Yeats's progress—and of art's—from decadence to power.

Too often dismissed or treated lightly as the cloying flower of a *fin-de-siècle* youth, Yeats's rose is far more important than is generally acknowledged. First of all, an understanding of his early struggle with himself and art is essential to an understanding of his later, greater triumph. As the central expression of that early struggle, the misty, melancholic poems on the rose help to provide us with the key to such an understanding.

For at the core of Yeats's rose lies an only partly conscious death-wish, a force which, in its emergence to full consciousness, was to play a vital role in the development of his life and work. In addition, predominantly subjective as it is, his rose marks a notable advance over nineteenth-century predecessors. For one thing, it embodies the first successful attempt since Blake to create in British literature a full-scale symbolic method. But beyond this it is the first successful attempt since Dante to express traditional as well as personal meanings in a single symbol. Because the fusion of personal with universal meanings has been essential to the development of the modern symbol, Yeats's complicated flower is of singular importance to an understanding of the symbolic literature of our time.

Behind Yeats's rose lay a medley of artistic and religious concepts. Through the influence of his father he had early been impressed by certain romantic and pre-Raphaelite poets, finding himself in accord with the romantic distrust of abstract reason and with the pre-Raphaelite emphasis on passion and an art freed of conscious moral purpose. But although for a time he wrote in the moody vein of the late nineteenth century, passion and beauty in themselves were insufficient for Yeats. Organization of experience into a meaningful pattern was also necessary, and for him such a pattern could be truly meaningful only if it were in some sense religious. Poetry could become itself a religion replacing the lost Christianity of his childhood, if the dreams it created could be actual truth. Seeking to believe in the truth of poetry, he entered the occult for the sake of art. In 1886 he joined the Dublin Theosophical disciples of Mme. Blavatsky, and two years later transferred his spiritual activities to the Rosicrucian Order of the Golden Dawn in London.

From Theosophists and Rosicrucians Yeats gained concepts fundamental to the symbolic theory he was formulating. Theosophists believed that the religions of the earth were all fragments of a once true and complete belief now being reassembled by Helena P. Blavatsky. The true faith, ancient Indian in origin, had posited an omnipresent Soul of the World, with which man could attain ultimate union through the rigorous perfection of his spiritual nature. Furthermore, man was believed to be identical in essence with the Oversoul, and therefore theoretically able to control the universe through the magical exploitation of his own psychic faculties. To theory the Rosicrucians added practice. Like Theosophists they believed man's spiritual goal to be a final, eternal union with the Oversoul. But while Theosophists frowned upon the use of magic, Rosicrucians deemed it a powerful agent in their quest for spirit. Following the ancient doctrine engraved on the Emerald Tablet of Hermes Trismegistus—"That which is above is like that which is below for the fulfillment of the wonders of the one thing"—Rosicrucians used material symbols for the magical evocation of spiritual forces.

These occult sources provided Yeats with the metaphysical basis for poetry he had been seeking. Accordingly, the symbolic theory that he practiced in his poetry and expounded in his prose relies heavily on occult belief. To begin with, he felt that the symbols of a poem, like those of practical magic, evoke divine powers. In his *Essays* he describes symbols as "the greatest of all powers whether they are used consciously by the masters of magic, or half-unconsciously by their successors, the poet, the musician, and the artist." [1] Moreover, symbols themselves emerge from the divine. For the mind of man is one with the Great Mind of the universe and the memory of man, one with the same Great Memory. In trancelike states "between sleeping and waking," the images that float up before the mind's eye come from a consciousness including but transcending the personal and are indications of spiritual mysteries: "Any one who has any experience of any mystical

[1] *Essays*, 2nd ed. (New York, 1924), p. 60. Future citations from Yeats's essays are to this edition.

state of the soul knows how there float up in the mind profound symbols . . . that our little memories are but a part of some great memory that renews the world and men's thoughts age after age, and that our thoughts are not, as we suppose, the deep but a little foam upon the deep" (*Essays*, p. 96). Since the imagination is ultimately inseparable from the universal, eternal consciousness, the genuine artist is inevitably a symbolist: "All art that is not mere story-telling or mere portraiture, is symbolic . . . for it entangles, in complex colours and forms, a part of the Divine Essence" (*Essays*, p. 183).

In the work of certain romantic predecessors Yeats found support for his own synthesis of occult with esthetic doctrine. Among English writers, Blake and Shelley in particular impressed him as visionaries expressing through symbols divine revelations. Of the French, with whom he was little familiar, he at least knew Villiers' symbolic drama, *Axël*, which he claimed to have read "slowly and laboriously as one reads a sacred book." But although he used symbols in the manner of earlier romantics to convey supersensual, visionary truths, Yeats differed significantly from most of his predecessors in deriving his symbols from external traditions. The occult provided a major source for symbols, and Irish myth or legend provided another. While it is true that Yeats used such symbols to convey primarily personal feelings, nevertheless their associations with objective bodies of belief or legend gave them not only added intelligibility but the added richness he sought therein: "It is only by ancient symbols, by symbols that have numberless meanings besides the one or two the writer lays an emphasis upon, or the half-score he knows of, that any highly subjective art can escape from the barrenness and shallowness of a too conscious arrangement, into the abundance and depth of nature" (*Essays*, p. 107).

The rose was sufficiently ancient and rich in meaning to

satisfy Yeats's requirements. In a note to the first edition of *The Wind Among the Reeds* (London, 1899), he traces its lineage: "The Rose has been for many centuries a symbol of spiritual love and supreme beauty . . . the western Flower of Life . . . and a symbol of Ireland" (pp. 74–76). Still more important, it was the central symbol of the Rosicrucians, betokening no less than the Divine Light of the universe. For Rosicrucians, believing man's aim to be the purgation of his spirit towards harmony with God, identified this process with the Great Work of alchemy and identified the rose found in alchemist writings with their own supreme symbol. Further, since the cross symbolized to Rosicrucians the temporal, material world of pain and sacrifice, the Rosicrucian conjunction of rose with cross expressed the final harmony of such contraries as matter and spirit, time and eternity, death and rebirth, man and God.

To Yeats, who was seeking "unity of being" or the integration of religious and temporal concerns, the Rosicrucian rose had particular appeal. Disturbed by discrepancies between his dreams and the external world, he sought reconciliation through this esoteric flower. As symbol of the eternal perfection beneath unpurged material appearances, it was applicable to his various ideals. In the first place, it could symbolize his conception of art; for if art is the expression of spiritual realities through material symbols, it is appropriately connoted by the symbol of that realm in which temporal things take on eternal aspects. The rose could also serve to justify and exalt at once a hopeless love and a dubious nationalism by becoming the symbol of Maud Gonne and of Ireland. In love with Maud Gonne but unable to win her, Yeats sought compensation in perceiving her as an earthly expression of the eternal Beauty that can never be fully attained in time. Involved in the Irish national movement, he sought to justify his nonpolitical absorption in esoteric mysteries on the grounds that the fundamental spirit of the nation could be penetrated only through the occult.[2]

These various meanings were expressed by Yeats's rose often simultaneously. Like Dante's rose, it expressed the temporal and eternal aspects of love, politics, and divinity; like Dante's, it attempted to reconcile these matters on a spiritual plane. But the reconciliation was doomed to failure. For unlike Dante, Yeats could neither objectify nor resolve his conflicts in genuine religious fashion. In fact, in some respects the occult heightened his difficulties. Irish nationalism called for political action, at least through the medium of literature, and he was deserting the concrete Ireland of the present for an obscure dream of the mystic past. Maud Gonne was involved in the national movement, and he was unable to fulfill her expectations as active participant in actual things. The Rosicrucian rose might offer Yeats a means of ordering experience on a spiritual plane, but at the same time it was luring him away from the genuine concerns of his terrestrial existence. Because of the conflict implicit in his rose, and because he was partly aware of that conflict, the complex flower of Yeats's early work is unique among the rose symbols of major writers in expressing less often reconciliation than the suspension of meanings in unresolved discord.

As Yeats's attempts to make peace with himself took altered forms, the rose correspondingly changed its hue. But the dis-

[2] Yeats felt that Irish legend and the occult were ultimately inseparable, the Irish symbols being local expressions of the one fundamental Soul of the World. In his dedication to *The Secret Rose* (London, 1897), he wrote: "My friends in Ireland sometimes ask me when I am going to write a really national poem or romance. . . . So far, however, as this book is visionary it is Irish." In his *Autobiographies* (New York, 1953), he was more explicit: "I had an unshakable conviction . . . that this philosophy [the occult] would find its manuals of devotion in all imaginative literature, and set before Irishmen for special manual an Irish literature which, though made by many minds, would seem to be the work of a single mind and turn our places of legendary association into holy symbols" (p. 153).

cord at its root remained. In the earliest rose poems appearing in *The Rose* (originally published in *The Countess Cathleen and Various Legends and Lyrics,* 1892), the Rosicrucian symbol is made thoroughly subjective. Steeped in the Platonism of such English poets as Spenser, Shelley, and Morris, and more in love with a beautiful woman than with Divine Spirit, Yeats identified the occult ideal with his own ideal of eternal Beauty.[3] But eternity, which provided a point of view, could neither satisfy earthly needs nor settle earthly problems. At the heart of Yeats's dilemma lay the fact that his longing for eternal life was actually inseparable from a longing for the tomb. Like Shelley, he sought a perfection that could not exist this side of death and so, in the poems of *The Rose,* sought eternal Beauty as a refuge from the trials of time. But the refuge remained unsatisfying because Yeats could no more be content with the best of an immaterial world than he could be with his immediate lot in the world of time. Unable to clarify or resolve his conflict between life and death-wishes, he reflected his dismay in his ambivalent rose. For the flower that embraces both time and eternity presents them not as harmonious but rather as separate realms unhappy for want of each other.

In "To the Rose upon the Rood of Time," the poem that serves as prologue to all the poems in *The Rose,* Yeats voices not only his general purpose but also his dominant mood of mournful uncertainty. The Rosicrucian flower is invoked as Muse that in the ensuing poems it may inspire the poet to sing "the ancient ways" of Ireland, its own sorrowful eternity, and the "eternal beauty" to be found in mortal things and mortal

[3] In making this identification Yeats remained within occult domains, since the Rosicrucian eternity was a general enough concept to encompass almost any supraterrestrial ideal. If man's mind in its profundity is one with the Great Mind, that which it conceives in visionary depths must be divine. Moreover, Villiers had in *Axël* associated the Rosicrucian rose with ideal love, and Stanislas de Guaita, whom Yeats met in Paris, had identified it with the poet's ideal beauty: "vos poèmes ont fait éclore l'amour de beau, comme une impérissable fleur" (*Rosa Mystica,* pp. 5–6).

love. The dominant themes and symbolic method of his art are to exist by grace of this encompassing rose. Yet at the same time the rose is held at a distance. For the poet fears that his desired, symbolic vision of the eternal reality beneath temporal appearances may carry him wholly beyond the bounds of earthly loves and intelligible words:

> Come near, come near, come near—Ah, leave me still
> A little space for the rose-breath to fill!
> Lest I no more hear common things that crave
>
> . . . .
>
> But seek alone to hear the strange things said
> By God to the bright hearts of those long dead,
> And learn to chaunt a tongue men do not know.[4]

The rose of the poem elsewhere is described as "sad" for the same reason that it is feared: eternity is a proud and beautiful thing but demands renunciation of temporal values on the "rood of time" and loss of communication through poetry and otherwise with the human world. Poetry's inspiration might be its defeat and life in the spirit mean death to the world.

The same sadness pervades the poems treating Yeats's love. And on one level most of the roses in the volume refer to Maud Gonne, whom Yeats perceives as a mortal manifestation of immortal beauty.[5] Presented as an idealized object of devotion and source of inspiration, she remains unattainable in the temporal world; and Yeats, who pursues a higher dream than he can reach, remains depressed by that which uplifts him. In "The Rose of the World" the rose is in one sense identified with Maud Gonne as the earthly woman whose beauty "passes like a dream." But Maud Gonne, as the embodi-

---

[4] *Collected Poems,* 2nd ed. (New York, 1951), p. 31. Unless otherwise indicated, future citations to Yeats's poems are to this edition.

[5] See A. Norman Jeffares, *W. B. Yeats: Man and Poet* (New Haven, 1949), p. 75. Maud Gonne informed Jeffares that the poems were on one level written to her, so that Yeats's statement in the *Autobiographies,* p. 153, that he symbolized love by the rose was equivalent to his saying that he symbolized his love for her.

ment of eternal Beauty, becomes, like Helen and Deirdre, a symbol to "the labouring world" of the ultimate ideal for which it lives—and dies:

> For these red lips, with all their mournful pride,
> Mournful that no new wonder may betide,
> Troy passed away in one high funeral gleam,
> And Usna's children died.   (*Poems*, p. 36)

The rose on this level, although divine, remains "lonely" and "mournful." For her devotees, being mortal, cannot share her solitary eternity, and "no new wonder may betide" in a world that has degenerated since the times of Helen and Deirdre, and that even at best can only repeat its utmost sacrifice of life to her.[6]

That eternity was not wholly comfortable to Yeats is apparent not only in the sorrowful "Rose of the World" but also in two poems that express directly a weariness with things occult. "The White Birds" presents the Irish Tirna nOg, fairyland where temporal joys remain unchanged until time ends, as an antidote to the remote, disembodied eternity of Rosicrucian dream:

I am haunted by numberless islands, and many a Danaan shore,
Where Time would surely forget us, and Sorrow come near us no
     more;
Soon far from the rose and the lily and the fret of the flames
     would we be,
Were we only white birds, my beloved, buoyed out on the foam
     of the sea!   (*Poems*, p. 41)

"The Rose of Peace" presents the rose as symbolic not of eternal but of mortal, temporal love. And in changing the meaning of his main symbol Yeats makes this a happier poem than any other rose poem in the volume. For as flower of

[6] The line, "Mournful that no new wonder may betide," may also carry an undercurrent of Yeats's own regret for his inability to make active sacrifice of himself to the cause Maud Gonne represented.

human love, this rose, and this alone, could end the eternal battle between heaven and hell, which is both the occult battle between spirit and matter and Yeats's personal battle between dreams and the actual world:

> And God would bid His warfare cease,
> Saying all things were well;
> And softly make a rosy peace,
> A peace of Heaven with Hell.   (*Poems*, p. 37)

Although here the desired reconciliation is to be effected through human means, it seems to be more welcome and more successful than any eternity has yet presented.

"The Rose of Battle," where the rose reverts to its usual role as eternal ideal, bears out this theme, although indirectly. God's battle of spirit with matter here appears to be never-ending. It is fought by "the sad, the lonely, the insatiable," who, like Yeats, can never have what they desire. But significantly the struggle would hold no glory and no refuge "For him who hears love sing and never cease / Beside her clean-swept hearth." The rose of the world is of the unhappy company waging everlasting battle on the "wharves of sorrow." For she is the spiritual counterpart of the temporal cross, and perhaps on another level, the mortal-immortal Maud Gonne, who at the time had also renounced human love for an ideal battle: "Beauty grown sad with its eternity / Made you of us, and of the dim grey sea." Divine as the battle may be, it is fought only by the sad and the loveless. Furthermore, it is doomed to defeat because those who are mortal must lose in order that spirit may win. Thus the questionable reward for its heroic participants becomes the cessation of suffering in the ultimate quiet of death:

> Our long ships loose thought-woven sails and wait,
> For God has bid them share an equal fate;
> And when at last, defeated in His wars,
> They have gone down under the same white stars,

We shall no longer hear the little cry
Of our sad hearts, that may not live nor die.

(Poems, p. 38)

The idealization of death in this poem is not unmixed with awareness that earthly love is a happier thing. And the same uneasiness that characterizes Yeats's attempts to sublimate time in eternity and earthly in ideal love, characterizes his attempt to transmute Irish nationalism into similar terms. Believing that the ancient myths and legends of Ireland symbolically embody the nation's spirit, Yeats had long been using in his poetry figures from Irish legends to symbolize occult concepts, and had long been unsuccessfully seeking to establish an Irish occult order for the dissemination of spiritual propaganda.[7] In "To Ireland in the Coming Times," he relates the occult rose explicitly to Ireland. His note to the original edition of *The Countess Cathleen* (London, 1892) throws light on his intentions: "The rose is a favourite symbol with the Irish poets . . . and is used, not merely in love poems, but in addresses to Ireland, as in De Vere's line, 'The little black rose shall be red at last' and in Mangan's 'Dark Rosaleen.' I do not, of course, use it in this latter sense" (p. 140). Yeats makes a clear distinction between his Irish rose and the usual national flower because he wishes to make it the flower of a non-political, mystic nationalism embodied in the mysteries of mythology and the souls of the people. Believing that "Dark Rosaleen" herself is in reality the descendant of an ancient Celtic goddess,[8] he is able to relate her to the Rosicrucian

[7] Richard Ellmann, *Yeats: The Man and the Masks* (New York, 1948), pp. 118–26.

[8] *The Wind Among the Reeds*, pp. 76–77: "If the rose was really a symbol of Ireland among the Gaelic poets, and if 'Roseen Dubh' is really a political poem, as some think, one may feel pretty certain that the ancient Celts associated the Rose with Eire, or Fotla, or Banba—goddesses who gave their names to Ireland—or with some principal god or goddess, for such symbols are not suddenly adopted or invented, but come out of mythology."

rose of eternal beauty in accord with his theory that all genuine symbols refer to the same underlying truth.

In the poem he attempts to justify his pursuit of Beauty's "red-rose-bordered hem" on the grounds that he is pursuing Ireland's fundamental spirit. It was, after all, eternal Beauty who first "made Ireland's heart begin to beat," and she who will at the end of time transfigure Ireland "in truth's consuming ecstasy." Yeats even attempts to justify his love as fit subject for a poetry contributing to true nationalism: "While still I may, I write for you / The love I lived, the dream I knew." For the woman he loves is, like Ireland, an earthly manifestation of her who will redeem all things and nations that embody herself. Nevertheless, the tone of the whole is uncertain and defensive. Written for the benefit of a posterity who he fears will misunderstand his esoteric nationalism, he claims a presumably disputed equality with the patriotic poets, Davis, Mangan, Ferguson:

> Know, that I would accounted be
> True brother of a company
> That sang to sweeten Ireland's wrong,
> Ballad and story, rann and song;
> Nor be I any less of them,
> Because the red-rose-bordered hem
>
> . . . .
> Trails all about the written page.   (*Poems,* p. 49)

And the motivation of the whole poem is made explicit in the title given it in the original edition: "Apologia . . ."

Yeats's uneasiness about Ireland was involved with unhappiness about his love and uncertainty about the effects of the occult on his art and life. He found the occult necessary to the ordering of his inner experience and to the symbolic art he was creating of that experience. At the same time it was increasing the disorder of his life in the world. His energies were devoted to esoteric practices rather than to political action, his art was not only of no immediate aid to the nationalist movement but was threatened by the obscurity of "a tongue men do not know," and Maud Gonne was not in sympathy with his preference for dreams over actions. The situation, in fact, formed a kind of vicious circle. Outer dissatisfactions heightened his need for spiritual compensations, while increased absorption in things spiritual enhanced his distress among things of this world. Neither time nor eternity was sufficient in itself to Yeats; he could neither renounce the world nor renounce his longing to renounce it. And since his desires were incompatible within his particular situation, he was unable to attain the joy and harmony he sought.

Yet temporal sorrows were part of the eternal plan. In 1893 Yeats was initiated into the high grade of Adept in the Order of the Golden Dawn and learned the full significance of the Rose Cross symbol. The initiation ceremony took place in the "tomb" of Father Christian Rosenkreutz, a vault made to represent the universe. Here the initiate was bound upon the cross of suffering and took a solemn vow to apply himself to the Great Work: "so to purify and exalt my spiritual nature that with the Divine Aid I may at length attain to be more than human." The ritual death to material things and rebirth in the spirit, symbolized by the ceremony itself, was reflected in the decorations of the initiatory vault. On the floor was a Rose Cross surrounded by blackness and on the ceiling a great Rose alone set against contrasting white.[9] Presenting with impressive immediacy the significance of suffering, this initiatory ceremony may have given Yeats greater hope for the resolution of his conflicts through ardent pursuit of the Rosicrucian rose. Certainly it is more than coincidence

---

[9] For detailed accounts of the symbolic rituals of the grades of the Order, see Aleister Crowley, "The Temple of Solomon the King," *The Equinox*, I (September, 1909), 239–334, and II (March, 1910), 135–280; Irving Regardie, *The Golden Dawn*, 4 vols. (Chicago, 1937), *passim*.

that in his subsequent writing he shows a markedly increased preoccupation with things occult.

In the stories of *The Secret Rose,* all of which were written in or after 1893, the flower of the poet's eternal ideal has become almost wholly indistinguishable from that of the Rosicrucian's Divine Spirit. It is true that Yeats's earlier roses had also leaned heavily on the occult. But in them the occult was so much identified with private romantic yearnings or with Shelleyan-Platonic Beauty that they could to a great extent be understood without special knowledge of esoteric beliefs. This is not true of the stories and poems written after Yeats's initiation. Even his cover design for *The Secret Rose,* first published in 1897, is entirely esoteric. Among other abstruse symbols, it presents a Rose Cross in the midst of the Kabba-listic Tree of Life.[10] Furthermore, the stories themselves, although suffused with Yeats's earlier mood of infinite and sorrowful longing, reveal a significant change in temper. The attempt to deny or transcend earthly wishes appears to be gaining the upper hand, for the poet is now less conscious of conflict, more single-minded in his pursuit of an exalted if tragic ideal that mingles eternity with death.

In the first two stories the cross of suffering is thoroughly explored. The outcast in "The Crucifixion of the Outcast" has endured isolation and sorrow throughout the world for the sake of an eternal vision: "And I have been the more alone upon the roads and by the sea because I heard in my heart the rustling of the rose-bordered dress of her who is . . . more lovely than a bursting dawn to them that are lost in darkness." [11] Crucified in the end for defying cruel monks, he, like a forsaken Christ, learns the final agony of desertion even by the beggars to whom he has given his last

[10] The full cover design is reproduced and interpreted in Richard Ell-mann, *The Identity of Yeats* (New York, 1954), pp. 64–65, 75.

[11] *Early Poems and Stories* (London, 1925), pp. 341–43. Future citations from Yeats's stories are to this edition. (Note the phrase "bursting dawn" above for possible associations with Yeats's Order of the Golden Dawn.)

meal. The Rosicrucian knight in "Out of the Rose" endures a similarly dismal fate. He too has had a vision that has determined his life: "He had seen a great Rose of Fire, and a Voice out of the Rose had told him . . . that none of those who had seen clearly the truth could enter into the Kingdom of God, which is in the Heart of the Rose, if they stayed on willingly in the corrupted world; and so they must prove their anger against the Powers of Corruption by dying in the service of the Rose" (*Stories,* p. 332). Renouncing the world for the sake of God's battles, this knight suffers earthly and spiritual hardships throughout life and dies in recovering a drove of stolen pigs for a band of ungrateful peasants who immediately forsake him.

In both stories it is sorrow that gives rise to the quest for the rose. The heroes are Yeatsean self-projections: an outcast gleeman who has found life barren by contrast with the ideal in his heart, and a knight with the melancholy "face of one of those who have come but seldom into the world, and always for its trouble, the dreamers who must do what they dream, the doers who must dream what they do" (*Stories,* p. 334). Finding sorrow in the contrast between life and the dream, they seek to actualize the dream by renouncing in life all that is incompatible. But the result of their quest must be as sorrowful as its cause. Since the heart of the dream is an eternity of spirit, the quest for the dream symbolized by the rose is in the last analysis a quest for physical death. The cross of suffering is the cross that temporal life must be to those who have glimpsed the eternal rose.

The death-wish, previously apparent in many poems of *The Rose,* has been carried to its Rosicrucian conclusion in the first two stories of *The Secret Rose.* The difference is slight but real. In the poems the ideal for which men died was conceived of in terms of eternal Beauty; in the stories it has become the more inclusive, more occult, eternal Spirit. The motivation has remained essentially unchanged, but the quest for a Rosicrucian solution to life's problems has intensified. This becomes still more evident in the last three stories of *The Secret Rose,* all of which were written in 1896. In them Yeats turns from the cross of suffering, a depressing thing when considered alone, to explore its counterpart and ful-fillment, the rose of eternal life. For if one accepts the world as a place of interminable frustration and renounces all desire for temporal fulfillment, one may find at least hope in con-templation of the rebirth to follow death. Although not wholly free of former elements of conflict, the last three stories of the volume, comprised in the *Rosa Alchemica* group, reflect the growing dominance of occultism over Yeats's mind.

Because they are told by a narrator, Owen Aherne, who has fled from the rose to the Catholic Church, the stories appear on the surface to repudiate the occult. However, symbol and tone make the narrator's choice seem of dubious wisdom. The usual battle of matter with spirit is now expressed through warring religions. The Catholic cross, unaffiliated with the true rose, becomes symbolic of surrender to external authority and the conventional world, while the alchemical rose flaunts its opposing doctrine of obedience to the laws of one's inner-most, divine nature. Eliphas Lévi, a Rosicrucian leader who much influenced Yeats, had abandoned Catholicism for the occult and had written in his *History of Magic* that the rose expressed all Renaissance protests against medieval Cathol-icism: "It was the flesh protesting against the oppression of the spirit . . . it was humanity aspiring to a natural religion, full of love and reason, founded on the revelation of the harmonies of existence of which the Rose was for initiates the living and blooming symbol. . . . The conquest of the Rose was the problem offered by initiation to science, while religion toiled to prepare and establish the universal, exclusive, and definitive triumph of the Cross." [12] Yeats's stories, despite the narrator's point of view, seem almost an elaboration of that text.

In "The Tables of the Law" the occult doctrine of the individual as microcosm of the macrocosm is developed. Owen Aherne, discovering the law of the universe through discovering the law of his own nature, is horrified to find that he can no longer fill a place in a society built on Christian foundations. But purple-robed spirits, representing the Order of the Alchemical Rose, proclaim the supremacy of a sphere of existence terrifying to those who wish peace in this world: "He has charged even his angels with folly, and they also bow and obey; but let your heart mingle with our hearts, which are wrought of divine ecstasy, and your body with our bodies, which are wrought of divine intellect" (*Stories*, p. 515). "The Adoration of the Magi" treats the belief that the occult divinity is symbolically expressed in the mythologies of all religions. The Christian emphasis on a single manifestation of God is contrasted, to its disfavor, with the innumerable manifestations acknowledged by the Order of the Alchemical Rose: "when people are good the world likes them and takes possession of them, and so eternity comes through the people who are not good or who have been forgotten. Perhaps Christianity was good and the world liked it, so now it is going away and the immortals are beginning to awake" (*Stories*, p. 524).

"Rosa Alchemica" develops these occult concepts more fully. Aherne, who is at first attracted to esoteric symbols by an esthetic appreciation, soon finds his appreciation deepening to spiritual desire. In this state he accompanies the occultist, Michael Robartes, to the temple of the Order of the

[12] *The History of Magic*, tr. A. E. Waite (New York, 1930), p. 351. In "The Last of the Romantics," *Sewanee Review*, LV (1947), 297–323, Hiram Haydn points out the Rose-Cross opposition and its relation to the passage from Eliphas Lévi, but he gives it a different interpretation in relation to the body of Yeats's work.

Alchemical Rose, wherein spiritual mysteries are manifest. On the ceiling of the temple is a great rose and on the floor a cross, reminiscent of the decorations in the Rosicrucian initiatory vault. The meaning of these symbols is brought out by a mystic dance in which the crucifix, symbol of the Christian emphasis on a single God, is ritualistically obliterated by the Rosicrucian rose: "I saw that the floor was of a green stone, and that a pale Christ on a pale cross was wrought in the midst. I asked Robartes the meaning of this, and was told that they desired 'to trouble his unity with their multitudinous feet.' The dance wound in and out, tracing upon the floor the shapes of petals that copied the petals in the rose overhead" (*Stories*, p. 492). Occult concepts also decorate the temple walls. On these walls the Christian subordination of the individual's will to God's is opposed in a symbolic painting wherein Christian angels battle gods; "the gods glimmering like rubies and sapphires, and the angels of the one greyness, because . . . they had renounced their divinity, and turned from the unfolding of their separate hearts, out of love for a God of humility and sorrow" (*Stories*, p. 491).

This battle of spirit with matter or rose with cross had been presented by itself in the companion stories. In "Rosa Alchemica," however, it is seen as only one phase of a great spiritual event. The cross of temporal things and a temporal religion is to be ultimately transfigured in the kingdom of the spirit. Eliphas Lévi, in the *History of Magic*, had concluded his discussion of the Catholic-Rosicrucian opposition by considering reconciliation on an occult basis: "The reunion of the Rose and the Cross, such was the problem proposed by supreme initiation, and, in effect, occult philosophy, being the universal synthesis, should take into account all the phenomena of being" (p. 351). Yeats's story had begun with hints of a similar reunion. His narrator was aware that the alchemists had hit upon the ultimate solution and hidden it in symbols because it might appear destructive: "all must be dissolved before the divine substance, material gold or immaterial ecstasy awake . . . the birth of that elaborate spiritual beauty which could alone uplift souls weighted with so many dreams" (*Stories,* p. 469). The Alchemical Rose then symbolizes a great rebirth that is to follow the crucifixion of all present things. And the rebirth in question will transfigure not only the individual but the entire social and religious order.

In his desire for universal rebirth Yeats was following fellow occultists who believed that imminent actual wars were about to destroy corrupt civilization and usher in a golden age.[13] These extravagant prophecies made it possible for him to identify his inner stresses and failings with the stresses and failings of his world and to seek his personal redemption in the redemption of the whole material order. The *Rosa Alchemica* stories do retain, in their narrative framework, traces of earlier fears that the occult may be harmful to life and art. But the fears are much overbalanced by wonder and an almost hypnotic fascination. For the dominant mood of these stories is awe and the dominant themes are intensely occultist. In fact, the narrator's very terror upon confronting eternity's dangers seems to imply increased belief in the power of things esoteric. Rose poems in Yeats's next volume, *The Wind Among the Reeds* (1899), only serve to confirm this impression. The spellbound hope for universal rebirth expressed in "Rosa Alchemica" becomes the major theme of these poems, while indications of doubt and conflict become even less evident.

The poems are for the most part more difficult than their forerunners, despite Yeats's long-standing anxiety lest the occult becloud his art. As recently as "Rosa Alchemica" his narrator had claimed to have "passed through strange experiences, which have changed me so that my writings have grown less popular and less intelligible" (*Stories,* p. 465).

[13] Ellmann, *Man and Masks,* pp. 97–98.

And Yeats had early predicted, in regard to the poems of
The Rose, "that for a time I could rhyme of love, calling it
The Rose, because of the Rose's double meaning . . . but
that I must some day—on that day when the gates began to
open—become difficult or obscure." [14] Yet now that those
gates were beginning to open and his art was becoming correspondingly obscure, he expressed little concern. Perhaps
he felt that, since he had chosen to follow the "red-rose-
bordered hem," obscurity was inevitable and therefore point-
less to lament. Perhaps he felt that after all obscurity was
not so great a price to pay for transcendent vision. But it is
more likely that he gained support for his own growing
esotericism from further acquaintance with the French.

Since his knowledge of the French language was poor,
Yeats was directly familiar with very few French works.
However, through his friendship with Arthur Symons in the
late 1890s, he did gain an indirect knowledge of the French
symbolist movement. In the *Autobiographies* he suggests that
it was Symons's translations from Mallarmé that "may have
given elaborate form to . . . the latter poems of *The Wind
Among the Reeds.*" But it seems a good deal more likely that
what influence there was came less from Symons's watered-
down renditions that resemble neither Mallarmé nor Yeats
than from the introduction Symons gave him to French aims
and theories. For Yeats helped Symons with the writing of
The Symbolist Movement in Literature (1899). [15] Reading
in Symons's manuscript of writers engaged in expressing the
unseen by visible symbols, he recognized their efforts as
parallel to his own. Reading further of Mallarmé's preoccupation with the formal arrangement of words themselves to
"create an atmosphere by the actual suggestive quality of
their syllables," he enlarged his own symbolic theories. In

---

[14] *Autobiographies,* p. 153. "To the Rose upon the Rood of Time" had
expressed the same anxiety.
[15] Ellmann, *Man and Masks,* p. 140.

"The Symbolism of Poetry" (1900) Yeats stressed the supreme importance of form to the expression of supersensual truths: "All sounds, all colours, all forms . . . call down among us certain disembodied powers, whose footsteps over our hearts we call emotions; and when sound, and colour, and form are in a musical relation . . . to one another, they become as it were one sound, one colour, one form, and evoke an emotion that is made out of their distinct evocations and yet is one emotion" (*Essays*, p. 193).

These ideas are put in practice in *The Wind Among the Reeds.* Because his themes were becoming more esoteric than ever, Yeats required a method of expression correspondingly more abstruse. The new poems, to a greater extent than any in *The Rose,* replace surface meaning with combinations of symbol, sound, rhythm, and atmosphere meant to convey indefinable mysteries. It is true that the rose still carries associations with personal sorrow, love, and Ireland. But, as might be expected, these old associations are now placed in a new perspective. For Yeats is chiefly absorbed by the coming spiritual millenium, and is accordingly less concerned with the occult as remedy for personal moods than with personal moods as symbolic harbingers of the victory of Spirit in God's long battle. Suggesting through indefinite verse the nebulous infinite, Yeats created in Ireland a symbolic medium comparable to that of the French for purposes of expressing "the trembling of the veil of the temple" he believed was affecting the entire age.

Old themes and symbols took on new coloring in the light of what lay behind the veil. Love for Maud Gonne, once symbolic of man's insatiable longing for ideal Beauty, came to symbolize the necessity for universal redemption. "The Lover Tells of the Rose in his Heart" appears on the surface to be no more than a slight and sentimental love lyric. But appearances are often deceptive in *The Wind Among the Reeds.* Beneath the poem's simplicity lurks Yeats's current preoccupation with the universal rebirth to follow a universal deluge. The image of his beloved, which "blossoms a rose" in the poet's heart, is meant to be identified with the Rosicrucian rose of eternal Spirit as well as with the conventional flower of earthly love. Since the vast ugliness of the temporal world is wronging that idealized image, the poet longs for the spiritual regeneration that will redeem all present things:

The wrong of unshapely things is a wrong too great to be told;
I hunger to build them anew and sit on a green knoll apart,
With the earth and the sky and the water, re-made like a casket
    of gold
For my dream of your image that blossoms a rose in the deeps of
    my heart.   (*Poems,* p. 54)

"The Poet Pleads with the Elemental Powers" is a more complicated development of the same basic theme. In a note to the poem Yeats associates his "Immortal Rose" with the divine flower of the major religions, with the secular flower of beautiful women, and with the particular flower of Ireland derived from some ancient Celtic goddess.[16] In the text of the poem it is associated with Maud Gonne as well: "Encircle her I love and sing her into peace/That my old care may cease." Here, as in *The Rose,* Maud Gonne, Ireland, and the Divine Spirit are identified and expressed through a single, multi-leveled symbol. But tone and purpose have now altered in accord with Yeats's new hopes. The Immortal Rose has been plucked from the Tree of Life by mysterious Powers, who have thereby entrammeled the eternal in the temporal "nets of day and night." And the poet's concern is no longer with the justification of his personal nationalism or the sublimation of his personal love, but with the return of the cosmic rose to her harmonious place in the scheme of things: "But let a gentle silence wrought with music flow/Whither her footsteps go" (*Poems,* p. 69).

[16] *The Wind Among the Reeds,* pp. 74–78.

In "The Blessed" the rose is related to intense human passion. Recalling Blake in manner and matter (and incidentally suggesting the classical rose of Dionysus), the poem associates holiness with the irrational pursuit of emotion, here symbolized by drunkenness:

> O blessedness comes in the night and the day
> And whither the wise heart knows;
> And one has seen in the redness of wine
> The Incorruptible Rose,
>
> That drowsily drops faint leaves on him
> And the sweetness of desire,
> While time and the world are ebbing away
> In twilights of dew and of fire.   (*Poems*, p. 66)

The rose, of course, is not itself identified with a state of drunken passion, but such passion is presented as a means to spiritual vision. And the vision in question involves not only an Incorruptible Rose but also the ebbing away of all corrupt temporal things. The great spiritual rebirth that Yeats so eagerly awaited was to be attained through no act of intellect but through the unhampered human heart.

"The Secret Rose" elaborates these ideas. By far the most important rose poem in the volume, it gathers into itself the themes of all the rest. The poet opens with a plea:

> Far-off, most secret, and inviolate Rose,
> Enfold me in my hour of hours; where those
> Who sought thee in the Holy Sepulchre,
> Or in the wine-vat, dwell beyond the stir
> And tumult of defeated dreams; and deep
> Among pale eyelids, heavy with the sleep
> Men have named beauty.   (*Poems*, p. 67)

The rose is here described as "far-off, most secret, and inviolate" because its full significance cannot be comprehended until one has died to things as they appear to be. The poet's "hour of hours" is the hour of his death and rebirth, and the "defeated dreams" of Christianity, the wine-vat, and love turn out to be the various passions that can lead men through temporal defeat to eternal triumph. For the dominant theme is again that of a great spiritual regeneration, and the means to regeneration is again a passion so intense that men will renounce the material world for it.

The poem goes on to illustrate the passionate pursuit of ideals that have led ultimately to the rose. Among men chosen as illustration are not only the Magi, who pursued the occult directly through magic, but also Conchubar, Cuchulain, Caolite, and Fergus, who pursued it indirectly through Christ, love, heroism, and wine, respectively. The preponderance of Irish heroes over any others indicates that the rose is Irish as well as universal, and that the anticipated redemption will be national as well as international. Yeats is still attempting to synthesize personal with occult values, and in this poem seems for the first time to be doing it with some success. Encompassing Yeats's own ideals of love, Ireland, magic, religion, and heroism, the legendary questers of the poem, like the poet himself, hopefully await the coming redemption of all things in the temporal world. The poem, despite the question mark, ends on a more positive note than Yeats had yet expressed in connection with the rose:

> I, too, await
> The hour of thy great wind of love and hate.
> When shall the stars be blown about the sky,
> Like the sparks blown out of a smithy, and die?
> Surely thine hour has come, thy great wind blows,
> Far-off, most secret, and inviolate Rose? (*Poems*, p. 67)

"The Secret Rose," which had headed the volume of stories by the same title before its inclusion in *The Wind Among the Reeds*, gives relatively full expression to Yeats's occult themes of the late 1890s. Enabling him to transmute personal sorrow into universal hope, the occult was proving itself to be temporarily beneficial. Since the cosmic triumph of Spirit was to bring about his particular salvation as well, he could perceive his troubles as an integral part of a transcendent pattern. The imminent annihilation of all existing things, which must precede the rosy millenium, could hold few terrors for a man who found little in his immediate lot to praise. And grave dissatisfactions with his life and self could be distinctly minimized when seen against a background of universal corruption and a foreground of universal hope. In fact, it may have been this more definite trend in his thinking that now made possible his completion of *The Shadowy Waters* (1900), a play on which he had been working indecisively for many years.

Since Yeats had been writing and rewriting this play on and off from 1885 through 1889, it includes most of the major concerns of his early work. Its hero, Forgael, is, like Yeats, a dreamer and an artist. Through the visionary powers of imagination he is in touch with the spiritual world; through the playing of a magic harp, symbolic of Yeats's conception of poetry, he casts spells over his listeners. The play's heroine, Dectora, is a proud and beautiful woman, remarkably like the Helen and Deirdre figures Yeats had identified with Maud Gonne. Its theme is once again the quest for an ideal level of being wherein unsatisfied earthly needs will find eternal spiritual fulfillment. And again mortal passion is seen as an intimation of all that can never be realized in the mortal world:

> It's not a dream
> But the reality that makes our passion.
> As a lamp shadow—no—no lamp, the sun.
> What the world's million lips are thirsting for
> Must be substantial somewhere.[17]

[17] *The Collected Plays,* 2nd ed. (London, 1952), p. 151.

Axël, treating a similar theme, contributed much to the conception of Yeats's well worked-over plan. Although the characters are Yeats's own, the intent is analogous to Villiers' and is likewise founded on Rosicrucian doctrine. Yeats substitutes a predominantly Irish symbolism for the occult symbolism of Villiers, but the concepts evoked are similar. And, too, in some versions Dectora appears with a rose embroidered on her breast. And in the acting version Yeats inserted a passage making explicit the correspondence between his or any other symbols and those of the occult:

> I have but images, analogies,
> The mystic bread, the sacramental wine,
> The red rose where the two shafts of the cross,
> Body and soul, waking and sleep, death, life,
> Whatever meaning ancient allegorists
> Have settled on, are mixed into one joy.[18]

It is to the eternal harmony signified by the red rose that the lovers in *The Shadowy Waters* aspire. Like the lovers in *Axël,* Forgael and Dectora have "everything that life can give/In having one another," but choose to renounce supreme earthly happiness for still greater glories. The play closes on their ecstatic decision to sail westward in quest of a temporal death that will presumably be a spiritual rebirth.

The Shadowy Waters applies to Yeats's personal problems the same expectations of rebirth that he had applied to universal issues in *The Wind Among the Reeds.* The play, like the poems, is more positive in tone than his earlier work. Although eternity still demands the renunciation of all time, there is more exaltation and less gloom involved in the sacrifice. And taken together, the play, the poems, and even the *Rosa Alchemica* stories indicate that for a few years Yeats had found some measure of hope in turning to the indefinite

[18] *Ibid.,* p. 152.

future for the unity of being he had ceased to seek in the present. But the strange balance he had reached was clearly a dubious blessing and one that would presently prove to have been entirely precarious. More escapist than ever, his intensified occultism was to a dangerous degree an exercise in self-delusion. However he may have tried to universalize his dreams by relating them to an impersonal religious doctrine, he had not achieved the objective ordering of experience that might have sustained him through a personal crisis. While Maud Gonne was beyond the reach of mortal man, it might be possible to love her in immortal fashion. But when in 1903 she married Major John MacBride, the complexion of things took on a new coloring. The material world had won a major victory over the Rose of Battle, and Yeats was forced to acknowledge that for him that rose had proved an impoverished sublimation for personal lack.

Fundamentally, of course, it was not the occult as such that had turned out to be destructive to Yeats's life and art. In later years he would succeed in forging out of spiritual mysteries a healthy and powerful poetry and vision. But what had been destructive in his early work was the use he chose to make of esoteric doctrine. The self-projected death-wish that lay only half concealed beneath the uneasy cover of immortal life had remained throughout at the very core of Yeats's difficulties and roses. For although in the earlier writing his death-wish was clearer because more conscious, it continued under the guise of eternity to cast a hypnotic pall over the later. Dissatisfied with himself and unhappy in his love, he had exploited the Cross-Rose pattern as a means of personal escape and an excuse for personal failure. For a time he could delude himself into believing that failure, flight, and life-denial were synonymous with eternal Spirit, but self-deceptive dreams could not survive the shock of Maud Gonne's very real and temporal marriage. Unable any longer to maintain an impossible balance between longing and possession or eternity and time, he had to face at last the desperate necessity of coming to terms with actual life if he wished to really live at all.

Accordingly, in his subsequent writing Yeats labored towards a more objective outlook and technic. And in his rehabilitation of experience and art, he left behind him the unharmonious rose of his indefinite, introverted youth. Rarely in the later poems does the flower appear at all, and when it does it is looked upon with a new detachment. Seldom even a symbol, it sporadically crops up to convey old meanings in simple, metaphoric fashion. "The Rose Tree" employs it only as a metaphor of Ireland; "The Three Bushes" employs it only as a metaphor of human love; "The Mountain Tomb," although a poem about Father Rosicross, employs it only as a simple token of the glorious past: "Bring roses if the rose be yet in bloom." Even on those two occasions when it is again a genuine symbol, the rose is held at a notable distance. In *A Vision* the flower that was once supreme has been significantly relegated to the most subjective quarter of the Great Wheel.[19] In "Meditations in Time of Civil War" it symbolizes not a remote eternity but rather those qualities of poetry and imagination that can still blossom on the "stony ground" of Yeats's distress in a war-torn society.

The characteristics of the rose that Yeats repudiated were for the most part characteristics of nineteenth-century literature that were to be repudiated in the twentieth century. The nebulous quality of mood and reference and the predominant subjectivity of the symbol were typical of the softer aspects of romanticism. Typical also were the longing for an unattainable, escapist ideal and the attempt to associate that ideal at once with absolute Beauty and with personal melancholy. Seeking to discover eternal realities in personal needs, Yeats,

[19] *A Vision* (London, 1937), p. 66. As symbol of subjectivity as opposed to objectivity, the rose here symbolizes as well beauty as opposed to truth, value as opposed to fact, and the like, in contrast to its former role as symbol of the eternal reconciliation of all antitheses.

like many of his predecessors, had succeeded in projecting his particular problems into generalized concepts of the absolute. When he looked back on his early work many years later he added a note to the poems of *The Rose*: "The quality symbolized as The Rose differs from the Intellectual Beauty of Shelley and Spenser in that I have imagined it as suffering with man and not as something pursued and seen from afar." [20] Whatever may have been the case with Shelley or with Spenser, symbolism was for Yeats at first a highly developed romantic medium for confusing private sentiments with cosmic principles.

Furthermore, his method as well as his outlook was in many ways typical of nineteenth-century romanticism. The poetry of *The Rose* was a development of factors in the English tradition, and that of *The Wind Among the Reeds* paralleled in important features the French symbolist movement. In the earlier poems the Platonic ideal of beauty, as filtered through English poetry, was given the symbolic complexity of Blake by its fusion with the Rosicrucian concept of a spiritual eternity imperfectly reflected in material appearances. Into this mystically Platonic rose, Yeats poured personal emotions with a lyrical directness that differed from that of Shelley or even of Dowson in degree of complexity more than in kind. By the time of writing *The Wind Among the Reeds* Yeats had increased his knowledge of French symbolist theory as well as of Rosicrucian practice, and this helps to account for his attempts to transmute the rose of personal idealism into the more remote and mysterious symbol of vaster powers or realities. Creating out of subjective moods an indefinable sense of cosmic mysteries, Yeats approached in these poems the effects of symbolists whose language he was unable to read.

But Yeats's rose did more than exemplify the manner and matter of nineteenth-century symbolists. For Yeats differed from most of his romantic predecessors in deriving his symbols

---

[20] *Collected Poems*, p. 447. This note is dated 1925.

from traditional sources and attempting to relate them to traditional meanings. Believing that his personal emotions were manifestations of the one Great Memory or Soul of the World, he sought to convey this relationship through symbols long significant in the mind of man. At the same time that his rose is clouded by remote esoteric beliefs or uncertain private emotions, it also gains richness and body by traditional associations with love, beauty, and Ireland. Beyond this, it gains some portion of the universality of great art and provides at least an initial step towards the integration of private emotions into a larger, more objective ordering of experience. Although despite tradition the rose poems are overly subjective, they cannot be dismissed as no more than overly subjective. In so far as Yeats tended to rely on the fact that the rose was traditional and rooted in the Great Mind as an excuse for stressing its relevance to his personal difficulties alone, he represented a passing phase of romanticism. But in so far as he attempted to enrich personal emotions through traditional associations, he anticipated one of the major and most essential developments of the contemporary symbol.

5

THE

CONTEMPORARY

SYMBOL

The lessons that Yeats was learning in Ireland at the turn of the century were soon to find their parallels among symbolist writers in England. Although specific causes of discord differed, a comparable need to make peace with the world produced comparable effects among English writers. Threatened with war, mechanism, and materialism, many poets could no longer afford romantic flight to private dreams, while the private dreams themselves, in inevitable reflection of daily life, were taking on the more terrible qualities of nightmare. Seeking to comprehend or to redeem their lives and times, writers of the twentieth century were, like Yeats, compelled to transmute the symbolism of personal longing into a means for expressing relationships between inner values and the outer world. Though the artist still felt himself an exile from the commercial age he lived in, he now saw the need for understanding its import if he wished to understand his own or other human lives. As a result the subjective rose, from which Yeats had turned to the objective mask, was to become in subsequent decades a symbolic link between self and mankind.

Various factors conspired to make symbolism the dominant method in present-day literature. Some of these factors were carry-overs from the nineteenth century; others seemed new but in retrospect could be traced to nineteenth-century roots.

Certainly the materialism of the ruling middle class and the corresponding mechanization of society had continued to lacerate the artist seeking intangible beauties and truths. In addition, the chaos of wars wherein mechanism harried its own creators had arisen to mock fundamental beliefs in love and the hope of a future. The waning of religion in a world whose need for it had increased drove some who could find no gods to the edge of absolute negation. And a mounting sense of abandonment in a power-ridden, money-ridden era drove others to embrace political creeds that in the end deepened their disenchantment. Such prevailing social conditions made the condition of the artist desperate in respect to both his art and his humanity. Before he could remedy his condition he had to come to terms with the external world, and it was in so doing that he developed the symbol. For symbolism, making possible the integration of private with social meanings, of material with spiritual values, was perhaps the most adequate literary medium through which to express the complex problems of poets in a complex age.

Reading the French with greater understanding than their *fin-de-siècle* forebears, writers during the second decade of this century began adapting French means to their own ends. Since private idealism alone was insufficient to their needs, they applied symbols from public sources to contemporary social or personal problems. Seeking to comprehend their present, they placed it in relation to past ages for contrast or comparison. Seeking to comprehend themselves, they applied symbols of universal significance to their particular conditions. In doing so they created a symbolism neither so traditional as Dante's nor so personal as Blake's. Something of a cross between the two, modern symbols cover a wide range from the primarily subjective to the primarily objective. A rose, for example, sometimes alludes to the rose of Dante or of the classics as a means of conveying the likeness or distance between our times and those, or as a means of conveying the private attitudes of a particular writer towards the Christian or pagan view. The latter motive tends to produce a more personal flower than the former. But whatever the proportion of inner to outer, modern symbols usually avoid the extremes alike of medieval authoritarianism and of romantic hyper-subjectivity.

In creating a symbolism that could be at once personal and social, subtle and intelligible, modern writers were aided by developments in modern thought. The great upsurge of interest in symbols among psychologists, anthropologists, and philosophers, as well as among literary men, made what might once have been abstruse now available to the public. Freud, for instance, had helped men and writers to strenuous consciousness of the unconscious, and Frazer had revealed basic similarities in men's mythological beliefs despite disparities in race, era, and civilization. Moreover, Jung, although less widely followed, had related the archetypal symbols of myth to the individual conscious and unconscious mind. The stream of consciousness quite naturally became a stream of symbols in which personal meanings were merged with universal, while the symbols of ancient myth or religion came to refer to issues as recurrent in human life as the religious impulse itself. Because they drew on so many sources, modern symbols tended to be more complicated than those of the highly subjective nineteenth-century poets. But at the same time, because their sources were largely available to the public, modern symbols were often more easily comprehended and analyzed. Equipped with refurbished goals and advanced methods of achieving them, twentieth-century writers made of symbolism a less limited if perhaps less mysterious medium than it had hitherto been.

The gains for literature were undoubtedly greater than the losses. The mystery of the wholly private, almost wholly ineffable experience had led to the bafflements of Mallarmé and the quicksands of decadence. Modern symbolists for the most part avoided such self-consuming hazards, while at the same time retaining the visionary powers of their past. To a great extent they brought to literature new materials and new methods which made possible an art that could span the distance between dreams and the world. This development was essential if their writing was to progress at all. For although modern writers differed from their immediate forebears in seeking to relate to their era and in seeking objective systems of value that might impose order on disintegration, nonetheless the solutions they offered to the problems of their times remained fundamentally romantic. Whether religious, humanistic, pessimistic, or simply sensitive, their attitudes, like their world, revealed nineteenth-century origins. And beneath the complexities and developments of modern life and modern symbols remained nineteenth-century motives of transcendent longing or despair. A continuing awareness of life's futilities and horror became the present wasteland of dry sand and drier bones. A continuing need to believe in love, beauty, or redemption became the present rose of multi-foliate hope.

It is true that before the First World War, British roses were rarely symbolic and were even more rarely affected by the times. Overlooking Yeats's example, poets who had less to say expressed themselves in simpler ways. Bourgeois material-ism had confirmed romanticism, but havoc had not yet deepened its tone. Such Georgian poets as John Masefield could still retreat in nineteenth-century fashion from a desensi-tized urban society to bucolic areas where roses blossomed as metaphors for life's enduring beauty: "Dust-footed Time will never tell its hour,/Through dusty Time its rose will draw men on." Imagists like F. S. Flint could center their attention almost entirely on formal innovations, seeing in a rose no less nor more than the precise embodiment of a mood: "Into the dark of the arch the swan floats;/and the black depth of my sorrow/bears a white rose of flame." Even such a poet as

Walter de la Mare, achieving symbolism through combinations of atmosphere, dream images, sound, and rhythm, could create suggestive roses that grow neither in our present nor in any specifiable past: "Oh, no man knows/Through what wild centuries/Roves back the rose."

But as the world became more disturbing, writers found it more difficult to ignore. The country suffered as well as the town, the past seemed ironic when compared to the present, and the outlook of artists was affected by that which they looked out upon. The symbolic method, reemerging after 1910 under the auspices of France, Freud, and personal necessity, attempted to bridge the widening gulf between time and the timeless. In this attempt the rose, which through all time had encompassed man's highest hopes of earth or heaven, was of supreme importance. Its prevalence in the works of modern British symbolists had been equalled only by its prevalence in the works of medieval Europe; the key roles that it played in such leading writers as Yeats, Joyce, or Eliot had been equalled only by those it played in the *Roman de la Rose* or Dante. Our age, in despair of itself, sought the complex, intangible values that the Middle Ages had, and, in its attempt to express or discover a positive, possible hope, reemphasized the symbol of countless centuries of hope. In fact, the flower that since Isaiah had signified the fecundity promised to redeem the world's wilderness was the one unavoidable choice of writers seeking universal symbols through which to express their hope for redemption from the wastes of their lives or times.

For just as the wasteland can be said to be a prime symbol of our era, so the rose can be said to be its prime antithesis. Since by the twentieth century the rose had become the accepted flower of almost every positive value, it is not surprising that in modern literature it blossoms in abundance where despair has been routed or defied. A symbol essentially of fulfillment, the rose operates now as always on either the religious or the secular plane. Of course, within these general areas it serves as the flexible vehicle for a wide range of desires and beliefs. As such it runs the whole gamut from Virginia Woolf's efforts to find final meaning in subjective, evanescent human emotions to T. S. Eliot's efforts to find that final meaning in an objective, eternal spiritual order. Nor is the rose's symbolic function limited to the expression of positive attitudes. Through its deficiencies or corruptions it also sometimes expresses the absence of adequate values in the twentieth-century world. But lament for the absence of values is an inverse way of expressing values. And whether denial or affirmation is at the root of an artist's rose, the flower almost without exception embraces some sort of judgment made on existing conditions in the light of an ideal standard.

Roses expressing a negative judgment through their own failure to bear healthy blossoms are less common but not less worth notice than the abundant modern roses directly expressing a positive hope. Typical of and more explicit than most of the faulty roses in question is that in Robert Graves's short poem, "The Florist Rose." Here the poet perceives the artificially nourished hothouse rose as an emblem of our world. Unnatural in its manner of life as well as in its sleek appearance, this flower, like the machine, belongs to a man-made age of commerce that has lost its roots in the common soil:

> She of the long stem and too glossy leaf,
> Is dead to honest greenfly and leaf-cutter:
> Behind plate-glass watches the yellow fogs.
> Claims kin with the robust male aeroplane
> Whom eagles hate and phantoms of the air,
> Who has no legend as she breaks from legend—
> From fellowship with sword and sail and crown.[1]

---

[1] *Collected Poems* (London, 1948), p. 110.

Again from time to time in Edith Sitwell's early poems roses are used to emphasize the unnaturalness of our age. Less explicit than Graves's, her roses are generally more complex. That in "Romance," for instance, expresses not only the universal decay of love, joy, beauty, and faith through the literal and figurative death of the heart, but also on another level suggests the steady decline of the ages from a golden past to what in our present appears to foreshadow ultimate nil:

> The green rains drip like the slow beat of Time
> That grows within the amber blood, green veins
> Of the rich rose, and in the rose-shaped heart,
> —Changing the amber flesh to a clay wall.
> Then comes the endless cold
> At last, that is the Zero, mighty, old,
> Huge as the heart, but than the worm more small—[2]

Ailing or inadequate roses, used as symbols of social distress in Robert Graves and Edith Sitwell, find their counterparts on the plane of the individual life in poets who are chiefly concerned with private salvation or damnation. Dylan Thomas, for one, uses a declining rose to express a whole complex of personal feelings about the relation of life to death. In "The force that through the green fuse drives the flower," the force that creates and destroys is sex, and this force is made complex by Thomas's usual alliance of physical with spiritual death. As creator of life, sex is the source of inevitable death, while as original sin, it is the cause of spiritual as well as physical destruction. Moreover, the force pervades the entire natural order, linking the poet's personal destiny to that of all living things. Evoking conventional but appropriate associations with mutability, the rose of the poem becomes a symbol through suggestions of both Freudian and transcendental meanings:

[2] *The Canticle of the Rose* (New York, 1949), p. 112.

The force that through the green fuse drives the flower
Drives my green age; that blasts the roots of trees
Is my destroyer.
And I am dumb to tell the crooked rose
My youth is bent by the same wintry fever.[3]

Following Thomas in exploring the conscious or unconscious mind for symbols of the human condition, Henry
Treece and Peter Yates also discovered blighted roses. Treece's
themes are on the whole more limited than those of Thomas.
His laments for dying roses, despite frequent verbal pyro-
technics, recall the traditional laments over human evanescence of Arnold's "Requiescat" or Housman's "fields where
roses fade." Thomas's self-identification with sex, sin, and
cosmic death becomes Treece's simple plaint: "For death
upon the rose is my death too." In his "Elegy Unending"
Treece uses the rose frankly as no more than a token of love
for the deceased: "A rose is in the hand/A tear is in the
eye. . . ." And in the "Never-Ending Rosary" he treats in
complicated language an equally uncomplicated theme. Here
the poet in a maze of words is made sorrowfully aware that
the sunset, perceived as a rosary, typifies the waning of time
and therefore the final futility of all human aspiration: "Then
what my gain, if scorpion terrors lurk/To tear my hamlet-
heart out on the rose?" [4]

Peter Yates, who was also impressed by mutability and by
Thomas, brought to the subject of death more original attitudes than did Treece. Since death in Yates's poems is the
final reality, life takes on the shape of a nightmare in which
tortured beings vainly seek in illusions escape from their
underlying knowledge of destiny. The symbol of a carnal
rose supports Yates's recurrent symbols of bones, winter,
stone, and mirrors in conveying life's inexorable horror. The

---

[3] *Collected Poems* (New York, 1953), p. 10.
[4] *Collected Poems* (New York, 1946), pp. 21, 30 respectively.

rose of "The Impure Rose," for example, resembles that of
Thomas in signifying sex, creator of life, as well as the terrible life-death cycle thereby originated. Although lacking
Thomas's religious associations with sin, Yates's rose is also
impure, as life, corrupted by death, is impure when compared with the ideal. The flower that grows and declines
with the seasons suggests the futility of the life cycle. It
further suggests to Yates the dark, doomed wings of Icarus,
who, like all of mankind, found death in his flight to life:

> How soon you fall! Chimerical dark wings
> Descending in your ruin like the rain
> Perpetual. See how the feathers fly
> And whirl, down the vast alleys and the wastes
> Of life unlivable: dark falling leaves! [5]

Modern roses of death or despair of course derive much of
their value from the flower's prevailing alliance with the ways
of life and hope. The ailing rose of an ailing society or the
doomed rose of a doom-ridden man would lack their import
as symbols of loss if the rose were not normally positive. While
this has been true in all ages, it is more notably true in ours.
Since modern roses of sin and sorrow tend to go beyond
those of the past in extremities of anguish, the number and
force of our roses maintaining affirmative roots become significant as a measure of our still surviving hope. It is surely a
healthy sign that even in the troubled present the rose has
continued to be far more often linked with attempts to resolve
man's problems than with the deceptiveness of such attempts.
A recurrent vehicle of hope, it has served as the private and
public flower of values that contribute to the growth of man
and the world. For many writers such values exist on the
human level alone, while for others mortal life derives its
final meaning from its relation to an eternal, spiritual plan.
But whether public or private, mortal or immortal, the rose

[5] *The Motionless Dancer* (London, 1943), p. 28.

in modern writing most significantly appears as the repeatedly chosen symbol of an ultimate, possible fulfillment.

Among British writers who sought and found final meanings on the temporal plane, Virginia Woolf, E. M. Forster, Elizabeth Bowen, and Henry Green all used symbolic roses to express what they valued most. Their values were different as their views on man and society were different, yet not so different that the flexible rose could not encompass each alike. Virginia Woolf, to begin with, was the most subjective of these writers, and so used the rose throughout her novels as a minor but recurrent symbol of a highly personal fulfillment. Almost devoid of social significance in her major novels, the flower appears in intense moments during which her characters realize the ineffable meanings of their lives. The moments are moments of true vision expressing Mrs. Woolf's own conviction that ecstasy, solitude, love, and death are interchangeable aspects of life, and that only by accepting the kinship between things that seem diverse can the individual attain his highest possible fulfillment. Her rose is a symbol of affirmation but her affirmation embraces both anguish and ecstasy. For in the end it makes little difference whether it is "a rose or a ram's skull" carved over the door to Jacob's room. The universal symbols of fruition and of death refer in Virginia Woolf to the same reality.

The complex and contradictory nature of this reality is unknowable to the intellect and so must be reached intuitively and expressed through symbols. In *Mrs. Dalloway* (1925) the rose becomes one of many symbols conveying the basic harmony between such seeming discords as love and aloneness, life and death. Both Mrs. Dalloway and Septimus are associated with roses at significant points throughout the novel. Mrs. Dalloway's roses, like Mrs. Dalloway herself, at first seem to be related to all that is life-affirming. In a sudden moment of ecstasy the fulness of her life appears to her as a rose: "It was her life, and, bending her head over the hall table, she bowed beneath the influence, felt blessed and purified, saying to herself . . . how moments like this are buds on the tree of life, flowers of darkness they are, so she thought (as if some lovely rose had blossomed for her eyes only)." Again, later in the novel, her husband gives her roses, which recur in her thoughts through the rest of the book as reminders of happiness and which symbolize his real but inarticulate love for her: "He was holding out flowers —roses, red and white roses. (But he could not bring himself to say he loved her; not in so many words)." [6]

There are at the same time, however, undertones of isolation and death in Mrs. Dalloway's roses, "the only flowers she could bear to see cut." Her husband substitutes roses for the verbal expression of love he desires but finds impossible, while the rose of her own ecstatic fulfillment is a private flower of darkness. The hint of death and aloneness in Mrs. Dalloway's roses is sharpened by their relation to those of Septimus, who is finally to become her surrogate in suicide. For Septimus is also given roses in place of words. But his roses are dying and the desired communication they symbolize is not with the wife who gave them but with a dead man, the friend who had lost his life in that war in which Septimus had lost his mental balance: "The roses, which Rezia said were dead, had been picked by him in the fields of Greece. 'Communication is health; communication is happiness, communication'— he muttered." [7] Since communication with the dead means death, Septimus presently kills himself and thereby affords Mrs. Dalloway a final comprehension of the essential beauty and mystery in the oneness of life with death. The theme of death as a force giving meaning to the ecstasy in life is carried from Septimus's roses to Mrs. Dalloway's, just as in the general scheme of the novel it is carried from Septimus's suicide to the party that is Mrs. Dalloway's offering to life.

[6] *Mrs. Dalloway* (New York, 1925), pp. 43, 178–79 respectively.
[7] *Ibid.*, p. 141.

Roses in *To The Lighthouse* (1927) also show negative qualities enhancing affirmation. Mr. Ramsay recites poetry: "The China rose is all abloom and buzzing with the honey bee." And these lines inspire in Mrs. Ramsay an ecstatic revery that clarifies unstatable things. Coming just a few pages before Mrs. Ramsay's death and marking the culmination of the whole first section of the book, her revery at this time expresses through the feminine rose an attainment of ultimate truth similar on a smaller scale to Mr. Ramsay's concluding attainment of the masculine lighthouse. If the lighthouse in the sea symbolizes the union of time and eternity, male and female, intellect and emotion, so also the earlier rose symbolizes the reconcilement of opposites. Mrs. Ramsay, reading poetry, feels as though she were climbing upwards under red and white petals, "so that she only knew this is white, or this is red." Altogether exalted, she exchanges a glance with her husband in which their solitudes seem to dissolve in momentary union. On the strength of this moment she achieves, through Shakespeare's rose of love in absence, a symbolic vision in which human solitude is transcended in love and the sorrow of human life is transcended in ecstasy: " 'Nor praise the deep vermilion in the rose,' she read, and so reading she was ascending . . . on to the top, on to the summit . . . the essence sucked out of life and held rounded here—the sonnet." [8]

In *To The Lighthouse* and *Mrs. Dalloway,* Virginia Woolf's finest novels, she is occupied almost exclusively with the individual's inner world. Perhaps because the social order was still at least tolerable, she was able to turn from it to values she felt were more essential. But as the Second World War approached and outer pressures increased, Mrs. Woolf became disturbed by society's effect on man. The roses that blossom in her last two novels place the values of the private consciousness in the context of the external world. In *The*

[8] *To The Lighthouse* (New York, 1927), pp. 178–82.

Years (1937) that world is one that grows more shabby with the passage of time. The rose appears throughout as a symbol of the superior past through its relation to the mother of the main characters, a woman whose name was Rose and whose teacups and portrait are trimmed with roses. Appropriately, Virginia Woolf's flower of a once mixed but ecstatic reality now conveys Martin's somber vision. As the novel draws to a close, he perceives the mountains of aspiration as falling petals on the river of mutability and death: "Through his half-open eyes he saw hands holding flowers. . . . And were they flowers the hands held? Or mountains. . . . Then petals fell. . . . They fall and fall and cover all, he murmured . . . that was a white rose; that was a yellow rose. . . . And petals fell. There they lay . . . boats on a river. And he was floating, and drifting, in a shallop, in a petal, down a river into silence, into solitude." [9] It is true that this vision inspires Martin to propose a toast to the human race. And his toast relates his falling roses to the shower of petals thrown over Rose, his sister, named for their mother, who has devoted herself to mankind. But Rose's rosy homage in the context of the declining years indicates only that human values still keep a spark of hope alive.

Finally in *Between the Acts* (1941), written after the outbreak of war, Virginia Woolf depicts the public and private betrayal of hope. The social significance of this novel is made entirely explicit: wartime England has desolated the promise of the nation's earlier days. The rose of the Anglo-Saxon and medieval periods, personified in the pageant upon which the novel centers, can no longer come to blossom in the twentieth century's loveless wastes. It is this barren state of affairs that frustrated Isa, the principal character, apprehends in a moment of vision that has lost all trace of ecstasy: " 'Where do I wander?' she mused. 'Down what draughty tunnels? Where the eyeless wind blows? And there grows nothing for the

[9] *The Years* (London, 1937), pp. 457–58.

eye. No rose. To issue where? In some harvestless dim field where no evening lets fall her mantle; nor sun rises. All's equal there. Unblowing, ungrowing are the roses there.' " [10] Although even this final novel ends on a dubious note of hope, its tone is essentially that conveyed by its ungrowing rose. But the desolation involved, while unreassuring, is unsurprising. Virginia Woolf's earlier roses of personal fulfillment had blossomed only in delicate moments of ecstatic intuition. They were, like their author herself, bound to decline and then cease to endure in a world that crushes the finer perceptions beneath the weight of war.

But the quest for values that absorbed and destroyed Virginia Woolf had less deleterious effects on writers who built on firmer foundations than the tenuous refinements of private feelings. While love in some sense is always involved in modern roses that seek redemption, the forms love takes are manifold. In E. M. Forster, more concerned with the external world than was Mrs. Woolf, the individual's fulfillment requires social reorientation. Although not notably partial to flowers, Forster in *The Longest Journey* (1907) uses a significant rose to convey certain of his basic ideas. Symbolic of Rickie's conception of life, it expresses much that Forster believed in. For Rickie, a dreamer caught between the two worlds of desiccated social convention and the truth of his mother's spirit, is destroyed by the former. But in dying to save the life of his half-brother, Stephen Wonham, the natural son of his mother's love, he unknowingly spares for the future the reality he fails to find for himself. The symbolic rose near the end of the novel is created by Stephen out of burning paper. It symbolizes to Rickie the reality he has sought in humanity, literature, his wife, and the memory of his mother: "Still he saw the mystic rose and the tunnel dropping diamonds. He had been driven away alone, believing the earth had confirmed him. He stood behind things at last, and

[10] *Between the Acts* (New York, 1941), pp. 154–55.

knew that conventions are not majestic, and that they will not claim us in the end." [11]

Forster's ideal here is complex, intangible, but attainable. It involves a humanity pursuing real values of love, integrity, and freedom of spirit; it necessitates surmounting class-conditioned actions that stifle the innate, positive attributes of men. It is not to be attained by Rickie's romantic dreaming or by Stephen's opposite earthy qualities alone, but rather demands a balance between their separate natures. Rickie, disillusioned with Stephen and, still more mistakenly, with his mother, dies believing that "that mystic rose and the face it illumined meant nothing." But Stephen, who had created the mystic rose in the first place, had been able to kneel in the water and so to follow its progress well beyond Rickie's remoter view: "It vanished for Rickie; but Stephen, who knelt in the water, declared that it was still afloat, far through the arch, burning as if it would burn forever." [12] Since Rickie's death has saved not only Stephen's life but also his spirit, Stephen goes on to fulfill the prophecy of his enduring rose. For he, like others in Forster, fathers a notable child, the hope of the future, named for their mother, in whom the rose of Rickie's earth is confirmed.

Forster then sought and in theory found ways and means of surmounting the sterility of upper middle-class England. Elizabeth Bowen sought ways of expressing it and also found a rose. Her novels and stories alike concern themselves with the need for love and with the distortions of that emotion in her immediate world. "Look at All Those Roses" (1941), title story of a collection on England between two wars, expresses her usual themes through an unusual garden of roses. The roses here carry a frightening irony used to expose the disease of an era that clings to the decayed romanticism of the past. For Lou, the central character, like so many

[11] *The Longest Journey* (Norfolk, Conn., 1922), p. 314.
[12] *Ibid.*, p. 309.

others in Elizabeth Bowen, sees life "in terms of ideal moments" and is therefore unable to accept the real. Driving to London with Edward, a lover whom she lives in neurotic dread of losing, she is impressed by a garden of roses in front of a fading country house. The place becomes in her twisted fancy the ideal home she thinks she lacks, a home in which she could find with Edward the ideal love she thinks she wants. But the car breaks down, she decides to remain there while Edward goes to the village for help, and the disease at the heart of the roses, like that at the heart of Lou's ideals, becomes increasingly evident.

The house and garden turn out to be run by an austere, unapproachable woman, who lives there in isolation with her hopelessly crippled child. While the house with its "extinct paper and phantom cretonne" is dead, the roses, like their keepers, seem to command an ominous life: "Most pretty scenes have something passive about them, but this looked like a trap baited with beauty. . . . Hundreds of standard roses disturbed with fragrance the dead air. In this spell-bound afternoon, with no shadows, the roses glared . . . frighteningly bright." [13] It is in such a place, amid such roses, that Lou is able to reach fulfillment. Lying on her back in the garden, she attains her ultimate ecstasy. But the ecstasy in question is an "ecstasy of indifference," divorced from beauty, hope, or human affirmation. In fact, through her rosy vision Lou at last becomes aware that the true end of her nervous desires is the final absence of all desires, that the true end of her anxious love is the final absence of all love. Moreover, the irony grows inescapable when Edward returns from the village with gossip. The house is the scene of suspected murder and the corpse is probably under the roses with which Lou had felt her greatest kinship. Symbols of evil, murder, extinction, and a moribund life cut off from the living, the roses expose the hypnotic but terrible nature of

[13] *Look at All Those Roses* (New York, 1949), p. 175.

twisted human love and of an ingrown romantic craving that no longer accords with the present world.

Love is then the value expressed by the roses in Elizabeth Bowen's work—not a love that is mixed with time as it is in Virginia Woolf or a love that is mixed with social ideals as it is in E. M. Forster, but a simple, positive love between people sharing each other's lives. Of course, this love is expressed inversely through the roses of those who cannot achieve it, but the meaning of the story is clear: only through healthy, outgoing love can Lou's or anyone's world be saved. A similar theme with more ramifications is again expressed by roses in Henry Green's novel, *Back* (1946). As symbolic as Miss Bowen's story but considerably more direct, *Back* embraces both the terror and wonder in human love. It is built around the rose, for the girl Charley Summers had loved was named Rose and neither woman nor flower is ever absent from his mind. A genuine symbol, the rose acquires associations with death, woman, mother, rebirth, all of which are directly related to Green's over-all concept of love. For the novel treats Charley's pain and salvation after his return from the Second World War minus his leg, his emotional balance, and the woman he loves. And Charley's particular struggle is given universal meaning through the rose that is both a specific woman and a symbol of redemptive human love.

Three passages in particular develop the book's symbolic themes. Associations between love and death are made at the outset in a cemetery filled with climbing roses wherein Charley seeks the grave of Rose. The roses, growing amid tombstones and nourished by the dead, suggest the endless cycle of love and mourning, life and death. In addition, they suggest that cycle's special relation to Charley, whose life has centered in an ideal Rose that has nearly been the death of his mind and body: "He might have been watching for a trap who had lost his leg in France for not noticing the gun beneath a rose. For climbing around and up those trees of mourning, was rose after rose, while, here and there . . . a live wreath lay fallen on a wreath of stone, or on a box in marble colder than this day . . . wherein the dear departed encouraged life above in the green grass, the cypresses and in those roses gay and bright." [14] The life cycle, of which death is a part, includes rebirth. The tendency to abandon himself to dreams and feelings, which had come close to being Charley's destruction, will become his salvation. For the cemetery scene, with its emphasis on mourning, finds its counterpart in the garden of a bombed out villa where Charley finds in Rose's sister, Nance, the reawakening of his love.

Nance, confused in Charley's suffering mind with Rose because of her close resemblance to her sister, begins in the garden to revive his failing spirit. The garden's roses, like Charley's love for Rose, have been withered by autumn and the war. They recall in wording and arrangement those of the graveyard where Rose lies: "briers that had borne gay rose, after rose, after wild rose, to sway under summer rain, to spatter the held drops, to touch a forehead, perhaps to wet the brown eyes of someone idly searching these cypresses for an abandoned nest whence fledglings, for they go before the coming of a rose, had long been gone, long ago now had flown." But there is a counterside to desiccation. Sunset in the garden creates for Charley live roseate flames on the bare rose briers: "the briers wreathed from one black cypress to another were aflame, as alive as live filaments in an electric-light bulb, against this night's quick agony of the sun." Further, it creates for him another rose of the girl he is just beginning to love: "her breath an attar of roses on his deep sun-red cheek, her hair an animal over his eyes and alive, for he could see each rose-glowing separate strand." [15]

Marriage to Nance, the third and last symbolic climax of the book, completes Charley's cycle of death and birth.

[14] *Back* (New York, 1950), p. 3.
[15] *Ibid.*, pp. 207–8.

Through Nance the rose of his love is reborn: "And because the lamp was lit, the pink shade seemed to spill a light of roses over her in all their summer colors. . . . 'Rose,' he called out, not knowing he did so, 'Rose.' " [16] Having found an equivalent to his first, lost love, Charley has found happiness and also peace. For his rose, who fulfills his need for help as well as love, plays the roles both of mother and of wife to him. His persistent fusion of Nance with Rose points up his emotional needs and problems. But at the same time this fusion of the two women, and the transference of identical needs from one to the other, seem meant to suggest that Nance and Rose share alike certain qualities basic to love and to women. The rose thus becomes a universal symbol of the regenerative power of woman's love, a symbol in which death, love, life, sex, and mother are united and reconciled. Its specific application to the struggles and fulfillment of a nerve-shattered veteran of the Second World War gives it, in addition to its universal values, a particular meaning for our war-shattered times.

The elaborate development of the rose in *Back* is perhaps second only to that in *Ulysses* in expressing the supremacy of human love. It may even be significant that Green's roses, like Joyce's, sometimes seem to echo through imagery of light Dante's final mystic rose, thereby further reinforcing on the human plane the importance of the force that moves the heavenly spheres. But whether or not echoes of Joyce or Dante are intended, Green's use of a highly suggestive symbol has given his rather commonplace characters universal meaning as bearers of the theme of love's redemptive powers. Roses in Virginia Woolf, E. M. Forster, and Elizabeth Bowen had also had something to say about love. Green's use of the flower is more extensive than theirs, more intricate and more entirely essential to the expression of his novel's over-all meanings. It is not, however, different in kind. All four alike reveal in one

[16] *Ibid.*, p. 246.

way or another the adaptability of the rose to present-day ideals of personal fulfillment. All four reveal to one degree or another the present-day attempt to use the symbol as a bridge between the private individual and the public world in which he lives.

The modern rose of personal, secular fulfillment has almost always been related to human love. Although the shapes of love have varied, as in the writers mentioned, now as in all ages the rose's roots remain the same. But the flower has roots in religious love as well, and to some modern writers the supernal has been needed to give meaning to the run-down human world. The traditional meanings offered by the Christian faith have appealed to those who could accept them or could see no other hope. Still others, who have found Christianity lacking, have created their own transcendental systems. In either case, the rose of writers spiritually inclined often demonstrates not only the integration of personal with social meanings found in secular writers, but also an added integration of traditional religious meanings with both. There is of course much range in degree of traditionalism. At one end of the scale is the highly subjective rose of D. H. Lawrence's personal creed; at the other end is the deliberately derivative, Dantesque rose of Charles Williams's Catholicism. And somewhere in between one finds the loosely Christian flowers of George Barker or the later Edith Sitwell. Nonetheless, even Lawrence's romantic transcendentalism, personal and unorthodox as it is, draws, as some nineteenth-century predecessors did not, upon public or traditional stores of meaning to enrich the significance of private symbols.

As Lawrence's work progresses, his rose increasingly takes on the values of a personal creed revealed to the unconscious and expressed through symbols. Seeking a cure for the disorders of the individual and the world, Lawrence preached the reversal of established attitudes. Intellect he held responsible for both the mechanism of science and the Christian denial of body in the interests of soul. These in turn he held responsible for the multiple ills of the world. Like writers a hundred years before him, Lawrence sought a return to nature and the natural in human beings, defying in the process both the "moral" laws of the Church and the "mechanical" laws of a scientific, materialistic age. And like the early romantics, he believed in the basic goodness of man. But a century had passed between Lawrence and his precursors, a century bringing advances in psychiatric thought. Lawrence, who knew about Freud, replaced consciousness with the unconscious as his measure of values and sought his return to natural harmony through the fundamental kinship between men and things revealed in the blood's darker passages. Furthermore, while indebted to Freud for the concept of the unconscious, he rejected Freud's conception of what was located there. In place of Freud's "slimy serpent of sex . . . and excrement," as he termed it, Lawrence identified the unconscious with the individual soul, and the individual soul with the universal flow of life.

The unconscious expressed itself in symbols, and among the many flower symbols in Lawrence are significant roses. Suggestive from the outset, his roses grow richer as his work develops. In the earlier writings, they express certain aspects of human love. More conscious than unconscious, they are also more natural than transcendental. A white rosebush, for instance, appears in *Sons and Lovers* (1913) as a symbol of Miriam's nature and hence her kind of love. Throughout the book she has felt more kinship with flowers than with people, so that in her search for communion with Paul she shows him her favorites: "Point after point the steady roses shone out to them, seeming to kindle something in their souls. . . . Paul looked into Miriam's eyes. . . . Her soul quivered. It was the communion she wanted. He turned aside, as if pained. . . . She looked at her roses. They were white, some incurved and holy, others expanded in an ecstasy. . . . There was a cool scent of ivory roses—a white, virgin scent. Something made him feel anxious and imprisoned." [17] These roses, which appear near the beginning of their relationship, foreshadowed their difficulties. The virginal, spiritual quality of Miriam, her efforts to absorb Paul's soul in hers, and his efforts to escape an exalted love that makes him feel degraded, are all symbolically conveyed by the pure and holy roses with which Miriam feels akin. The roses here help to express the bond between two human beings but have not yet gone beyond that to relate man's love to vaster things.

The same holds true of Lawrence's story, "The Shadow in the Rose Garden," in *The Prussian Officer* (1914). Here again symbolic roses communicate the mystery of conscious human love but do not carry on to the still greater mysteries of the unconscious and the cosmos. In this story it is the tragedy of loss that is explored. A woman who has made a loveless marriage wishes to recapture former ecstasy. She returns to the rose garden where she and a lover, long since reported dead, had often been together: "She drifted down the path, coming at last to a tiny terrace all full of roses. She was shy of them, they were so many and so bright. They seemed to be conversing and laughing. She felt herself in a strange crowd. It exhilarated her, carried her out of herself. . . . She sat quite still, feeling her own existence lapse. She was no more than a rose, a rose that could not quite come into blossom, but remained tense." [18] Approaching ecstasy, her mood is shattered by the shadow of her lover who appears in the garden and whose fate, worse than death, is insanity. It was this that had been intimated by the laughing roses with which she could not quite come into communion. For, her lover being more lost than the dead, she can never again blossom into a rose. Beneath the shadow of madness, loss, and disillusion, the beauty of the roses is transfigured by horror, while the

[17] *Sons and Lovers* (New York, 1922), pp. 189–90.
[18] *The Prussian Officer* (London, 1914), p. 196.

horror in turn helps to convey the discrepancy between the past and the present, the ideal and the reality, our dreams and their fulfillment.

The rose of these early writings is clearly an effective and genuine symbol. It differs from Lawrence's later roses in being less clearly a vehicle for his personal, semireligious mixture of sex and mysticism. In the poems, where symbols are planted, the growth of Lawrence's rose is mirrored. Those written early employ it simply as a metaphor for sex. This is implicit in "Love Storm," where the sex act is described through images of wind, hawk, and rose. It is explicit in "Rose of All the World," where the importance of sex is questioned:

> How will you have it?—The rose is all in all,
> Or the ripe rose-fruits of the luscious fall?
> The sharp begetting, or the child begot?
> Our consummation matters, or does it not?

But "River Roses" is more suggestive. The "dark wild roses" of a "simmering marsh" seem to associate sex with vast and unconscious primeval life forces. And in "Grapes," a later poem, the rose is elaborately related to Lawrence's fully developed beliefs. A symbol of modern love, the traditional Western rose of the world is contrasted with the primitive grape to suggest the decline of the modern spirit under the coordinate pressures of intellect and Christian faith:

Ours is the universe of the unfolded rose,
The explicit
The candid revelation
But long ago, oh, long ago
Before the rose began to simper supreme,
Before the rose of all roses, rose of all the world, was even in bud,

· · · ·

There was another world, a dusky, flowerless, tendrilled world

· · · ·

Of which world the vine was the invisible rose,

Before petals spread, before colour made its disturbance, before eyes saw too much.[19]

Despite the insipid nature of the usual modern rose, Lawrence elsewhere made the flower a symbol of his own idea of fulfillment. In *Women in Love* (1920) symbolic roses emerge at the two most important points in the novel, having first been prepared for by Birkin's contrast between the *"fleurs du mal"* of present-day corruption and the "roses, warm and flamy" of creative affirmation. The book focuses on the love relationships between Birkin and Ursula, Gerald and Gudrun; and the climax of each of these relationships is notably deepened by roses. The first symbolic rose appears just before Birkin proposes to Ursula. The scene is a pond in which is reflected the "inviolable moon," a reflection that Birkin tries vainly to annihilate with stones. And the moon is in turn for several pages identified with a rose, symbolic of life's ultimate oneness from which the individual cannot escape: "gleam after gleam fell in with the whole, until a ragged rose, a distorted, frayed moon was shaking upon the water again, reasserted, renewed . . . at peace." [20] Accepting reality or the oneness expressed by the indestructible rose, Birkin at last accepts Ursula. In his relationship with her he comes close to achieving the proper balance between selfhood and union needed for spiritual fulfillment.

The second rose conveys a like concept in more elaborate fashion. It precedes not the union but the breakup between Gudrun and Gerald, but their breakup is the result of Gerald's incapacity for union. The couple are staying at a mountain

[19] *Collected Poems* (London, 1932), pp. 272–73 ("Rose of All the World"), 268 ("River Roses"), 361–63 ("Grapes"). In *St. Mawr* (Leipzig, 1932), as in "Grapes," Lawrence contrasts the rose of Christian civilization with primeval vegetation: "Only the pink wild roses smelled sweet, like the old world. . . . The roses of the desert are the cactus flowers . . . set among spines the devil himself must have conceived in a moment of sheer ecstasy. Nay, it was a world before and after the God of Love" (p. 202).
[20] *Women in Love* (New York, 1922), p. 283.

resort and the peaks of snow surrounding their dwelling appear at sunset "like the heart petals of an open rose." This analogy is sufficiently important to be carried throughout the book's final chapters. By means of it Lawrence is able to associate his symbolic rose with the transcendental wholeness of life Gudrun senses at the heart of the snowy peaks: "She felt that there . . . in the navel of the mystic world, among the final cluster of peaks . . . was her consummation. If she could but come there, alone . . . she would be a oneness with all, she would be herself the eternal, infinite silence, the sleeping, timeless, frozen center of the All." [21] From this oneness Gerald is debarred, for he, unlike the others, is a victim of mines and mechanics. To him the snow brings death but not transfiguration.

Finally, in *The Man Who Died* (1928), Lawrence, who was also dying, again expressed through roses his philosophy of life. Opposing ascetic Christianity with his private religion, he resurrected Christ through a priestess of Isis. Opposing the rose of the Virgin and Paradise with his own rose of sex and natural harmony, he set up his private transcendental beliefs in direct defiance of the Church. For Christ, who has not died but merely lost consciousness on the cross, is in despair in Lawrence's myth because of the nature of mankind. Needing emotional rebirth, he finds it in the priestess of Isis. By making love to her he attains a thing "beyond prayer . . . the deep, interfolded warmth, warmth living and penetrable, the woman, the heart of the rose!" Moreover, Christ's union with

[21] *Ibid.*, p. 467. The whole concept is made somewhat clearer in Lawrence's *Twilight in Italy* (London, 1916), where snowy peaks again create a kind of rose: "On the length of mountain-ridge, the snow grew rosy-incandescent, like heaven breaking into blossom. . . . In the rosy snow that shone in heaven over a darkened earth was the ecstasy of consummation. Night and day are one, light and dark are one. . . . Where is the transcendent knowledge in our hearts, uniting sun and shadow, day and night, spirit and senses? Why do we not know that the two in consummation are one; that each is only part; partial and alone forever; but that the two in consummation are perfect, beyond the range of loneliness or solitude?" (pp. 50–53).

the priestess gives him the spiritual fulfillment needed for a true mystic awareness of life's ultimate harmony. In a vision that seems intended at once to evoke and oppose Dante's, Christ himself embraces Lawrence's view of the scheme of things: "the man looked at the vivid stars before dawn, as they rained down to the sea. . . . And he thought: 'How plastic it is, how full of curves and folds like an invisible rose of dark-petalled openness. . . . How full it is, and great beyond all gods. How it leans around me, and I am part of it, the great rose of Space. I am like a grain of its perfume, and the woman is a grain of its beauty. Now the world is one flower of many petalled darknesses, and I am in its perfume as in a touch.' " [22]

Lawrence was in many ways a Rousseauistic romantic impressed by modern interests in psychiatry, anthropology, and mystic creeds. In twentieth-century fashion he drew symbols from Freud, myth, or Christianity to clarify and deepen his own nineteenth-century primitivist and transcendental views. The result is a style and substance richer and more suggestive though in the end no less romantic than was common among his predecessors. His semimystical rose of life's essential wholeness, blossoming in the depths of the primitive unconscious, could be attained through sexual union or solitary ecstasy but never through rational thought or its products. Other writers wished to preserve the civilization Lawrence abandoned and the intellect Lawrence despised. Some who, like Lawrence, required a supraterrestrial creed to give significance and hope to an unregenerate world turned to the form of transcendentalism preached by the Western Church. Finding there the Christian rose that Lawrence repudiated, they made of it a symbol in which romanticism was tempered, to a greater extent at least than in Lawrence, by objective, traditional views.

Two poets, for example, of Dylan Thomas's generation, disturbed by the Second World War, expressed through symbols

[22] *The Man Who Died* (New York, 1928), pp. 95–96.

their horror and hope. Seldom orthodox, the poems of Lawrence Durrell and George Barker are nonetheless colored by
Christian attitudes which are sometimes conveyed by Christian roses. Although it is scarce in Durrell's work, the flower
appears as a major symbol in two poems in *A Private Country*
(1943). The first, "In Crisis," treats the devastations of love
by war and culminates in a rose:

> Empty your hearts: or fill from a purer source.
> That what is in men can weep, having eyes:
> That what is in Truth can speak from responsible dust
> And O the rose grow in the middle of the great world.

Encompassing purity, sympathy, and truth, the rose sums up
the themes of the poem. It conveys the idea that love alone
can redeem us and suggests through imagery and meaning
Isaiah's Messianic rose. "Letter to Seferis the Greek" presents a similar view of our present through the medium of
a correlative past. Greece under pall of invasion, snow, and
death is the contemporary wasteland, while the prophetic rose
with which the poem concludes is the contemporary hope:

> With the unsuspected world somewhere awake,
> Born of this darkness, our imperfect sight
> The stirring seed of Nostradamus' rose.[23]

The Nostradamus allusion is to a prophecy that is unlike
Isaiah's in forecasting doom: "Attica which . . . now is the
Rose of the World . . . shall be in ruins." [24] It is understood
that our world has already fulfilled the prophecy. But Durrell
goes a step further than Nostradamus did, using his rose in
Messianic fashion as symbol of the great rebirth that shall yet
follow upon this death.

[23] *A Private Country* (London, 1943), pp. 28, 72 respectively.
[24] *The Complete Prophecies of Nostradamus,* ed. H. C. Roberts (New
York, 1947), p. 155. The prophecy literally states that in Attica a bridge
shall be in ruins, but the editor interprets this prophecy to signify the
downfall of Attica itself.

Durrell's roses proclaim that love, in the sense of Christian brotherhood, is the world's one hope for redemption. Barker, considering a similar hope, came to relate it more explicitly to traditional Christian faith. Already in *Calamiterror* (1937) the roses of his opening and closing sections carry Christian overtones, although their religious implications are still tentative. The first rose seems to refer to Christ's particular mission as well as to any sacrifice of self for humanity:

> The hand that lifts the intimating rose
> With infinitesimal machinery is
> The instrument that digs and dies and buries
> Itself and self; from whence arose
> The hand that elevates another,
> Whose area like a world displayed
> Supports the race like a feather;
>
> . . . .
>
> Through apertures in his own tomb
> The one who won against his shade
> Contemplates the successors for whom
> Out of his hand the world was made.

And the beliefs for which some men have died, betrayed by the calamiterror of war, become in the end bleeding roses, which are perhaps meant to suggest the medieval flower of martyrs: "What flower then shall the red tree in my heart wear / But the red tongues of the rose, which speak and bleed." Moreover, the tragedy of *Calamiterror* can, through the imitation of Christ, become the triumph of *Lament and Triumph* (1940). The rose in "Holy Poems" symbolizes love's redemption in a context that is now unmistakably Christian:

> Andromeda world, fixed to God's rock,
> Who, what am I to drop down from the sky
> Shaking a word's sword, capped with a rose,
> Booted with birds and gloved with love,
> To crack that world and free a world:

The dove that nestles in the green breast,
O world within a world! [25]

More important than Durrell's or Barker's, Edith Sitwell's later poems, written during and after the Second World War, offer the Christian hope through symbols that derive much of their life directly from medieval tradition. So impressed was Miss Sitwell by the rose in particular that she filled her poems of the 1940s with important roses and appropriately entitled her 1949 volume of collected poems *The Canticle of the Rose*.[26] The most important of her late roses have explicit religious affinities, while others that do not are related to the religious by similarities of theme and phrasing. The flower has, moreover, retained the levels of meaning that it carried in Miss Sitwell's earlier work, enriching and deepening those meanings with the new Christian associations. Crushed by war, her once declining rose has undergone its last agony; watered by Christ's blood, it now awaits resurrection. On the one hand, the rose of natural joy in primal innocence, love, and hope has become a mocking memory in a world that has forgotten love: "So what can I give to her? Civilization's / Disease, a delirium flushed like the rose" ("Poor Young Simpleton," p. 177). On the other hand, the natural values lost through the worship of mammon can be redeemed through the resurrection brought about by forgiveness:

Then came the Pentecostal Rushing of Flames, God in the wind
    that comes to the wheat,
Returned from the Dead for the guilty hands of Caesar
Like the rose at morning shouting of red joys
And redder sorrows fallen from young veins and heart-springs,
Come back for the wrong and the right, the wise and the foolish,

[25] *Calamiterror* (London, 1937), pp. 11, 52 respectively; *Lament and Triumph* (London, 1940), pp. 29–30.
[26] Citations from Miss Sitwell's poems below are to the New York, 1949, edition, since her 1954 volume of collected poems (despite the addition of a section entitled *Gardeners and Astronomers*) contains no additional notable roses.

Who like the rose care not for our philosophies
Of life and death, knowing the earth's forgiveness
And the great dews that comes to the sick rose; . . .

("Harvest," p. 161)

More extensive is the treatment of the rose in "The Two Loves." Here the flower becomes a multi-leveled symbol of sorrow and salvation, mortal love and God. At the outset God's fire of love is sought as an antidote to the fire of hate that has ravished the present war-torn world: "I thought the seeds of Fire should be let loose / . . . The light that lies deep in the heart of the rose." And the fire is identified with the rose because the rose is the parent source and symbol of love either in God's heart or in the heart of man. But man has perverted love to destruction by setting his heart upon the wrong things. The rose of God's love becomes the rose of his sorrow and at the same time the rose of our salvation. For the Passion of Christ has made possible redemption in which the fire of death becomes the fire of purgation:

I see Christ's wounds weep in the Rose on the wall.
Then I who nursed in my earth the dark red seeds of Fire—
The pomegranate grandeur, the dark seeds of Death,
Felt them change to the light and fire in the heart of the rose. . . .

(p. 232)

Moreover, the rose is an image of Christ not only in his passion but also in his Incarnation. The poem ends in a passage celebrating Incarnation, which is seen as a symbol of life's fundametal mystery: the embodiment of eternal spirit in mortal flesh, of infinite love in finite man:

And of One who contracted His Immensity
And shut Himself in the scope of a small flower
Whose root is clasped in darkness . . . God in the span
Of the root and light-seeking corolla . . . with the voice of Fire
    I cry—
Will He disdain that flower of the world, the heart of Man?

(p. 233)

"The Canticle of the Rose," significantly both title and concluding poem of her 1949 volume, represents the culmination of the rose symbol in Edith Sitwell's work. The opening stanzas recall "The Two Loves" in phrasing and meaning:

The Rose upon the wall
Cries—"I am the voice of Fire:
And in me grows
The pomegranate splendor of Death, the ruby garnet almandine
Dews: Christ's Wounds in me shine!

I rise upon my stem—
The Flower, the whole Plant-being, produced by Light
With all Plant-systems and formations. . . . As in Fire
All elements dissolve, so in one bright
Ineffable essence all Plant-being dissolves to make the Flower.

My stem rises bright—
Organic water polarized to the dark
Earth-center, and to Light."

Below that wall, in Famine Street,
There is nothing left but the heart to eat . . .

(p. 279)

The various aspects of Incarnation—flesh and spirit, sin and redemption, love, creation, and the divinity of all things—are here, as in "The Two Loves," expressed through the rose. The symbol has, moreover, been enriched by associations with the "Rose of the World" of two intervening poems. In "A Hymn to Venus" it was the flower of earthly love that made manifest the sun's revitalizing fire:

An old woman speaks:

"Lady, beside the great green wall of Sea
I kneel to make my plea

To you, great Rose of the world. . . . Beyond the seeds of petri-
    faction, Gorgon of itself,
Behind the face bright as the Rose—I pray

To the seeds of fire in the veins that should
Hold diamonds, iris, beryls for their blood; . . .   (p. 249)

In "The Shadow of Cain" it was the flower of creation, confused by Dives with material wealth:

Once hold

The primal matter of all gold—
From which it grows
(That Rose of the World) as the sharp clear tree from the seed
    of the great rose—

Then give of this, condensed to the transparency
Of the beryl, the weight of twenty barley grains:
And the leper's face will be full as the rose's face
After great rains.   (p. 277)

And both world-roses are now comprised in "The Canticle of the Rose." For Christ's "Rose upon the wall" is at once the fire of all love and the true primal matter of all existing things.

This ultimate rose grows upon a wall, for no flower can thrive in the soil of a world that has turned the sun's fire to atomic destruction and the sun's gold to material greed: "Below that wall in Famine Street, / There is nothing left but the heart to eat." Yet above our darkness the rose of Christ still offers its eternal promise of rebirth:

But high upon the wall
The Rose where the Wounds of Christ are red
Cries to the Light—
"See how I rise upon my stem, ineffable bright
Effluence of bright essence. . . . From my little span
I cry of Christ, Who is the ultimate Fire
Who will burn away the cold in the heart of Man.
Springs come, springs go. . . .
'I was reddere on Rode than the Rose in the rayne . . .'
'This smell is Crist, clepid the plantynge of the Rose in Jerico.' "
    (p. 280)

Comprising the various meanings of Miss Sitwell's later roses, this final passage of poem and volume has closed on two quotations of admonishment and promise. The first, from *Anturs of Arthur,* is spoken by Guinevere's mother's ghost, who has risen from hell as a tormented warning against pride and lack of charity. The second is from a Wyclif sermon that interprets Christ's healing of a blind man near Jericho as an exhortation to follow Christ in merciful works to sin-blind humanity. Jericho, etymologically explained as "the smelling that men should have," is identified with Christ's rose, whose fragrance should guide mankind.[27] The message is simple though the poem is complex: following the rose will be the world's cure.

Having turned in her later work from expressions of her age to attempts to cure it, Edith Sitwell turned for inspirational sources from French symbolists to medieval Christians. As the notes to the poems indicate, the all-fructifying sun, symbol of the divine Creator, and the fructified rose, symbol of the incarnate Christ, claim medieval origins. Less mannered, less concerned with verbal elegancies than before, the later poems show a gain in human sympathy and the later symbols a gain in both complexity and clarity. For the symbols and themes, not so much new as more developed, have been often carried over from early work to later but have been deepened in the process by religious meanings. And the religious meanings, being public and traditional, have made the poems more intelligible as well as more profound. Enriched by her awareness of the relation between our present and the whole past, her rose preaches Christ's eternal message to the contemporary world. The flower of love and sorrow, of life and death on the natural level, has become the eternal flower of mercy and redemption. Edith Sitwell, on a course akin to T. S. Eliot's,

[27] See "The Anturs of Arthur at the Tarnewathelan," in *Three Early English Metrical Romances,* ed. John Robson (London, 1842), pp. 32–33; *Select English Works of John Wyclif,* ed. Thomas Arnold (Oxford, 1869), I, 39.

has moved from the wasteland of our present to the fulfillment of eternity.

At the same time, her rose differs from that of Eliot and other modern medievalists in blossoming outside of the Catholic influence. Despite its interaction with the divine sun, it shows no specific traces of Dante, nor are those roses acknowledged in her notes taken from Catholic texts. Miss Sitwell's flower is Christian and as such derives from the origins of Christianity, but it postulates nothing about God or man beyond the scriptural message of Christ. Essentially Protestant, her rose relies on the individual's response to its message and in this respect is to be distinguished from the rose of writers whose medievalism took on a Catholic coloring. For some, who were distrustful of unguided human nature and its romantic products, sought a return to the objective, authoritarian system established by the Catholic Church. Whether they traveled as far as Rome or stopped at Canterbury, writers like Graham Greene, Charles Williams, or T. S. Eliot show a greater reliance on the ordered structure of religion than on the vagaries of the unstructured private heart. In consequence their roses, drawn from Catholic tradition, express to one degree or another the established dogmas of the medieval Church.

Graham Greene, not preeminently a symbolist but a writer who uses occasional symbols to enhance the effectiveness of his work, uses a rose in *The Power and the Glory* (1940). The flower is unobtrusive but important, appearing at three key points in the novel and serving as the one true symbol of fruition in a book filled with rats, parched land, and dust. For the story takes place in a modern wasteland, a Mexican state from which religion has been outlawed, and here as in all deserts the flower blooms where faith survives. It is a flower in a song that the state's last priest, hunted and fleeing for his life, hears at moments when his duties triumph over his desires. He hears it first, at the outset of the story, as he fore-goes a chance of freedom to attend a dying woman; he hears it next in a desolated village as he listens to confession in the teeth of danger. Ironically these moments blossoming in roses are moments of anguish for the frightened priest, who feels that his actions hold no hope of heaven because he is a drunk-ard, father of a child. But when in the end he gives up all thought of freedom, here as at the outset to attend the dying, the flower blooms for him as his first hint of joy: "The oddest thing of all was that he felt quite cheerful. . . . He began to whistle. . . . 'I found a rose.' " [28]

Greene's rose is Catholic, flowering at moments when a Catholic priest renounces self for God. It gains its value from association with the whole tradition of the Catholic rose. But while it punctuates the priest's fine moments, suggesting a beatitude that he is not aware of, it remains a relatively simple flower. At once more involved and more specific in its doc-trinal suggestions is the rose in Charles Williams's *All Hal-lows' Eve* (1945). For Williams, an Anglo-Catholic convert, employs a rose that is elaborately patterned on Dante's. The novel, a religious melodrama, expresses through the super-natural machinery of ghosts, black magic, and attendant spirits the struggle between Catholic good and evil; it builds to a climax in the Dantesque rose. Beginning as "a faint roseal glow in the waters," this rose expands through the book's con-cluding pages to become the full-blown flower of the Catholic cosmos. Its appearance in the midst of torrential rain associates it with both the end of the world and the spiritual rebirth from the waters of baptism symbolized by the rain. Its appear-ance to the novel's three major characters associates it with the moral import of their lives.

To Simon, who embodies and magically controls the forces of evil, it appears as a terrifying confusion of blood, hell-fire, and hate, and enfolds in its center two phantoms of evil that

<hr>

[28] *The Power and the Glory* (New York, 1946), p. 245.

are at once agents and projections of himself: "the hate seemed to swell in a nightmare bubble within the rose which was forming round them, cloud in cloud, overlying like petals . . . and beyond him he could see only his multiplied self. . . . The smell of blood was in his nostrils; the touch of burning on his flesh; this was what the crimson must be to him." To the spirit of Lester, whose purgation results in the victory of love over the evil in herself and others, the rose with its accompanying phantoms undergoes transfiguration: "The color of it—rose or blood or fire—struck up the descending lines of rain and was lost somewhere in that empty upper sky above her; but below it was by now almost a wall which moved after those forms; and absorbed and changed the antipathy they diffused; and all the freshness of the waters and the light was free and lovely." To Simon's daughter, Betty, saved by baptism and Lester's love from the powers of his evil, the heart of the flower, untainted by phantoms and smelling of roses rather than blood, becomes an apocalyptic vision: "It was she who saw, as the driving torrent dwindled and passed, a fume of crimson rising, as if the rain had so fallen on the shaping rose that it sent up a cloud as of the smell of rose-gardens. . . . She saw a small pool of crimson in the light and that too vanishing, till it was no more than the level of dark wine in a wine cup, and within it, before it vanished, she saw the whole City through which she had so often passed, vivid and real in that glowing richness." [29]

Williams's rose thus comprises within itself damnation, purgation, and salvation. Although it differs from Dante's in embracing more than heaven (the three selves involved in Simon's rose even suggesting Dante's Satan), it is nonetheless clearly related to Dante's in form and substance. The image of a rose evolving in cloud on cloud of light is in itself reminiscent of the *Paradiso*. More important, Dante's rose,

[29] *All Hallows' Eve* (New York, 1948), pp. 265–66, 258, 267 respectively.

crowning the Catholic scheme of things, had also implied God's justice as well as his love. And perhaps most important, Betty's ultimate vision of the earthly City become divine recalls Williams's own interpretation of Dante. In *The Figure of Beatrice,* Williams had written that Dante had intended his culminating flower to encompass the transfiguration of Florence, type of human society, into the eternal City of God: "The image of the City of Florence had existed all this time in the background. . . . In the *Commedia,* it is only at the end of the Way of Affirmation, and of its rejections, purgations, and indoctrinations, that . . . the humility and charity of all the City burns sensitively on human eyes." [30]

Dante's symbol is also basic to the two most significant modern roses. Differing from Williams in subtlety and power, T. S. Eliot and James Joyce also differ from each other in using Dante to opposite ends. Joyce, while accepting such positive values as charity and rebirth, rejects the Catholic supernatural premise and applies Dante's values to human life. Eliot, on the other hand, overlooks much of the human in Dante but reflects in the rose a romantic image of medieval religion. Each exemplifies the contemporary quest for positive values to redeem the wasteland, a quest which, if it is successful, inevitably ends in God or man. Beyond this, each represents the culmination in modern literature of one or the other of these alternatives. For Joyce has surpassed all his contemporaries in making of the rose a flexible vehicle for uniting personal, social, and traditional secular meanings. And Eliot has equally surpassed all modern religious writers in making of it a flexible vehicle for uniting private and public spiritual beliefs. That Dante's rose should be basic to each of these major writers is appropriate to their lives and themes, and also to our world.

For the modern use of Dante's rose relates our flowers of affirmation to the supreme flower of affirmation in Western

[30] *The Figure of Beatrice* (London, 1943), pp. 39, 48.

literature. It shows that our age has not lost touch with the basic traditions of the Christian era, and that our values, though diverse, have a harmonious core. Whether secular or religious, the values of faith, hope, and love pervade the roses that unite our writers with each other and with the past. The Dantesque rose alone, of course, does not convey this kinship. Through flowering at the end of either road to joy, it merely serves to confirm an impression built up by other factors. The flower that grows apart from Dante in so many modern writers has equally expressed our quest for affirmation. It has equally expressed our quest for a positive concourse between the private individual and the world in which he lives. Dante's flower is supreme among pre-modern roses, as Joyce's and Eliot's are supreme among the roses of today. But the flower has had to prove its value for our century, as for others, through its subsidiary role in a diversity of works as well as through its leading role in the major writings of a few.

6

ELIOT

AND

TRADITION

The rose that dominates much of the later work of T. S. Eliot symbolizes the goal of his quest. Searching the past for redemption from the present, he found in the medieval Church a tradition that would harmonize contemporary discords, and in the medieval Catholic rose an objective correlative for contemporary feelings. Just as his view of the world as a wasteland epitomized for many their growing pessimism about things, so his rose of divine resolution has become an expression of our times. Eliot's rose is not wholly modern, since it traces its roots to the Middle Ages, but what he has done is to make modern the symbol of an earlier day. Clearly the present quest for communion between inner and outer worlds could be fulfilled for the religious in the Anglo-Catholic Church; and the present quest for redemption from the wasteland of our time could be fulfilled for now and eternity in the Anglo-Catholic rose. For the rose is the obvious symbol of whole and enduring resolution, and one which in addition unites today with the Western past. Combining the romanticism of a yearning, nostalgic, insatiable age with the absolute, authoritarian standards of medieval times, Eliot has created a symbol suited to religious present needs.

He has also created a symbol suited to his private needs. For Dante had set a literary precedent relevant to Eliot's problems. The rose as such, which in Eliot's work is related to religious matters and heavily colored by Dantesque attitudes, does not appear before *The Hollow Men* and does not assume its full significance before the close of "Little Gidding." But Anglo-Catholicism was for Eliot the appropriate conclusion to prior concerns leading to his conversion, so that the genesis of his rose is traceable to his earlier writings. In fact, reinterpretation of former experience in the light of later understanding has given the development of Eliot's work its appearance of inevitability. Furthermore, the variations on the sterility theme, which dominates the poetry written before *Ash Wednesday,* show a gradual movement in the direction of religion. In *Prufrock* Eliot contemplated the contemporary loss of values, and in some of the 1920 poems he deplored the contemporary loss of faith. Pessimism, deepening into despair, led in *The Waste Land* to that quest for spiritual rebirth that subsequently became a specifically Christian phenomenon. His prevalent images of desiccation together with those of hesitant hope, carried from poem to poem throughout Eliot's career, conveyed through their own changes his changing attitudes and feelings.

It was almost inevitable that these images should gather layers of symbolic complexity in accord with the increasing complexity of his themes. And in time, drawing on several sources, Eliot did evolve his own particular brand of symbolism. Since his problems were shared by many, and since he was able to perceive them against a social background, his symbols and expressions have become central to our age. It was in the attempt to transcend the limits of his personality that he turned to metaphysical poets, Elizabethan dramatists, modern imagists, and French symbolists, all of whom he felt had achieved one sort of objectivity or another. Imagists and symbolists had replaced the direct statement of feeling with its indirect expression through concrete entities, metaphysical poets had united emotion and intellect, and Elizabethan playwrights had transmuted private experience into the impersonal life of drama. Eliot, seeking objective correlatives for the externalization of emotion in art, combined these influences in practice as in theory. His early work, in which precise images convey definite feelings, showed an advance over imagism. For Eliot substituted multiple images for the single focal image of most imagist verse and integrated these images within a dramatic framework. Going beyond this, he added social to personal levels of meaning and gave to the whole an intellectual as well as emotional significance.

Still later, when Christianity brought eternity to bear on temporal things, objective correlatives had to be sought for transcendental experiences. Eliot's images themselves then sacrificed their precision of outline to limitless symbolic suggestion. Yet there is no sharp break between the early imagery of despair and the later symbolism of salvation. Transformed, reinterpreted, or enriched with new meanings in accord with the development of Eliot's thought, his prevailing image patterns of sterility and flowering carry through the whole body of his work. The contemporary wasteland that dominates the early poetry, when perceived from an orthodox Christian standpoint, becomes the Dark Night of spiritual purgation. Glimpses of flowers, sunlight, and water, which had seemed mirages in our vacant desert, turn out to have been hints of eternal reality. It is true that negative symbols tend to dominate his work after Eliot's conversion as well as before. Nevertheless fertility symbols, and especially the rose, become increasingly important as spiritual glory assumes the position of eternal truth.

Flowers in the early poems support themes later to be included and transcended in the Christian rose garden. Generally associated with the failure of love, they express moods of frustrated desire. The sunlight and flowers in "La Figlia Che Piange" (1917) provide the setting for love's end:

> Weave, weave the sunlight in your hair—
> Clasp your flowers to you with a pained surprise—

Fling them to the ground and turn
With a fugitive resentment in your eyes.[1]

The rain and flowers in "Dans le Restaurant" (1920) contribute to the tone of an interrupted early love experience:
"J'avais sept ans, elle était plus petite. / Elle était toute
mouillée, je lui ai donné des primevères" (p. 31: "I was seven,
she was smaller. / She was all wet, I gave her primroses"—
J. P. S.). And the lilacs and hyacinths in "Portrait of a Lady"
(1917) point up the deficiencies of both the lady and her
uncharitable commentator. For the lady is ironically killing
lilacs as she assumes a love of life, and the commentator is
maintaining the dubious self-esteem which generally serves
him as a refuge from emotional demands:

> Except when a street piano, mechanical and tired
> Reiterates some worn-out common song
> With the smell of hyacinths across the garden
> Recalling things that other people have desired.   (p. 10)

The early poems are relatively simple; their flowers serve
largely to accentuate the lack of flowering in our world. But
by the time of *The Waste Land* (1922) flower imagery has
assumed a greater complexity than before, becoming related
to levels of reality and conflicting attitudes towards rebirth.
The quest for a rebirth that could redeem the wasteland is expressed partly through the contrast of rock and dry sand with
vegetation nurtured by spring rains. But the revival of life in
spring is regarded ambivalently. Although it is recognized as
a kind of hope, it is also feared as a disturbance of the lethal
calm of despair:

> April is the cruellest month, breeding
> Lilacs out of the dead land, mixing
> Memory and desire, stirring
> Dull roots with spring rain.   (p. 37)

---

[1] *The Complete Poems and Plays* (New York, 1952), p. 20. Future
citations from Eliot's poems are to this edition.

Stirring regret for unfulfilled promise, lilacs and memories cruelly emphasize our present sterility. For the memory of ecstasy is in the wasteland a memory of failure. Love, for example, had seemed to offer a reality transcending life and death, but the moment had passed leaving in its wake only the void of surrounding things:

> —Yet when we came back, late, from the Hyacinth garden,
> Your arms full, and your hair wet, I could not
> Speak, and my eyes failed, I was neither
> Living nor dead, and I knew nothing,
> Looking into the heart of light, the silence.
> *Oed und leer das Meer.*   (p. 38)

The Hollow Men (1925), like the preceding poems, emphasizes sterility. Here, however, for the first time Eliot's themes of emotional failure and fear of rebirth are given Christian overtones, and the flower imagery linked with these themes appropriately becomes the Christian rose. Although it appears only once in the poem, the rose is a symbol of central importance, as it is the poem's final expression of spiritual redemption:

> Sightless, unless
> The eyes reappear
> As the perpetual star
> Multifoliate rose
> Of death's twilight kingdom
> The hope only
> Of empty men.   (p. 58)

The hollow men dread above all things "that final meeting/In the twilight kingdom" (p. 57). They fear the eyes that are one with the rose, eyes of a love they have failed to meet.[2] Providing a clear allusion to Dante's, Eliot's multifoliate rose

---

[2] In "Eyes that last I saw in tears" (1924), a poem closely associated with *The Hollow Men* in imagery and meaning, the eyes were explicitly related to betrayed human love; but Eliot had not yet made the Dantesque alliance between human love and divine.

suggests Divine Love's enduring bloom. Through this symbol the fading star of the hollow men's existence and the eyes that serve a judgment on their living death become a part of the final realm in which such images are transfigured for those able to perceive them. The fading star of spiritual death shines in "death's other kingdom" as the perpetual star of eternal life. The eyes, recalling Beatrice's, suggest not only love's betrayal but the spiritual grace that could, if accepted, lead from the "dead land" to God's rose.

Following the guidance shunned by the hollow men, Eliot in *Ash Wednesday* (1930) moved towards the rose. This poem, more than any of his other works, shows the influence of Dante in symbols and significance. In fact, in his Dante essay, written the preceding year, Eliot had commended Dante for the type of poetry he himself was soon to undertake. Firstly, Dante had grounded his work in tradition, and Eliot preferred such objective grounding to the poetry of purely subjective vision: "That is the advantage of a coherent traditional system of dogma and morals like the Catholic: it stands apart, for understanding and assent even without belief, from the single individual who propounds it." Secondly, Dante had used his traditional system and symbols in just such a manner as Eliot was now striving to approach: "One can feel only awe at the power of the master who could thus at every moment realize the inapprehensible in visual images." [3] About to write a poem treating inapprehensibles, Eliot saw in Dante a striking precedent for transcendentalizing his own increasingly intricate imagery. And since images that attempt to encompass no less than cosmic truth inevitably take on the magnitude of symbols, Eliot's pursuit of Dante led him down a spiritual path not only to Catholic thinking but to symbolic art.

Moreover, in its specific symbols as well as in its over-all method, *Ash Wednesday* clearly reveals the influence of

[3] *Selected Essays* (New York, 1932), pp. 219, 228.

Dante. The winding purgatorial stair, the Word at the still center of the turning World, and the Lady as the bestower of the grace that leads to salvation find their evident counterparts in the *Comedy*. Further, Eliot's Lady is allied with Dante's Beatrice and Virgin figures in being accompanied by imagery of whiteness and light, and identified with symbols of Garden and Rose. Perhaps less definable than Dante's but meant to convey analogous meanings, Eliot's symbols are likewise expressions of spiritual progress and its goal. Guided by grace of the Lady up the purgatorial stairs, the soul will at last attain the Garden of the heavenly Rose wherein "the unspoken word, the Word unheard," is understood. But Eliot, unlike Dante, is only at the beginning of the way and writes not of a vision remembered but of one desired. Suspended between sense and spirit, doubt and faith, death and rebirth, he seeks through purgation the transfiguration of temporal desert into eternal Garden.

The Lady, who is the central figure in the poem, is the means of uniting earth and heaven. The Rose and the Garden with which she is identified symbolize that ultimate union. In fact, although it appears in only one section of the poem, the rose encompasses a good deal of the significance of the whole. The litany of the rose sung by the bones in section II shows the influence of Remy de Gourmont's "Litanies de la Rose." Eliot's litany is, however, opposite in import to Gourmont's. For Gourmont's rose, a symbol of sex and particularly of sexual disappointment, slowly expands to become a symbol of entire disillusion both with earthly things which are inadequate and with Catholic dreams which are untrue. Eliot, on the other hand, evokes Gourmont's nihilistic, sexual, and anti-Catholic flower in order to emphasize by contrast his Anglo-Catholic beliefs. In Eliot's litany disillusion with the earthly and sensual is also expressed, but only to be dispersed by a proper direction of spiritual energies. His litany opens, as does Gourmont's, with a series of paradoxes. But for Eliot such apparent antitheses serve to illumine an ultimate harmony:

> Lady of silences
> Calm and distressed
> Torn and most whole
> Rose of memory
> Rose of forgetfulness
> Exhausted and life-giving
> Worried reposeful
> The single Rose
> Is now the Garden
> Where all loves end . . .   (p. 62)

Seen under the aspect of eternity, the concepts cease to be paradoxical. On one level the calm and distressed Lady or Rose suggests the Virgin, whose mortal sufferings led to her immortal glory and whose ever-present concern for man is his most immediate source of spiritual life. On another level she is related to Beatrice, who was distressed by Dante's errors, yet calm in her recognition of God's eternal Mercy and Justice. Since in suggesting Dante's rose she also suggests the Church, the paradoxes seem to imply at once the Church's earthly persecutions redeemed in divine glory and the spirit of the eternal Church Triumphant unimpaired by the corruptions of the Church in the present world. This last is supported by a line that Eliot deleted from an early edition, referring to his "single Rose" as having "worm-eaten petals" and thereby suggesting George Herbert's poem, "Church-Rents and Schisms," in which a worm at the heart of a rose is used to signify Church corruptions.[4] Moreover, as Virgin or Church, the Rose of memory and forgetfulness aids man to forget earthly trials and temptations but to remember indications of grace and the message of Christ. In short,

---

[4] This analogy is pointed out by E. E. Duncan-Jones, "Ash Wednesday," in *T. S. Eliot: A Study of his Writings by Several Hands,* ed. B. Rajan (New York, 1949), p. 47. Duncan-Jones suggests that the line was deleted because it limited the rose's meanings.

if man follows the guidance of the embracing Rose, he will at last attain the Garden in which all seeming earthly paradoxes are resolved in harmony.

Eliot's reconciliations are in orthodox fashion ultimately subsumed under the concept of Love. For Divine Love brought redemption from original sin and hence from the seeming discords which that sin had perpetrated. In his Dante essay Eliot had spoken of "the contrast between higher and lower carnal love, the transition from Beatrice living to Beatrice dead, rising to the Cult of the Virgin." [5] And in *Ash Wednesday* through the media of grace—Beatrice, Church, and Virgin—man rises from carnal to spiritual love. The "single Rose" becomes the Garden "where all loves end," as earthly love leads to love of the Virgin and love of the Virgin leads to God. The technic of paradox, applied to the Lady herself at the litany's outset, is applied to her function as director of man's love in later lines:

> Terminate torment
> Of love unsatisfied
> The greater torment
> Of love satisfied
> End of the endless
> Journey to no end
> Conclusion of all that
> Is inconclusible . . .   (p. 62)

Love, which is futile when wrongly directed, becomes man's means of attaining the goal of his being when Mary's grace guides it to the final Garden: "Grace to the Mother/For the Garden/Where all love ends" (p. 62).

The Lady's Garden, in which the Rose takes root, does not fade out after the litany but, on the contrary, runs through *Ash Wednesday*. Retaining the meanings it carried in the litany, it serves as reclamation of the poet's spiritual desert and promised goal of his purgatorial sufferings. The lure of earthly

[5] *Selected Essays*, p. 235.

gardens, suggesting Eden, has led to disillusion and spiritual dryness. But through purgation, aided by the Lady's grace, the temporal desert can be made eternally fertile in the final Garden:

> Will the veiled sister between the slender
> Yew trees pray for those who offend her
>
> .   .   .   .
>
> In the last desert between the last blue rocks
> The desert in the garden the garden in the desert
> Of drouth, spitting from the mouth the withered apple-seed.
>
> (pp. 65–66)

Eliot's dominant symbols of sin, penitence, and redemption are here used in more traditional fashion than is usual in his subsequent work. But the basic Christian pattern, which he was later to assimilate and express in terms of his personal experience, has already been established. Alternating between purgatorial means and divine ends, the poem contrasts symbols of desolation and darkness with those of fruition and attainment. When in *Four Quartets* Eliot's system of salvation was to be fully worked out and individualized, it was still to be expressed through a modified form of this traditional symbolic pattern.

For the desert on the one hand and the rose on the other corresponded at once to Eliot's own feelings and to the two dominant strains in Christian teaching. Dante, for example, had come to perceive the human object of his love as an expression of the divine and his earthly ecstasy as an intimation of eternal glory. St. John of the Cross, in contrast, had approached God through rejecting all sublunary loves and had perceived the Dark Night of complete desolation as the first stage of the purgatorial journey. Representing what have been termed the affirmative and negative ways to God,[6] these

---

[6] In *The Figure of Beatrice*, pp. 8–10, Charles Williams discusses the two ways, attributing their origins to the writings of Pseudo-Dionysius and St. Athanasius.

writers appealed to the two poles of Eliot's experience. The wasteland of spiritual desolation conformed to St. John's Dark Night of the Soul, while moments of transcendent intensity conformed to Dantesque intimations of glory. The alternation in *Ash Wednesday* between symbols of spiritual dryness and of flowering had already laid the foundations for Eliot's fusion of St. John with Dante. Immersed in the purgatorial Dark Night, the poet gained "strength beyond hope and despair" from his faith in the Lady's heavenly Garden. The Dantesque vision, it is true, had not yet been fully realized, for the poet had had no direct experience of the ultimate Garden. But the basic pattern was there, and in his subsequent poetry Eliot would develop associations between the Garden of divine beatitude and that of supreme earthly moments of bliss.

In the process the Dantesque symbols would be significantly altered. Imagery of natural experience would be merged with that of religious tradition in order to express the relation of temporal grace to eternal salvation. The result would be a symbolism less like Dante's in form and more like Dante's in effect than that presented in *Ash Wednesday*. "Marina" (1930), written shortly after *Ash Wednesday*, already represents an important step in this direction. Although Eliot replaces the spiritual Lady with a natural girl and the spiritual Garden with scenery from Casco Bay, Maine, he nevertheless comes closer to the Dantesque experience in this poem than he had in its more traditional predecessor. Pericles' discovery of his lost daughter, serving as objective correlative, becomes symbolic of rebirth through grace and of the attainment of spiritual fulfillment:

> This form, this face, this life
> Living to live in a world of time beyond me; let me
> Resign my life for this life, my speech for that unspoken,
> The awakened, lips parted, the hope, the new ships. (p. 73)

The poem resembles *Ash Wednesday* in its use of a feminine messenger of grace and in its imagery of nature's flowering. But it goes beyond the earlier work in two important ways. It presents harmony rather than conflict between the worlds of sense and spirit, and it expresses the momentary attainment of that which before had been only desired.

Conveying a religious theme through secular symbols, "Marina" paved the way for the rose gardens of *The Family Reunion* and the *Four Quartets*. In these works the medieval Rose and Garden of *Ash Wednesday* reappear but are now modified by elements drawn from personal experience and the sensory world. Aspects of fertility imagery harking back to Eliot's non-Christian poems are fused with their traditional counterparts, the religious rose and garden harking back to Dante. It is this fusion of private with public emotions and of modern with traditional meanings in a single set of multi-leveled symbols that has helped Eliot provide appropriate religious expression for the sensitive individual in the contemporary world. Sunlight and flowers, which he had formerly associated with the failure of love and the obstacles to rebirth, retain their former meanings but are enriched and reinterpreted in terms of a transcendental perspective. Children and birds, which had appeared in his pre-conversion poems as distressing reminders of an unfulfilled promise, have wholly replaced the spiritual Lady as inhabitants of the garden and messengers of grace.

In "Burnt Norton" (1935), where the rose-garden symbol is introduced, its relation to childhood is most fully developed. Presided over by spirit children, this garden represents the point where things as they were merge with things as they might have been. Like earlier symbols of flowering in Eliot, that of the rose garden recalls a past opportunity and thereby reminds us of our present condition by also recalling our failure to follow that once-offered good. For because the op-

portunity requires childhood innocence, it has long been lost
to adults in our far from innocent world:

> Footfalls echo in the memory
> Down the passage which we did not take
> Towards the door we never opened
> Into the rose-garden . . .   (p. 117)

Nonetheless, earthly failure, looked at from a different angle,
can become a means to eternal redemption. It is true that we
cannot relive our lives on any physical or literal level. But
we can return on a timeless level to the point at which we
once could and still can take a new spiritual direction.

Children in Eliot had previously been associated with nostalgic memories of untainted joy. In *The Waste Land* a memory of early sledding in the mountains emphasized by contrast
the sterility of the present: "In the mountains, there you feel
free./I read, much of the night, and go south in the winter"
(p. 37). In "Marina" the narrator's moment of ecstatic recognition gave rise to a fundamental, buried recollection: "Whis-
pers and small laughter between leaves and hurrying feet/
Under sleep, where all the waters meet" (p. 72). In the
"New Hampshire" fragment (1934), "children's voices in
the orchard" inspired regret for the loss of youth: "Twenty
years and the spring is over;/To-day grieves, to-morrow
grieves,/Cover me over, light-in-leaves" (p. 93). Now in the
religious context of "Burnt Norton" such hitherto secular
memories are related directly to spiritual goals. The children
hidden in the rose garden, similar to those in Kipling's
"They," are invisible to all who lack true qualities of spirit.[7]
At the same time they serve as necessary guides to the desired
spiritual condition. For through the pursuit of memory to the

---

[7] Helen Gardner, *The Art of T. S. Eliot* (New York, 1950), p. 160,
suggests that Eliot may have been influenced by Kipling's story. An
examination of the story itself reveals much imagery similar to Eliot's. In
it there is laughter of unseen children, an impression that the children
have just hurried off to hide, and references to "quick feet" and "feet
stealing across the dead land."

point of recapturing the childhood's ecstasy, one can reattain
its purity of vision:

> Dry the pool, dry concrete, brown edged,
> And the pool was filled with water out of sunlight,
> And the lotos rose, quietly, quietly,
> The surface glittered out of heart of light,
> And they were behind us, reflected in the pool.   (p. 118)

The lotos, Eastern symbol of creation, and the sunlight,
symbol of God in most religions, are, like the supernatural
children, perceived only in reflection. Yet such a reflection
of the divine in the earthly represents man's closest approach
in his lifetime to the ultimate reality. It is true that this vision
of the "heart of light" is as unsustainable as was that in *The
Waste Land*:

> Then a cloud passed, and the pool was empty.
> Go, said the bird, for the leaves were full of children,
> Hidden excitedly, containing laughter.
> Go, go, go, said the bird: human kind
> Cannot bear very much reality.   (p. 118)

Nevertheless this vision, unlike its forerunner, leaves behind
it not a gnawing emptiness but the awareness of an abiding
goal:

> Time past and time future
> What might have been and what has been
> Point to one end, which is always present.   (p. 118)

Because the divisions of time have meaning only within the
limits of time, the lost past is actually still present within the
enduring scope of eternity. And in the eternal present, which
is eternally present, our unfulfilled potentialities are realized
and the errors of all time redeemed.

The redemption of time can be achieved in time, but innocence is needed for the first vision. On one level Eliot's
emphasis on "what might have been" seems in the religious

context to relate the rose garden of early memory to the garden of Eden.[8] For in Eliot as in Blake the childhood innocence of the individual suggests a correspondence with man's original state of purity. "Our first world" is not only our early youth but also the earthly paradise. There the "heart of light" might have been perpetually apparent had the pool not been dried out by man's life-denying sin. It is because man's choice in Eden was erroneous that he must grow to maturity in a fallen world and know the timeless glory of his original condition only in brief moments with the aid of a force outside himself: "Through the first gate,/Into our first world, shall we follow/The deception of the thrush?" (pp. 117–18). The thrush as a symbolic messenger of grace leads to a vision that is deceptive in seeming everlasting. And yet this fleeting vision of things as they might have been is the hope that is left us in the fallen world of ultimately realizing lost opportunities.

For the transitory moment of grace, the rose garden vision of past purity and peace can sustain us through the Dark Night of our loss and so guide us by the way of purgation back to purity. Of course, we can never reattain the primal innocence of the garden of Eden. The way of innocence, "which is the way of ignorance" and of humility, has been forever lost to us through pride. However, the Redemption has made possible our resumption of purity on a different and still higher plane in the garden of God. A passage from "The Dry Salvages" helps to clarify Eliot's point:

> We had the experience but missed the meaning,
> And approach to the meaning restores the experience
> In a different form, beyond any meaning
> We can assign to happiness . . .   (p. 133)

In the childhood of the individual and the race we "missed the meaning," being innocent of the knowledge of good and

[8] See Sister M. Cléophas, "Notes on Levels of Meaning in *Four Quartets*," *Renascence*, II (1950): 105.

evil. Now, with maturity in the sinful world and with a proper understanding of spiritual good and evil, we can reapproach the original experience with wiser if with heavier hearts.

The reattained experience symbolized by the rose garden renders an apprehension of the timeless. By escaping the usual temporal limitations, one attains for a brief moment a sense of the ultimate ordering of things. Essentially mystical, the experience in question is also essentially ineffable. It involves an entire release from anxiety, a release from the concerns of yesterday and tomorrow, a sense of peace and of the harmony of things that goes as far beyond ecstasy as it goes beyond words:

> The inner freedom from the practical desire,
> The release from action and suffering, release from the inner
> And outer compulsion, yet surrounded
> By a grace of sense, a white light still and moving. (p. 119)

Illuminating this world and the next, the white light of transcendent vision turns out to be the Thomistic Divine Love, Unmoved Mover of the universe. This Love exists in its perfection "at the still point of the turning world," the silent center of the whole creation. For Eliot's conception echoes Dante's, whose Unmoved Mover was also expressed by a still point of intensest light round which revolved the nine concentric spheres. And Dante's God was made manifest in a rose as Eliot's is made manifest in a rose garden, where for a moment eternal reality is perceived beneath temporal sensory guise:

> Love is itself unmoving,
> Only the cause and end of movement,
> Timeless, and undesiring
> Except in the aspect of time
> Caught in the form of limitation
> Between un-being and being.
> Sudden in a shaft of sunlight

> Even while the dust moves
> There rises the hidden laughter
> Of children in the foliage
> Quick now, here, now, always—   (p. 122)

This final passage of "Burnt Norton" implies that it is imperfect human love that is the temporal expression of eternal Love. Moreover, love, which appears as desire in the temporal world, will be finally fulfilled in the eternity only glimpsed in the rose garden. The conception is basically that of *Ash Wednesday,* wherein the Lady's Garden represents the "End of the endless/Journey to no end." But neither here nor in the earlier poem is the kinship between human and divine love developed to any really adequate degree. It is in his next work, *The Family Reunion* (1939), that Eliot first makes reasonably explicit the whole question of the garden's relation to love and the nature of the garden's transcendental ecstasy. Since human love is an essential stage of the arduous journey to the divine, the play becomes of major importance to a full understanding of the rose garden. In it the garden retains its previous link with childhood, but now makes the vision of that which might have been attendant upon present love experience. Bearing analogy to Dante's *Vita Nuova,*[9] the play's alliance of childhood ecstasy with love is seen as a supernatural indication of the need for rebirth and the true nature of Love.

Harry, tormented by Furies for what he believes to be his share of guilt in his wife's death, goes back to Wishwood, the scene of his childhood.[10] In seeking "to return to the

---

[9] See Leonard Unger, "T. S. Eliot's Rose Garden," in *T. S. Eliot: A Selected Critique,* ed. Leonard Unger (New York, 1948), pp. 374–94. Unger traces garden imagery throughout Eliot's poetry, taking the point of view that the garden symbolizes an early sexual awakening comparable to that described by Eliot in his discussion of the *Vita Nuova.*

[10] The name of Harry's family home, Wishwood, is significant. He has come home wishing to recapture a childhood sense of freedom felt in a nearby wood: "It's absurd that one's only memory of freedom/Should be a hollow tree in a wood by the river" (p. 248).

point of departure/And start again as if nothing had happened" (p. 249), he is seeking to return to the rose garden point at which things as they were merge with things as they might have been. But the rose garden is a spiritual experience and cannot be attained through geography. Harry finds that although time has made very little impression on Wishwood, it has altered him; he learns that on the temporal plane you can't go home again. Thrown into despair by this discovery, he discusses the situation with Mary and is shown that the trouble is of his own making:

> But surely, what you say
> Only proves that you expected Wishwood
> To be your real self, to do something for you
> That you can only do for yourself.
> What you need to alter is something inside you
> Which you can change anywhere—here, as well as elsewhere.
>
> (pp. 249–50)

Mary's suggestion that emotional rebirth may render him the inner freedom he had thought to find in Wishwood gives Harry new hope as well as new wisdom. He is able now to experience his first intimation of the rose garden:

> You bring me news
> Of a door that opens at the end of a corridor,
> Sunlight and singing; when I had felt sure
> That every corridor only led to another,
> Or to a blank wall . . .   (p. 252)

Although the Furies immediately dispel this partial vision, its significance is not lost but is taken up again and completed in the scene with Agatha. Harry learns from Agatha that the cause of his inner torment lies not in his own wish to murder his wife but in his father's wish to murder his mother. This knowledge frees him from personal terrors: "The things I thought were real are shadows, and the real/Are what I thought were private shadows. O that awful privacy/Of the insane mind" (p. 276). He learns further from Agatha that she could have married his father in the event of his mother's murder but had sacrificed her happiness so that he might be born: "I only looked through the little door/When the sun was shining on the rose-garden . . . /And then a black raven flew over" (p. 276). The knowledge that Agatha has also had a partial vision through love of him renders Harry the fulfillment of that ecstasy he had only sensed with Mary:

> I was not there, you were not there, only our phantasms
> And what did not happen is as true as what did happen,
> O my dear, and you walked through the little door
> And I ran to meet you in the rose-garden.   (p. 277)

Things as they were have finally merged for Harry with things as they might have been. For a moment he has felt perfect communion with Agatha, making her sense of having been his mother seem as true as the actual fact that she was not.

At the same time, his emotion for Agatha is also that of a lover. Rose gardens since the *Roman de la Rose* have a way of evoking associations with sex. More specifically here, a letter from Eliot to his producer, E. Martin Browne, makes clear that Harry's vision of the rose garden with both Mary and Agatha is meant to carry sexual undertones. In it Eliot refers to the scene with Mary as the first time since Harry's marriage that he has felt attracted to any woman. The letter goes on to explain that it is this reawakening, incapable of developing owing to Harry's mental state, that leads him to his semi-filial, semi-sexual emotion for Agatha.[11] However, Harry's earthly vision of love's ecstasy is not to be taken as a goal in itself. Its value lies rather in pointing the way to a new level of being, as Agatha understands:

[11] MS letter to E. Martin Browne, dated March 19, 1938, in the Eliot collection, Harvard University. The originals of the entire Eliot-Browne correspondence are in the possession of Miss Emily Hale.

This is the next moment. This is the beginning.
We do not pass twice through the same door
Or return to the door through which we did not pass.
.   .   .   .   . You have a long journey.   (pp. 277–78)

For the Furies rush back to disrupt Harry's mood, here as in
the scene with Mary. But now, led by Agatha to understanding, Harry knows that they are messengers of grace and that
the torment they cause will be his soul's salvation. Calling
them "the bright angels," he will follow their guidance
through the purgation of ancestral sin to a permanent ecstasy.

Harry's rose garden is a development of that in "Burnt
Norton." The origin of his ecstasy in a moment of human
love makes explicit what had been hinted in the earlier work
—that human love is our best, if imperfect mirror of the divine.
Moreover, the rose gardens of poem and play are each symbolic of spiritual rebirth. The theme of rebirth is suggested
by the quest for a new point of departure to be found in the
rose garden of early ecstasy. In the play in particular this
theme is enhanced by echoes of *Alice in Wonderland*, where
passage, little door, and rose garden itself appear in a context connoting birth in Freudian interpretation.[12] In addition,
the spiritual implications of Harry's symbolic garden, conveyed by Eliot's religious framework, receive support from
relations to Dante, whose ultimate rose had also been reached
through pursuing a childhood vision of love. Enriched by
such allusions to the symbols of secular and religious experience, as well as by associations with flower imagery from his
own early writings, Eliot's symbol has fully assumed a central
position in a definite pattern of spiritual progress. Escape
from present suffering is first sought in the return to an
early point of departure for purposes of pursuing what might

[12] Louis Martz, "The Wheel and the Point," in *T. S. Eliot: A Selected
Critique*, ed. Leonard Unger, pp. 447–49, discusses the correspondence
with *Alice in Wonderland*, a correspondence which Eliot himself had
stressed in conversation.

have been as opposed to what has been. That point once reached in the moment in the rose garden, it is discovered that the things of time are redeemable only outside of time. But the garden, intimating the timeless, starts man out upon a new way of being that will lead him in the end to the eternal reality.

For after his vision of things divine through the medium of things earthly, Harry starts out in what appears on the surface to be a direction opposed to that indicated by the rose garden. He renounces entirely his new-found loves and the beauties of the natural world for the austerities of the spirit: "the worship in the desert, the thirst and deprivation, / A stony sanctuary and a primitive altar" (p. 281). These deprivations, however, are actually in fundamental accord with all that the garden had truly meant. In fact, the garden remains at once the inspiration and goal, the beginning and end of his arduous journey. What Harry has renounced are the human desires, imperfections, impediments that stand between him and the eternal reality manifested to temporal vision through the moment of grace in an earthly garden. The ecstasy in the rose garden, being too intense for human kind to bear, is quickly shattered by cloud, raven, or Furies. But it persists in memory as a perpetual reminder of the purgatorial purpose. A passage on the rose garden in "Burnt Norton" could serve equally well as a comment on Harry's experiences in *The Family Reunion:*

> Time past and time future
> Allow but a little consciousness.
> To be conscious is not to be in time
> But only in time can the moment in the rose-garden
>
> .   .   .   .
>
> Be remembered; involved with past and future.
> Only through time time is conquered.   (pp. 119–20)

The conquest of time can be achieved in time through the arduous process of atonement. In "Burnt Norton" the passages on the rose garden are followed by passages on a condition of "internal darkness, deprivation" similar to St. John's purgatorial Dark Night. And *The Family Reunion* makes explicit the link between the moment of ecstasy and the ensuing lifetime of abnegation. For through Agatha's explanations Harry comes to an understanding that makes possible his rebirth in the rose garden and his consequent departure on the long journey of purification:

> I know that I have made a decision
> In a moment of clarity, and now I feel dull again.
>
> . . . .
>
> But I know there is only one way out of defilement—
> Which leads in the end to reconciliation.
> And I know that I must go.   (p. 279)

Uniting St. John's way of negation with Dante's way of affirmation, Eliot has evolved a pattern of spiritual progress that unites the two principal paths to God in Christian teaching. Approaching the Creator through his creation, approaching divine through human love has become the rose garden moment of grace that starts man out upon his journey. Approaching God through ascetic denial of all distracting temporal wants has become the purgatorial process whereby man makes himself worthy of the moment of grace and of the eternal garden glimpsed in that fleeting moment. In Eliot's last three *Quartets,* which were written after *The Family Reunion,* this integration of the sunlit rose garden with the Dark Night in a purgatorial wasteland is given full and explicit development.

It is true that the rose garden symbol itself, in accord with the musical structure of the *Four Quartets,* is afforded less space than heretofore. Already treated in detail in "Burnt Norton," it is evoked only by incidental garden imagery in the three ensuing poems. But it appears in significant passages, and its meaning, remaining fundamentally what it was, is expanded and clarified by new contexts. "East Coker" (1940) shows the philosophical concepts of "Burnt Norton" applied to man's history. Treating the failure of the humanistic movement begun in the Renaissance, the poem stresses conditions of darkness. The darkness of a world in which wisdom has been lost in superficial knowledge and humility has been lost in the pride of self-reliance is juxtaposed with the darkness of spiritual purgation:

> O dark dark dark. They all go into the dark,
> The vacant interstellar spaces, the vacant into the vacant,
>
> . . . .
>
> And we all go with them, into the silent funeral,
> Nobody's funeral, for there is no one to bury.
> I said to my soul, be still, and let the dark come upon you
> Which shall be the darkness of God.   (p. 126)

But the purpose of turning from man's darkness to God's is ultimate light. St. John had written: "In order to reach the Union of Light, the soul must pass through the Dark Night." [13] And Eliot expresses a similar concept in the final line of his passage on darkness: "So the darkness shall be the light and the stillness the dancing" (p. 127).

This reference to the eternal goal is immediately followed by a passage recalling the moment in the rose garden:

> Whisper of running streams, and winter lightning.
> The wild thyme unseen and the wild strawberry,
> The laughter in the garden, echoed ecstasy
> Not lost, but requiring, pointing to the agony
> Of death and birth.   (p. 127)

Here for the first time the union between the negative and positive ways is made explicit. "Pointing to the agony / Of death and birth," the fleeting experience in the garden should serve as an exhortation to die to the desires of this life in order to be reborn on a plane where the ecstasy we know only

---

[13] *The Complete Works of St. John of the Cross,* ed. E. Allison Peers (London, 1934), I, 2.

in echoes has its reality. And the theme is further developed
in the poem's concluding passage. It is made clear that the
moment of vision is itself insufficient to eternal life and so must
be followed up by ceaseless spiritual effort. We must burn
not only with the intensity achieved in isolated moments of
vision, but also with the intensity required of a life spent in
loving atonement:

> As we grow older
> The world becomes stranger, the pattern more complicated
> Of dead and living. Not the intense moment
> Isolated, with no before and after,
> But a lifetime burning in every moment . . .   (p. 129)

The pattern of vision and purgation, intimated in "Burnt
Norton" and defined in "East Coker," is further developed in
"The Dry Salvages" (1941). Here for the first time it is related to the central conception in Christian belief. The rose
garden moment, described as a "gift," is clearly a revelation
of grace. As such it is an incarnation of the eternal in the
temporal:

> For most of us, there is only the unattended
> Moment, the moment in and out of time,
> The distraction fit lost in a shaft of sunlight,
>
>   . . . . .
>
> Hints followed by guesses; and the rest
> Is prayer, observance, discipline, thought and action.
> The hint half guessed, the gift half understood, is Incarnation.
>   (p. 136)

Capitalized, the term Incarnation indicates an identity between any manifestation of spirit in matter and the supreme
manifestation of God to man in the person of his Son. The
ecstasy in the rose garden is therefore related not only to any
human vision of the divine but also specifically to Christ, who
is the beginning and end of all vision. Sent through God's
grace to redeem sinful man, Christ represents the union of

such apparent contraries as death and life, matter and spirit, pain and ecstasy, time and eternity. An understanding of the rose garden moment thus becomes an understanding of no less than the central mysteries in the Christian universe:

> Here the impossible union
> Of spheres of existence is actual,
> Here the past and future
> Are conquered and reconciled, . . .   (p. 136)

Obviously, by the time of "Little Gidding" (1942) Eliot had explored pretty thoroughly the meaning for man's life on earth of the experience in the rose garden. Related to human and divine love, purgation, innocence, grace, and Incarnation, the rose garden had become a multi-leveled symbol of spiritual truth. But it yet remained for Eliot to express the complex relation between his garden of temporal vision and the eternal garden of Paradise, final goal of the whole pattern of love, grace, and purgation. In the last of the *Four Quartets* the main meanings of the preceding works are gathered up and completed on a new plane. Aspects of love, aspects of being, and the paradoxical interdependence of pain and ecstasy are now reconciled primarily by the symbol of fire. For the fires of purgation and the fires of grace turn out to be inseparable not only from each other but also from the rose garden of time and eternity. In fact, in the last analysis the temporal garden becomes in its eternal reality the culminating symbol at once of "Little Gidding" and of the *Four Quartets* as a whole.

The association of love, human or divine, with burning, and of the divine with the sun's heat and light-giving fire, is of course constant in religion and literature. Moreover, Dante's ultimate rose had been presented as inseparable from the divine sun to indicate that the rose, manifestation of God's love, is inseparable from the sun, creative power that makes love manifest. Accordingly, it is not surprising to find that Eliot's rose garden of earthly and spiritual love is identified in one way or another with figurative flame. In *The Family Reunion* the timeless flames apprehended in love's garden were compared with the flames of purgation:

> There are hours when there seems to be no past or future,
> Only a present moment of pointed light
> When you want to burn. When you stretch out your hand
> To the flames. They only come once,
> Thank God, that kind. Perhaps there is another kind,
> I believe, across a whole Thibet of broken stones
> That lie, fang up, a lifetime's march. I have believed this.
>
> (p. 274)

In "East Coker" the purgatorial flames were directly identified with the rose: "If to be warmed, then I must freeze / And quake in frigid purgatorial fires / Of which the flame is roses, and the smoke is briars" (p. 128). Now in "Little Gidding" it is revealed that the fires of ecstasy and of purgation issue from the same source and are one with the rose of Love.

At once the most timely and timeless of the *Four Quartets,* "Little Gidding" is set in the present war-torn world at the season of Pentecost. Bomber and Holy Ghost are associated with each other through the embracing symbols of dove and fire. Thus affiliated, they convey the message that our sole salvation from the fires of war lies in our choosing to undergo the fires of spiritual atonement:

> The dove descending breaks the air
> With flame of incandescent terror
> Of which the tongues declare
> The one discharge from sin and error.
> The only hope or else despair
>   Lies in the choice of pyre or pyre—
>   To be redeemed from fire by fire. (pp. 143–44)

If, warned by the bomber, we follow the Holy Ghost, the long process of purification will lead us in the end back to the beginning, to the ecstasy experienced in a childhood rose garden. The final section of "Little Gidding" evokes the symbol with which the *Quartets* had opened and which implicitly or explicitly had dominated each of them:

> And the end of all our exploring
> Will be to arrive where we started
> And know the place for the first time.
> Through the unknown, remembered gate
> When the last of earth left to discover
> Is that which was the beginning
>
> .   .   .   .
>
> And the children in the apple-tree
> Not known, because not looked for
> But heard, half-heard, in the stillness
> Between two waves of the sea.
> Quick now, here, now, always—
> A condition of complete simplicity
> (Costing not less than everything) . . .   (p. 145)

It is by now unmistakably clear that the experience in the rose garden, when finally comprehended, will turn out to be a beginning on a more fundamental level than childhood, Eden, or even the grace that leads to spiritual rebirth. For man's end is a return to the Love that is the source of his being, apprehended in earthly moments of intensity and achieved through purgatorial torment:

> And all shall be well and
> All manner of thing shall be well
> When the tongues of flame are in-folded
> Into the crowned knot of fire
> And the fire and the rose are one.   (p. 145)

It is on this final image of harmonious rose and flame that Eliot concludes his *Four Quartets*. Embracing as it does the final meanings of poems and cosmos, the image again reminds one of Dante and of the Dantesque pattern underlying Eliot's rose. For while his symbol, in its alliance with a personal

garden and a personal wasteland, has by now moved well beyond the derivative flower of *Ash Wednesday,* it has gained
in the process deeper meanings and a deeper if less obvious
affinity with Dante's. Both poets use the symbol to express
basic Catholic conceptions of grace, love, Christ, eternity, and
the Unmoved Mover that is the beginning and end of all
creation. Both rise through the rose to a vision, unsustainable
in mortal life, of the final flame or "heart of light" that is
God.

Eliot's medievalism is real and extensive. Not only do his
symbols and the meanings of his symbols bear affinity with
Dante's, but his symbols go as far as to bear interpretation in
terms of Dante's four-leveled method of allegory. The rose
garden itself simultaneously expresses natural ecstasy, divine
grace, Christ, and eternal God, meanings that correspond to
the literal, moral, allegorical and anagogical levels of medieval
interpretation.[14] Then in the overall pattern "Burnt Norton,"
with its stress on the nature of the rose garden moment, suggests the literal level or rose garden ecstasy per se. "East
Coker," with its stress on the pattern of grace and atonement,
suggests the moral meaning of the ecstasy for man's spiritual
life. "The Dry Salvages," with its stress on Incarnation, suggests the allegorical relationship between the experience and
Christ's mission to humanity. And "Little Gidding," with its
stress on the eternal counterpart to the temporal garden,
suggests the anagogical level or God's ineffable mystery manifested in created form. Such evident parallels are undoubtedly
more than coincidental, while so thoroughgoing a use of
medieval symbolic method gives to Eliot's religious poetry a
link with tradition and Church authority that carries it well
along the path towards the objectivity he sought.

[14] Sister M. Cléophas "Notes on Levels of Meaning in *Four Quartets,*"
Renascence, II (1950), 103–12, applies this method to the *Quartets* but
does not suggest that each of the poems itself represents one of the four
levels.

At the same time, however, the rose garden bears analogies with romanticism, analogies in some respects at odds with traditional Catholicism. The association of the rose garden with a childhood experience of spiritual ecstasy recalls the romantic conception of the child as a visionary creature still half in touch with his divine origin. Eliot's intimation of immortality, moreover, displays a still more widespread characteristic of romanticism: the dissatisfaction with things earthly and the consequent longing for things divine. In the Catholic scheme of things an opposite approach is generally acknowledged, man's longing for God being viewed as cause rather than effect of his disdain for earthly things. Though there may be as many paths to God as there are men who seek for him, it is important to recognize the private longing that transmuted Eliot's particular wasteland into the Christian rose in order to understand the private idealism that suffuses his particular flower. The private ideal was for Eliot happily identifiable with the Anglo-Catholic faith. Nonetheless, it retains in his poetry subjective qualities of nostalgia, melancholy, and transcendental yearning more typical of the nineteenth and twentieth centuries than of the objective era from whence it draws religious life.

The form through which his ideal is expressed is accordingly also a product of modern as well as medieval times. While many of his symbols, including the rose, are derived from Catholic tradition, and while the four-fold system of theological interpretation can be legitimately applied, Eliot's symbolic method itself owes a good deal to that of the French. His attempt to approximate music in the structure of the *Four Quartets* recalls the theory and practice of Mallarmé. And his conception of art as approaching through symbolic form the pure, ineffable ideal seems at times more akin to Mallarmé's indefinite suggestiveness than to Dante's precise, theological system:

> Words, after speech, reach
> Into the silence. Only by the form, the pattern
> Can words or music reach
> The stillness, as a Chinese jar still
> Moves perpetually in its stillness.   (p. 121)

Moreover, to the French symbolist influence Eliot has added a debt to contemporary methods. Following Freud and Freudian views of *Alice in Wonderland,* he has given his rose garden subjective undertones, enhanced by dreamlike hints of meanings stored in the unconscious since early childhood. Following the contemporary effort to reconcile inner and outer worlds, he has sought to correlate the wasteland and rose of private or religious conviction with the immediate state of twentieth-century society.

The end result of these combined influences, as filtered through Eliot's own personality, is a method at once original and important to modern literature. Eliot, it would seem, is less objective than he believes and is in many ways a product of the romantic movement he has largely rejected. But it is probably because rather than in spite of this that his has been a major contribution to contemporary symbolism. To a greater extent than any of his contemporaries he has adapted the symbols and technics of medieval Catholic writing to the twentieth-century world. In the process he has romanticized an essentially unromantic tradition. But in so doing he has met only the needed and inevitable requirements of an age that is chiefly romantic. Rivers of Protestantism and unbelief have flowed between Dante's time and ours. The individual in his unique complexity, in all of his labeled and unlabeled longings, and in the most hidden reaches of his psyche, has been exalted, analyzed, democratized between Dante's time and ours. If time is a river, it cannot flow backwards. And Eliot, for all his medieval longings, has had to accommodate himself to the age in which he happens to live in order that his art may reach that troubled age at all.

Accordingly, he has enriched public symbols with private meanings. In doing so he has made those symbols relevant to a world and time in which the private consciousness is sufficiently important to demand unique expression, yet sufficiently distressed to demand some public outlet. By giving private emotions validity in an objective belief that includes and transcends private desires, Eliot has solved for many a part at least of the modern problem. Traditional belief, made personal and immediate through a symbolism combining medieval and romantic elements, offers an organization at once definite and elastic for the diffuse distresses and discontents of the age. It offers the backbone needed to stiffen a romantic outlook that has in the past century and might again in ours become dangerously soft. And it offers a symbolic method that is relevant not just to Anglo-Catholicism but also to any expression of Christian experience in our era. In his adaptation of medieval tradition to contemporary times, Eliot has found a way of reconciling inner and outer worlds within a framework that promises to him and those who share his feelings a much desired redemption from the present day.

7

JOYCE

AND

SYNTHESIS

James Joyce, who had been brought up among traditions, set out on a quest opposite to T. S. Eliot's. While Eliot sought in the Church liberation from the world with its attendant limitations and evils, Joyce sought in the world liberation from the Church with its attendant bonds of family and nation. Tradition was too much a part of Joyce to be abandoned. But he was able to work out through rebellion and exile a synthesis of experience in which Catholicism supported a secular outlook, nationalism contributed to internationalism, and personal biases were transmuted to universal sympathy. Although his goals and values were the antitheses of Eliot's, as were his conceptions of human experience, he did for the contemporary secular outlook something comparable to what Eliot did for the religious. For Joyce, like Eliot, gave to his age an organized, objective image of itself in which the melting outlines of romanticism were once more brought into definite focus. And like Eliot he used for his secular purpose a combination of symbols and symbolic traditions drawn from modern, romantic, and medieval sources.

Among the many symbols in Joyce's works the rose is major in *A Portrait of the Artist as a Young Man* and *Ulysses*. In placing human love at the center of his cosmos Joyce relied heavily on the flower of love for the expression of his humanistic synthesis as well as of the various stages in its development. And because Church, Ireland, and woman were intrinsic parts of Joyce's views, the rose could embrace not only the axis but also the spokes of his wheel of life. Moreover, the flower of woman, love, nation, and religion was adaptable to public and private attitudes alike, and so could convey with relative ease Joyce's modifications of tradition. A symbol suited to so many simultaneous ends was exactly what Joyce's mind and method most required. For he was continually seeking to express both the interrelatedness of phenomena and the rich, universal conclusions that he drew from complex, individual experiences. Certainly the prime symbol of fulfillment in all literature could not be more appropriate to any writer than to one wishing to celebrate his personal faith in man. And Joyce, unlike many of his contemporaries, did come to accept the world around him and to present through the rose an affirmative vision of things not as they ought to be but as they are.

Affirmation, however, was the outcome of struggle. Consequently, the rose of the *Portrait* and *Ulysses* expresses stages and aspects of Stephen Dedalus's conflicts as well as their final reconciliation. Since Stephen's personal conflicts are ultimately united with Joyce's embracing vision of life, the same symbol is used to carry at once the unique and the general in Stephen's experience. The flower appears in both novels primarily as a female symbol. As such it expresses reactions to woman basic to Stephen's development. In addition, it expands beyond woman herself to embrace certain other major concerns that are only indirectly related to woman. As the Virgin's flower the rose is allied with Stephen's reactions first to Catholicism and later to his mother, who comes to represent his Catholic conscience. As the flower of mortal woman it embodies his changing views of earthly love or beauty. And cutting across both the religious and secular levels of meaning, it symbolizes artistic creation, which Stephen associates with birth and with

divine creation. Although all are expressions of ideals of fulfillment, certain of these meanings were at first in opposition.
Nor were they brought into final harmony until the traditions
with which they were linked had been reexamined and reinterpreted in the light of mature emotional experience.

The rose in the *Portrait* supports themes of conflict and
the struggle for harmony. Taking a place beside water and
birds as one of the novel's leading symbols, it plays a far from
negligible role in the elaboration of structure and theme.
Roses blossom at crucial stages of Stephen's development in
association with such major concerns as women, Catholicism,
art, and sometimes Ireland. Since his conceptions of all four
are ambivalent and inseparable, the use of a symbol able to
carry several levels of conscious and unconscious meaning is
essential to the full expression of his emotional state. Since
his emotional state itself is dynamic and fluctuating, the rose
takes on additional import in conveying vital changes in
attitudes and reactions determining his course on the road
to maturity. Further, Joyce, who was impressed by such
symbolic achievements as the four-fold allegory of Dante's
Comedy or the indefinite suggestiveness of early Yeats, found
in these precursors conspicuous roses used as symbols of
woman, religion, nation, and art. With traditional analogies
supporting and enhancing private concerns, he was able to
enrich Stephen's rose by introducing echoes of objective beliefs into the interplay of subtle subjective impressions.

The symbol's association with Stephen is made on the very
first page of the *Portrait*. This in itself is an indication of its
intended importance; for Joyce, who was notably exacting
about every word and the position of every word in his books,
was anything but negligent of his opening pages. Here Stephen
learns a song about a rose:

> *O, the wild rose blossoms*
> *On the little green place.*

He sang that song. That was his song.
O, the green wothe botheth.[1]

The little green place is clearly Ireland, while the wild rose growing there is Stephen, who is at this time in the blossoming stage, who specifically claims the song as "his," and who is to be rebellious, alone, and in his own terms "wild" throughout his Irish youth. With the green rose in the child's own version of the song, hints of Stephen's artistic leanings emerge. By altering the wording he shows incipient creativity, and by positing a green rose he creates in imagination that which does not exist elsewhere. As a flower whose color is that of Ireland and whose existence is dependent upon Stephen's imagination, the green rose of the child's initial artistic effort acts as a symbolic foreshadowing of the young man's final determination "to forge in the smithy of my soul the uncreated conscience of my race" (p. 299).

The green rose is also related to Stephen's emotional condition. Green is suggestive of fertility and therefore of potentiality, but at the same time implies present unripeness or immaturity. In this respect the flower is associated not only with Stephen's youth but also with his persistent desire to find an imaginative ideal in the unimaginative world. The association is made specific when, during Stephen's first school experience, the War of the Roses in his mathematics class calls his song to mind again: "But you could not have a green rose. But perhaps somewhere in the world you could" (p. 8). And his thought here is simply an early expression of the longing, which will dominate his adolescence, "to meet in the real world the unsubstantial image which his soul so constantly beheld" (p. 71).

For Stephen's fantasies of Mercedes, the "unsubstantial image" in question, always have a rose garden as their setting. The ideal of Mercedes was derived from Stephen's reading

[1] Citations from the *Portrait* and *Ulysses* (first published in 1916 and 1922, respectively) are to the Modern Library editions.

The Count of Monte Cristo and identifying himself with the novel's hero in his love for the girl Mercedes. In fact, Stephen's fantasy owes to Dumas almost every romantic detail: a lady who embodies all goodness and virtue, a love that will weather untold hardships, and, when his dream shall have been betrayed, a triumph no less glorious than the passion that provoked it. But Stephen's ideal is framed with roses, which do not appear in Dumas: "Outside Blackrock, on the road that led to the mountains, stood a small whitewashed house in the garden of which grew many rosebushes: and in this house, he told himself, another Mercedes lived" (p. 68). Since no rose garden is to be found in Dumas (although almost all else down to the whitewash is Dumas), Joyce undoubtedly adds it with symbolic intent. Through associating Mercedes with roses he is able to make more apparent her relation to other women in the *Portrait* who are also associated with roses. Further, his use of symbolism in the treatment of Mercedes enables him to express more than a single meaning and thus to suggest the complexity of young Stephen's attitude towards women.

The ideal lady in her rose garden is on one level reminiscent of Beatrice, who leads Dante to the rose of heaven and is herself enthroned on one of its petals. Other features of Stephen's fantasy support this association. The Count of Monte Cristo, with whom Stephen identifies himself, is named Edmond Dantes. In addition to the likeness of names, both Dante and Dantes were proud and angry exiles, intense moral idealists, and devoted lovers. In each, love for the lady remained chaste and unconsummated; in each it served as moral guide throughout an otherwise troubled life.[2] Then, reinforcing the clear Dantesque parallels to *The Count of Monte Cristo* (which Joyce, if not Dumas, was surely aware of),

[2] Dantes, throughout his long career of vengeance, regarded himself as a veritable agent of Providence sent to punish his betrayers. Mercedes, the chief motive behind his fierce justice, was alone able to temper his vengeful excesses when they threatened the life of her innocent son.

there are two further parallels to Dante, pointed up by Joycean modifications of Dumas. While Dantes is in his teens at the time of falling in love with Mercedes, Stephen, like Dante, is still a child. More important, while Dantes' Mercedes lives on a promontory, Stephen's lives on a road leading to mountains. The substitution of mountains for promontory seems deliberate: Dante's attempt to climb the holy hill when he lost his way in the dark wood of sense and his success in climbing Purgatory by grace imparted through Beatrice both find their echo in Stephen's later youth when he, lost in his own dark wood, experiences relief in remembering his early vision of purity: "In the pauses of his desire, when the luxury that was wasting him gave room to a softer languor, the image of Mercedes traversed the background of his memory. He saw again the small white house and the garden of rose-bushes on the road that led to the mountains" (pp. 111–12).

The alliance of Mercedes with roses that have perceptible Dantesque hues links her to other rose-women in the *Portrait* who are also in some sense Beatrice-like. Whether secular or spiritual, the later roses have roots in Mercedes' garden, for Stephen's childhood fantasy-woman embodies within herself the seeds of those to follow. First among her descendants is the Virgin herself. As a chaste, ennobling influence Mercedes plays a role in Stephen's consciousness (as does Beatrice in Dante's) which is similar in some ways to that of Mary. During his struggles with lust and guilt, when memories of Mercedes brought transitory balm, the idea of the Virgin was a still more potent source of inspiration and relief. Since the rose is traditionally symbolic of the Virgin as well as of womankind, Stephen's experience of penance, expressed in prayers to Mary, is rightly conveyed by the same flower that had been linked with his earlier female idol: "his prayers ascended to heaven from his purified heart like perfume streaming upwards from a heart of white rose" (p. 168). The use of rose symbolism for both Mary and Mercedes to evoke analogous moods of elevated serenity makes apparent a parallel between Stephen's divine and earthly ideals.

But the correspondence between ideals and roses is devious. While Stephen's conscious worship of chastity is at this time strongly colored by his unquestioning Catholicism,[3] his unconscious attitudes towards women are not wholly in accord with Catholic ideals. In a novel told entirely from Stephen's conscious point of view, such unconscious reactions must be conveyed primarily by symbolic indirection. The roses of Mercedes and the Virgin indicate Stephen's suppressed sensual desires as well as his acknowledged admiration for holiness. Mercedes' dwelling in a garden of rosebushes, through suggesting the idealized sexuality of the *Roman de la Rose,* clarifies the nature of the "strange unrest" Stephen felt when he "brooded upon her image" (p. 70). And the "heart of white rose" he offers to the Virgin at the end of the religious retreat ironically recalls his sensations at its outset: "Stephen's heart had withered up like a flower of the desert that feels the simoon coming from afar" (p. 123).

Such hints of unconscious sexual stirrings are reinforced by association with other symbols. Stephen's painful, ascetic attempts to transform the withered flower of his sensual nature into the purified white rose of the Virgin evoke the novel's recurrent associations of white, the color of Catholic purity, with cold, dank, unpleasant things.[4] More specifically, the Virgin's flower recalls the only other white rose in the *Portrait,* that worn by Stephen during the early War of the Roses in his mathematics class. On this occasion Stephen's white rose is defeated by the opposing red rose, just as later his religious ideal of chastity, associated with the Virgin's

---

[3] An unresolved Oedipus complex also seems to be influential. In Freudian theory guilt over unconscious incestuous desires often results in dichotomizing women into pure women, placed in the mother category, and women who are sexually attractive but therefore evil.

[4] See Hugh Kenner, "The Portrait in Perspective," in *James Joyce: Two Decades of Criticism,* ed. Seon Givens (New York, 1948), pp. 147–48.

white rose, was to be defeated by a victorious sensual ideal, associated with the more commonly secular red rose.

Red and white roses then symbolize Stephen's conflict between the flesh and the spirit. It is notable that Joyce assigned no color to the roses surrounding Mercedes, and this is possibly because she is Stephen's "unsubstantial image," the green rose of the child's still undesignated longing. Certainly the fantasy of Mercedes contains in embryo both the religious and the profane poles of Stephen's conflict, while his subsequent worship of the Virgin represents his first conscious choice between opposites. Since the choice is contrary to his nature, his repudiation of the Virgin in favor of a secular ideal is almost inevitable. Significantly his reversal, the climax of the book, is again reminiscent of Mercedes and this time culminates in a gigantic crimson rose.

Through his encounter with the girl on the beach Stephen is converted from the worship of things divine to the worship of things earthly. The importance of this inverted conversion is to a great extent conveyed by symbols which express opposition to Catholicism through association with a markedly secular rose. Throughout the experience Stephen's most frequent adjective is "wild," indicating both rebellion and release and echoing the "wild rose" with which he identified himself in infancy. The girl, recalling Mercedes, is suggestive of Beatrice: like Beatrice she has come as a messenger of ultimate truth, and like Beatrice she will guide Stephen by her eyes to his vision of ineffable glory. But going beyond Mercedes, the girl on the beach is a now avowedly sensual Beatrice, and the vision to which her inspiration leads will be an avowedly secular vision: "Her eyes had called him and his soul had leaped at the call. . . . A wild angel had appeared to him, the angel of mortal youth and beauty, an envoy from the fair courts of life to throw open before him in an instant of ecstasy the gates of all the ways of error and glory" (p. 200).

Stephen's "instant of ecstasy" follows almost immediately his experience of the girl. He is no longer near her (as Dante was no longer beside Beatrice in his final ecstasy), but "her image had passed into his soul for ever" (p. 200). Lying down upon the beach to calm his agitation, he is granted a vision of a rose of heavenly light, which is a temporal image of Dante's rose of God: "His eyelids trembled . . . as if they felt the strange light of some new world . . . fantastic, dim, uncertain as under sea, traversed by cloudy shapes and beings. A world, a glimmer, or a flower? Glimmering and trembling, trembling and unfolding, a breaking light, an opening flower, it spread in endless succession to itself, breaking in full crimson and unfolding and fading to palest rose, leaf by leaf and wave of light by wave of light, flooding all the heavens with its soft flushes" (pp. 200–1). Stephen's ecstasy is brief and Dante's is protracted. But one can acquire some conception of the close parallel between them (in light, water imagery, shapes and beings, vast opening flower) from Dante's description of the rose's first manifestation to him:

> Fassi di raggio tutta sua parvenza
> riflesso al sommo del Mobile Primo,
>
> . . . .
>
> E come clivo in acqua di suo imo
> si specchia. . . .
>
> . . . .
>
> si soprastando al lume intorno intorno
> vidi specchiarsi in piu di mille soglie,
> quanto di noi lassu fatto ha ritorno.
>
> E se l' infimo grado in se raccoglie
> si grande lume, quant' e la larghezza
> di questa rosa nell' estreme foglie?
>
> (*Par.* XXX, 106–17)

> It is composed wholly of rays
> reflected on the top of the Primum Mobile,
>
> . . . .

and as a hillside mirrors itself in water

. . . .

so, overlooking the light all around,
I saw, as in a mirror, on more than a thousand tiers,
all who have returned on high;

and if the lowest row gathers to itself
so much light, how great is the width
of the rose in its outermost petals!   —H. R. HUSE

Joyce's presentation of Stephen's climactic vision through symbols recalling the *Paradiso* stresses both the opposition and kinship between Stephen's experience and Dante's. Inspired by primarily sensual feelings, the crimson rose represents Stephen's supreme affirmation of the "wonder of mortal beauty," in direct contrast to Dante's white rose of spiritual beauty. At the same time the analogy with Dante's rose enhances the tremendous significance of Stephen's. It is notable that Stephen, like Molly Bloom and Anna Livia, is granted his moment of supreme affirmation in the borderland between sleep and waking when the relaxation of the critical intellect presumably facilitates cosmic insights.[5] His twilight vision of a Dantesque rose of mortal glory, symbolizing his new comprehension of life's meaning, clearly implies that Stephen's ecstasy has for him something of the transcendent import that Dante's had for Dante.

Beneath the experience, however, lurks an ironic undertone that becomes magnified in retrospect. The immediate effect of Stephen's conversion to the worship of mortal beauty is his realization of his true vocation. Dedication to art fills the place left vacant by his rejection of the priesthood and, after developing an esthetic theory applying Thomistic concepts to the art for art's sake doctrine, Stephen is ready to

[5] Cf. Yeats's "moment when we are both asleep and awake . . . in which the mind liberated from the pressure of the will is unfolded in symbols" (*Essays*, p. 193), and T. S. Eliot's visionary lady "who moves in the time between sleeping and waking" (*Ash Wednesday*).

write a poem putting theory into practice. The symbolic atmosphere surrounding the creation of this poem parallels that of his experience on the beach in almost every detail. Again inspired by a girl who is for the moment the center of Stephen's emotional universe, the poem is composed in a like state of visionary ecstasy expressed by clouds, water, light, and most notably another Dantesque rose. Since this experience is more extensive and complex than its earlier counterpart, a close analysis of the symbolism through which it is conveyed illuminates the real conflict underlying Stephen's attitude and the irony of his ecstatic conviction.

Stephen's second vision simultaneously encompasses the three main levels of meaning associated with the rose: religion, woman, and art. Like its predecessor it takes place in the borderland between dream and waking and unfolds in cloud-like rays of rosy light: "Over his limbs in sleep pale cool waves of light had passed. He lay still, as if his soul lay amid cool waters. . . . His mind was waking slowly to a tremulous morning knowledge, a morning inspiration. . . . In a dream or vision he had known the ecstasy of seraphic life. . . . The instant flashed forth like a point of light and now from cloud on cloud of vague circumstance confused form was veiling softly its afterglow . . . deepening to a rose and ardent light" (pp. 254–55). Here the *Paradiso* is recalled by the imagery of watery light at the outset as well as by the emerging rose. Just as Dante's rose of heaven first appeared as a river of light (E vidi lume in forma di riviera: *Par.* XXX, 61), so Stephen's second Dantesque rose now evolves from a dreamlike impression of light and waters.[6] The inescapable echo of Dante is again made partly to mark the comparison between Stephen's vision of mortal beauty and Dante's of heavenly beauty. But

[6] Water here also suggests rebirth, as has Stephen's wading in the first vision. His poem's completion uses similar imagery to indicate his rebirth as artist through acceptance of sex: "Her nakedness . . . enfolded him like water with a liquid life . . . the liquid letters of speech . . . flowed forth over his brain" (p. 262).

as a symbol of specifically creative ecstasy the rose of the *Paradiso* is still more suggestive. Not only does it culminate one of the world's greatest literary creations, but it also symbolizes therein the fulfillment of God's eternal creation. Stephen's exalted conception of the artist could scarcely have found more apt expression.

As the vision unfolds, further implications for art develop. Stephen's rose, like Dante's, becomes the Virgin's flower. And in accord with Stephen's usual conversion of the divine to the earthly, the Virgin herself becomes associated with his markedly secular theory of art. The art for art's sake doctrine, already presented explicitly in Stephen's talk with Lynch (pp. 241–50), is here presented by symbolic indirection. The Annunciation is made to symbolize artistic inspiration: "O! in the virgin womb of the imagination the word was made flesh. Gabriel the seraph had come to the virgin's chamber" (p. 255). And the Annunciation as symbol of poetic inspiration is presently complemented by the Eucharist, symbol of poetic composition: "transmuting the daily bread of experience into the radiant body of everliving life" (p. 260). Following Stephen's esthetic theory, artistic creation is presented as a dual process in which inspiration first makes the word flesh (i.e., gives rise to an "epiphany" or illuminating insight), and artistic discipline then makes the flesh word (i.e., gives the insight "wholeness, harmony, and radiance," thereby molding it into an esthetic form).

It is notable that these concepts, here associated with Dante's flower of heaven and Mary, are again associated with a rose by Stephen's remarks in *Ulysses*: "Desire's wind blasts the thorntree but after it becomes from a bramblebush to be a rose upon the rood of time. . . . In woman's womb word is made flesh but in the spirit of the maker all flesh that passes becomes the word that shall not pass away" (p. 385). Stephen, still identifying the artist with the divine

Creator, still associates the rose with the process of artistic creation. Although he has now substituted Yeats's "rose upon the rood of time" for Dante's rose of heaven, there is small difference in effect. For Yeats's rose of eternal Beauty, like Dante's rose of Eternity, symbolizes the beginning and end of art and life; and Yeats, like Dante, believed (or tried to believe) that art was a bodying forth of spiritual mysteries. Joyce, seeking symbolic expression for Stephen's secular esthetics, continues to choose the most transcendental of literary roses to emphasize the supreme importance to Stephen of his doctrine of earthly beauty in art.

Beauty has become Stephen's highest value in life as well. Since beauty throughout the *Portrait* has been associated with women at least as much as with art, and since the sensual charm of a woman has been directly responsible for Stephen's conversion to mortal beauty, it is not surprising to find yet another woman involved in his creation of a poem. Again the rose as the Virgin's flower is important, and here the opposition to Dante is most strongly marked. Stephen's girl, who has inspired his creative ecstasy, is a virgin and a Catholic, "her life . . . a simple rosary of hours" (p. 254). But in his fantasy she becomes a temptress awakening man's lust, a universal embodiment of all that is opposed to Mary: "That rose and ardent light was her strange wilful heart, strange that no man had known or would know, wilful from before the beginning of the world: and lured by that ardent roselike glow the choirs of the seraphim were falling from heaven. . . . Its rays burned up the world, consumed the hearts of men and angels: the rays from the rose that was her wilful heart" (p. 255). In the sacrilegious spirit of the *fin de siècle,* this passage recalls the "mystical rose of the mire" of Swinburne's "Dolores" or the "rose that is rooted in hell" of Arthur Symons's "Rosa Flammae." Stephen, still preoccupied with the religion he is repudiating, has used Dantesque imagery to translate his sexual desire into anti-Catholic terms and to create of its object an inverted Virgin who is as potent a force for damnation as Mary is for salvation. His conceptions of art and woman are at this time inseparable. Both are esthetic, sensual, and anti-Catholic, and both rest on the same infirm emotional foundation. Two further analogies complement the analogy with Dante in revealing the attitudes underlying Stephen's ecstasy. His idealized rose-woman, existing "from before the beginning of the world" and sending forth rays of beauty that "consumed the hearts of men and angels," echoes Yeats's "Rose of the World," who existed before there were angels "or any hearts to beat" and for whose beauty "Troy passed away in one high funeral gleam." Stephen's rose, like Yeats's, is at once the inspiration of his art, the particular woman to whom he is attracted, and the embodiment of his ideal of beauty; and Stephen, like Yeats, is constrained at this stage by highly subjective, romantic, and immature attitudes which he too is later to repudiate. A passage from Joyce's own early essay on James Clarence Mangan completes the picture. Writing of the moving spirit in Mangan's poetry, Joyce describes it as a feminine symbol of ideal beauty, a "flower of flowers" remarkably similar to Yeats's or to Stephen's: "the presence of an imaginative personality reflecting the light of imaginative beauty is . . . vividly felt. . . . Music and odours and lights are spread about her. . . . Vittoria Colonna and Laura and Beatrice . . . embody one chivalrous idea . . . and she whose white and holy hands have the virtue of enchanted hands, his virgin flower, the flower of flowers, is no less than these an embodiment of that idea." [7] It is significant that this essay was published in *St. Stephen's* for May, 1902, a few months before Joyce's winter flight from Dublin and there-

---

[7] Quoted in Herbert Gorman, *James Joyce* (New York, 1948), pp. 76–77. Joyce borrows "flower of flowers" from Mangan's "Dark Rosaleen," a version of the traditional Irish song, allusions to which are also present in Yeats's rose poems.

fore at approximately the time when the autobiographical Stephen was composing his poem.

Despite his elaborate conversion to mortal beauty, Stephen is still in much the same frame of mind as the child who dreamed of a green rose that couldn't exist. He had set out to discover his unsubstantial ideal "in the real world," but sought it in Virgin and anti-Virgin, heaven and hell, ironically ignoring the solid earth in between. His adherence to the lush, world-weary romanticism of the 1890s reflects the introverted adolescence of his present emotional orientation, while his use of Dante in expressing rebellion against the Church reveals his continuing preoccupation with the religion he has rejected. Turning from the spirit to the flesh, Stephen has simply substituted one side of his conflict for the other without working out a real resolution. His reaction to woman is now a purely sensual thing and his artistic ideal does not go beyond the esthete's hollow shell of formal beauty. He himself is dimly conscious of dissatisfaction when, at the very pinnacle of creative ecstasy, inspiration suddenly fails him: "The full morning light had come. . . . He knew that all around him life was about to awaken in common noises, hoarse voices, sleepy prayers. Shrinking from that life he turned towards the wall . . . staring at the great overblown scarlet flowers of the tattered wallpaper. . . . Weary! Weary! He too was weary of ardent ways" (p. 260). But he remains unconscious of the nature of his trouble, also hinted in this passage. The awakening of daily life causes Stephen's roses to appear overblown because he cannot yet come to terms with that life. He is suffering primarily from an egocentricity that excludes charity, and will achieve neither a true resolution of conflicts nor an adequate conception of art until his discovery of humanity, the subject of *Ulysses*.

A little epiphany towards the close of the *Portrait* illuminates Stephen's condition and serves almost as a forecast of his course in *Ulysses*. The epiphany is associated with a woman who is again a rose. Stephen and Cranly overhear a servant singing "Rosie O'Grady," and in Stephen's mind she is related to his conflicting conceptions of woman, the spiritual and the secular. He first envisions "the figure of woman as she appears in the liturgy of the church" (p. 288), thereby evoking the Beatrice-Virgin-Catholic aura of his earlier rose-women. The image passes and he thinks of his girl, the rosy temptress of his recent villanelle, whom he now feels he is losing to Cranly: "Yes; he would go. He could not strive against another. He knew his part" (p. 289). But the singer herself is actually a typical Irish servant, characteristic of the nation from which Stephen is about to flee, and so of the ordinary humanity from which egocentric Stephen holds himself aloof.

Cranly, well ahead of Stephen in tolerance and sympathy, unites all these women through the phrase, *"Mulier cantat"*; for in their fundamental kinship, which Stephen fails to comprehend, lies a potential resolution of his difficulties. Commenting on the lyrics of "Rosie O'Grady," Cranly attempts to point out to Stephen the charity that is lacking in his cold art and selfish life:

—There's real poetry for you—he said.—There's real love.—
He glanced sideways at Stephen with a strange smile and said:
—Do you consider that poetry? Or do you know what the words mean?—
—I want to see Rosie first—said Stephen.
—She's easy to find—Cranly said.

But Stephen is not yet ready to understand. Not until his comprehension of Molly Bloom, the ultimate rose of human life, will he learn what the words love and poetry mean and find his fulfillment "in the real world."

This comprehension will come in the course of a single day and will be once again associated with the rose. But it will not by any means come quickly or easily, since the day recounted in *Ulysses* is the longest day in literature and the rose in *Ulysses* is even more intricate than its counterpart in the *Portrait*. Carrying over from the earlier novel all prior associations, the flower acquires in *Ulysses* still more levels of meaning, which lead in the end to harmony but begin in former conflict. For despite his flight from the nets of Church, family, and nation, Stephen at the outset remains entrammeled by inner bonds. He has not yet been able to start the great book he plans to write, he feels exiled within Ireland but has found no place where he belongs, and he is haunted by guilt for denying mother and Church by refusing his mother's dying wish that he make his Easter duty. In attempting to turn his back on everything of which he has been a part, Stephen has at once intensified his internal conflicts and cut himself off from any real kinship with the external world. He is consequently in quest of an adequate father figure through whom he may attain a resolution of the discords between himself and surrounding society.

But before the discovery of humanity in Bloom that will lead to his ultimate vision of Molly, Stephen has finally to break through certain emotional fixations impeding his development. This is symbolically achieved in the brothel scene through the smashing of the chandelier, and is prepared for by the culmination of his conflict in attitude towards woman. As it had been in the *Portrait*, the rose here is important in making possible the simultaneous expression of both poles of Stephen's conflict. Shortly before the smashing of the chandelier, the group in Bella Cohen's brothel has been engaged in a wild dance to the accompaniment of the song of the factory lass, the "little Yorkshire rose." The prostitute Zoe, a Yorkshire girl, is specifically identified with that rose. But the song is also related to Stephen's conception of God. When Cissy Caffrey, another prostitute, and two soldiers enter singing it, Stephen exclaims: "Hark! Our friend, noise in the street" (p. 559). His remark recalls his early definition of God: "A shout in the street" (p. 35). And in the context of whoredom it also recalls his adaptation of Blake just prior to that definition: "The harlot's cry from street to street / Shall weave old Ireland's winding sheet" (p. 34).

This association of God with a harlot and its particular relation to Blake is significant. Throughout the *Portrait,* where the affinity with Blake is never explicit, Stephen had fiercely sought release from what Blake had termed "the net of religion." Throughout *Ulysses* Blake has been one of his principal heroes. Moreover, he is again to be at the forefront of Stephen's consciousness in the climactic smashing of the chandelier, conceived of in terms of shattering space and time, Blake's dream of freedom. Evoking the earlier writer's belief that Christianity's moral strictures have produced the distortions of human nature that lead to harlotry and general corruption, Stephen has previously conceived of our world as "an age of exhausted whoredom groping for its God" (p. 204). Now, at this time of emotional crisis, his Yorkshire rose of prostitution, like Blake's sick rose of repressed sexuality, has come to represent the ultimate product of an antinatural, inhibitory religion. In fact, the nightmare of history from which Stephen seeks release is in a significant sense Blake's nightmare of Christian tradition, just as the religion of humanity he will achieve in heaven's stead will parallel in important ways Blake's man-centered devotion.

In the brothel scene, however, Stephen's outlook is still muddled by conflict. Moreover, the situation is extremely intricate, for the whore represents not only the end product of Catholic tradition but also the end product of Stephen's anti-Catholic pursuits to date. He refers to his dance with Zoe as a "dance of death," and the death in question is meant to encompass both poles of Stephen's conflict. In the *Portrait* he had at first suffered intense religious guilt over his relations with harlots. He had then gone to the other extreme in repudiating the Catholic source of his guilt and establishing in its stead a sacrilegious estheticism. Now in the brothel scene that whole course of events reaches its conclusion. The comment, "Think of your mother's people," gives rise to Stephen's "dance of death" (p. 564), and the dance is immediately followed by the apparition of his mother's corpse surrounded by "virgins and confessors" chanting praises to the Virgin. Zoe, the Yorkshire rose, has evoked the image of his Catholic mother at once through guilty contrast and through essential kinship. For it is clear that in abandoning the rose of mother and Virgin for the rose of the esthete's earthly temptress, Stephen has in fact abandoned a kind of love for a kind of lust. But it is at the same time clear that his mother's Catholic values are as life-denying to Stephen as are his own anti-Catholic lusts.

In other words, what has happened is that Stephen has come to perceive the seeds of death at the core of his whole present outlook upon life. In place of a synthesis of experience he has wavered between conflicting extremes, each of which has proved for him to be equally stultifying. It is significant that the name Zoe is from the Greek ζωή, meaning life. And it is still more significant that Zoe is identified with a rose, hitherto always symbolic of Stephen's misguided affirmations. The harlot, who epitomizes lust, sterility, and death, has at last ironically revealed the true nature of Stephen's way of life. And yet it must be allowed that even a cankered rose can become indirectly fertilizing. For it is Stephen's perception of horror beneath his guilt-created conflict that drives him to the smashing of the brothel's chandelier. Repudiating at once Catholic and anti-Catholic extremes, he echoes Blake in his decisive, symbolic act of self-deliverance: "Time's livid final flame leaps . . . ruin of all space, shattered glass and toppling masonry" (pp. 567–68). Stephen has at last abandoned the sick rose of an inner conflict and freed himself from the nightmare of his own and Catholic history. He is ready now to encounter a new feminine image whose rose will provide him with a healthy, harmonious synthesis of life.

Stephen, it is true, never directly encounters Molly and never directly expresses his comprehension of Leopold. But as Joyce's stand-in for himself, Stephen is the artist who wrote *Ulysses*, the very existence of which testifies to his breadth of understanding. Moreover, Stephen does encounter and accept Leopold Bloom, while Bloom in turn leads Stephen to his symbolic vision of the window of Molly's room. This culminating vision, prepared for by Leopold, itself culminates in a rose, prepared for by the book's earlier roses. For Bloom's path, no less than Stephen's, is bestrewn with cankered blossoms which lead him also by inversion to the same healthy, final rose. Since it is Stephen's comprehension of his affinity with Bloom and hence with ordinary man that will make possible his ultimate vision, a full understanding of that vision requires an understanding of the likeness between Bloom's quest and Stephen's. Much has been made of the fact that Stephen is seeking a father and Bloom is seeking a son. But it is equally important to realize that they can find the son-father kinship in each other because each alike also seeks a woman who will be at once wife, mother, mistress, and deity. Furthermore, in pursuing this feminine image they pursue analogous paths. Bloom resembles not only Everyman but also Stephen and his counterpart, Dante. For he too is at first attracted by false images of lust and so also has to suffer Bella Cohen's sterile inferno before being ready to guide Stephen to Molly's flowering paradise.

From the outset the fact that Bloom's quest for fertility will be of major importance to *Ulysses* is made clear in part through his constant alliance with flower symbolism. Most striking as well as most obvious are his various surnames. Just as the name Dedalus is significant for its mythological associations with invention and flight, so the name Bloom is significant for its association with flowering. This is the more evident in that Bloom has changed his name from Virag, which means flower in Hungarian, and has chosen the pseudonym,

Henry Flower, for his correspondence with Martha. Moreover, in the Penelope episode Molly confirms the importance of names. Remembering her youth when before meeting Bloom she had pretended to be engaged to Don Miguel de la Flora, she considers her present name and pronounces it adequate: [8] "M Bloom you're looking blooming. Josie used to say after I married him well its better than Breen or Briggs does brig or those awful names with bottom in them" (p. 748). Although Bloom, recollecting that his name was changed, concedes the truth of Juliet's "What's in a name?" (p. 607), it is clear that in *Ulysses* as in Shakespeare's play the names are of consequence.

Of course, not only the name but the flower itself is important. Roses are primary in *Ulysses* but receive continual reinforcement from the numerous undesignated flowers that blossom throughout the book. Less complex than the rose, these flowers nonetheless help to confirm the importance of the fertility theme and so of its rosy culmination. Stephen, for instance, perceives the ever-renewing tide as a "flower unfurling" (p. 50) at about the same time that Bloom sees his genitals as "a languid floating flower" (p. 85). Wasteland visions such as Bloom's in the Lotus Eaters episode ("A barren land, bare waste," p. 61), or that in the Oxen of the Sun ("The rosy buds all gone brown," p. 390), are characterized by the absence of flowers; and during Bloom's death in the Circe chapter, "they cast dead sea fruit upon him, no flowers" (p. 532). In contrast, Bloom's final Utopian daydream is set in "Flowerville" (p. 699), while earlier his fantasy of the East had been conceived of in terms of flowers: "the garden of the world, big lazy leaves to float about on, cactuses, flowery meads. . . . Flowers of idleness. . . . Walk on roseleaves" (pp. 70–71). And in the Circe episode, as Henry Flower wearing Christ's face, he sings, "There is a

[8] The significance of names has been pointed out by W. Y. Tindall, "Dante and Mrs. Bloom," *Accent*, XI (1951), 91.

flower that bloometh" (p. 506), a song that Molly later associates with her first love for him (p. 744).

Such generalized expressions of fertility through flowers emphasize the importance of roses. For the traditional queen of flowers is queen of the flowers in Joyce's work. It is both the recurrent symbol of women, who carry the real burden of the fertility theme, and the particular symbol of Molly, who culminates and concludes the book. In fact, the leading women of the novel, all in a sense surrogates for Molly, are all identified with roses that foreshadow Molly's rose. Martha Clifford at the outset has sent Bloom a yellow flower; it provokes in him a train of thoughts associating Martha with roses. Gerty MacDowell with her rosebud mouth, rosepink ribbon, rosebloom complexion, and whiterose scent is also unmistakably related to a rose. The rose worn by Miss Lydia Douce, one of the barmaids in the Ormond Hotel, expands beyond a flower to become a leading symbol in the Sirens episode. Mina Purefoy, the woman in labor in the Oxen of the Sun, is identified with a rose of creation and procreation. And in the brothel scene, at the center of Bloom's womancity, a fountain is found in the midst of mammoth damask roses.

All of these roses remind Bloom of Molly, in part by their likeness but more by their contrast. In fact the rose, more than any other single symbol in the book, carries the highly significant theme of sterile lust versus fertile love. Though its full import has not been recognized this is not a new theme in Joyce. "The Dead" had treated it directly by showing the contrast in feeling between the man who had loved Gretta Conroy and the man who had married her. And the *Portrait* had treated it indirectly by showing the sterile nature of Stephen's goals and desires as they developed within a person not yet capable of love. Now in *Ulysses*, concluding Stephen's quest through the medium of Bloom, Joyce treats the theme on a larger scale. Stephen remains the uncharitable person he

had been throughout the *Portrait* until his final communion
with Bloom, which implies an inevitable change. For Bloom,
although lacking in much, is not lacking in charity, nor could
Stephen find in him the lost father were Stephen himself not
being reborn. Love or charity in *Ulysses* is of course broader
than the man-woman relationship. But woman in narrow and
broad aspects is vital to the theme of love. Bloom is unfaithful
in thoughts to Molly, and Molly unfaithful in deeds to
Bloom. Yet deeper than sexual infidelities, which Joyce invariably shows to be sterile, are the bonds of fertile love that
give their lives and marriage substance and that indirectly give
Stephen the wholeness of vision he requires.

The rose is material to the expression of the complexities
of this theme. It will in the end be symbolic of Molly's love
for Bloom and is throughout the book symbolic of Bloom's
love for Molly. His love is at first expressed inversely through
contrast with its opponent, lust. For the flower shared in common by all Bloom's extramarital lures is invariably deficient in
comparison with Molly's. Martha, for example, fastened hers
to her letter by a pin. "No roses without thorns" (p. 77),
thinks Bloom. This further reminds him of a jingle he'd over-
heard two prostitutes singing: "O, Mairy lost the pin of her
drawers" (p. 77). And the jingle in turn leads directly to the
Biblical Mary-Martha theme, whereby Marion Bloom through
likeness of names is contrasted favorably with Martha Clifford,
as Christ had favored Mary's choice.[9] Pin, jingle, and Mary-
Martha comparison recur in the Nausicaa episode (p. 362),
this time to the detriment of Gerty MacDowell, who is closely
linked in Bloom's mind with Martha. Moreover, Martha's
question, "Do tell me what kind of perfume does your wife
use" (p. 77), is here at last answered by Bloom's contrast between the cheap rose perfume Gerty wears and Molly's better

[9] Gospel of Luke 10:38–42. I am indebted for this observation to a discussion with Virginia Mosely.

choice: "That's her perfume. . . . Roses, I think. She'd like scent of that kind. Sweet and cheap: soon sour. Why Molly likes opoponax" (p. 368).[10] Nostalgia for Molly, everywhere present, is dominant in the Sirens chapter. Here the rose worn by Lydia Douce, barmaid in the Ormond bar, contributes much to the lonely reminiscence the music arouses in Bloom who has been estranged from his wife for ten years. The very first mention of Miss Douce's rose in the opening lines of the episode relates her flower directly to Molly: "A jumping rose on satiny breasts of satin, rose of Castille" (p. 252). The allusion here is to *Rose of Castille*, the opera written by an Irishman about a Spanish queen, an opera associated by Bloom with his own Spanish-Irish rose.[11] But the thought of Molly saddens Bloom, who because of his estrangement from her identifies himself with Ben Dollard's rendition of *The Last Rose of Summer*: "Last rose Castille of summer left bloom I feel so sad alone" (p. 253). And his sense of loss is deepened by the arrival of Blazes Boylan, Molly's current paramour. Boylan, who had earlier appeared on the scene to the tune of the Yorkshire Rose (p. 250), now receives tribute from Miss Douce, "preening for him her richer hair, a bosom and a rose" (p. 260). Depressed by these reminders of Molly's infidelity, Bloom has nonetheless been protected from the charms of Miss Douce, the rosy siren, by his nostalgic recollections of the rose he values most.

His haunting nostalgia for Molly and consequent dissatisfaction elsewhere is to be deepened by horror in Bella Cohen's brothel. Here where Bloom's guilt and anxiety come simultaneously to a head, the deficiency of other roses is also finally culminated. The Yorkshire prostitute, Zoe, instrumental in

---

[10] Flower scents throughout *Ulysses* are associated with women, a further indication of the woman-flower analogy. It is notable that while Bloom likes perfumes Molly wears for him, he calls that worn in infidelity "foul flowerwater" (p. 63).

[11] The opera title is the answer to Lenehan's riddle: "What opera is like a railway line" (p. 130). Its association with Molly is pointed out by Tindall, "Dante and Mrs. Bloom," pp. 90–91.

revealing to Stephen the blight at the heart of his roses, plays the same vital role for Bloom. The episode in question is brief but significant. Zoe evokes in Bloom his fantasy of the woman-city, at the center of which "mammoth roses murmur of scarlet winegrapes." But the roses here are tinged with night-mare: "A wine of shame, lust, blood exudes." And when Zoe bites his ear, her gold-stopped teeth and garlic breath reveal to Bloom the real sterility underlying his fantasy: "The roses draw apart, disclose a sepulchre of the gold of kings and their mouldering bones" (p. 468). In other words, for Bloom as for Stephen, the whore as a symbol of sterility is a symbol of death and serves to bring home the bleak reality at the root of all roses unwatered by love.

Bloom and Stephen, in the same place and during the same hour, have reached a similar understanding. Moreover, they have followed what are in some ways analogous paths. Because Bloom's love has been frustrated and Stephen's has been blocked up at the source, each has become an unsatisfied wanderer drifting down sterile paths beguiled by the cankered blossoms of deceptive lusts. The analogy of wanderers seek-ing in error a healthy rose is suggested again in the Ithaca chapter when Bloom is perceived by Stephen in the very same roles in which Stephen has long perceived himself: "Ever he would wander, selfcompelled, to the extreme limit of his cometary orbit, beyond the fixed stars and variable suns . . . and after incalculable eons of peregrination return an es-tranged avenger, a wreaker of justice on malefactors, a dark crusader . . . with financial resources (by supposition) sur-passing those of Rothschild or of the silver king" (p. 712). Bloom roaming "beyond the fixed stars" inevitably recalls Dante, while the wealthy "estranged avenger" is none other than the Count of Monte Cristo. Both Dante and Monte Cristo have been associated for Stephen at once with each other, with himself, and with his quest for an ideal rose. Their identification here with Bloom is surely made in part to confirm the continuous parallel between Stephen's flowery travels and Bloom's.

The parallel itself is of course important because in it are involved some of the principal themes of both the *Portrait* and *Ulysses*. The search for love as opposed to lust, or fertility as opposed to sterility, unites Stephen's quest with Bloom's; and the likeness of quests in turn makes possible Stephen's recognition of kinship with Bloom, a recognition that enables him to follow Bloom to an ultimate fulfillment. There are luckily also certain differences, also confirmed by the roses. Bloom, who must act as father and guide to Stephen, must be wiser and morally superior. And throughout both novels it is certainly clear that self-centered Stephen is deceived into seizing each loveless rose as truth, whereas Bloom is invariably aware that all other roses fall short of the one he has left at home. In sum, the situation clarified by the roses is twofold. It is because Bloom's quest is so much like Stephen's that Stephen can recognize in Bloom a redeeming affinity. But it is at the same time because Bloom is faithful to Molly after his fashion, because he possesses the ordinary human charity Stephen lacks, that he is able to guide Stephen to the rose of harmony Stephen seeks.

That Stephen's final vision should again be associated with a rose is not only appropriate but inevitable; for Molly Bloom, the flower in question, comprises within herself characteristics sought but imperfectly realized in Bloom's and Stephen's earlier blossoms. That her rose should suggest on the natural level the significance of Dante's rose of God is equally essential; for Molly embodies at once the goal of Stephen's complex quest and the ultimate resolution of the perplexities of life. Just as the vision that had formed the climax of the *Portrait* had evoked Dante's rose to affirm Stephen's limited faith in mortal beauty, so now the vision that forms the climax of his entire journey evokes Dante to affirm his larger faith in mortal love. Moreover, the Dantesque analogy suggested by Molly's rose has been prepared for not only by that in the *Portrait* but also by lesser Dantesque analogies throughout *Ulysses* itself. For example, in the Aeolus episode Stephen had quoted from the *Inferno* lines on the lust of Paolo and Francesca, and then from the *Paradiso* lines describing the rose of love (p. 137). In the Ithaca episode he had quoted from Psalm 113 the very passage that Dante had quoted when describing his fourfold technic in the *Epistle to Can Grande*: "*In exitu Israêl de Egypto* . . ." (p. 682). And Stephen's quotation from the psalm is significantly followed first by a contemplation of the heavenly bodies and next by his pseudo-mystical, pseudo-ineffable vision of Molly as pointed out to him by Bloom: [12]

How did he elucidate the mystery of an invisible person, his wife Marion (Molly) Bloom, denoted by a visible splendid sign, a lamp?
With indirect and direct verbal allusions or affirmations: with description: with impediment: with suggestion.   (p. 687)

In addition, Dante's rose had been the flower of the Virgin, and Marion Bloom is on one level identified with Mary. This analogy, suggested directly by the correspondence of names, is reinforced indirectly by associations between Molly and her surrogates. To begin with, both Martha and Gerty are related to Mary. Bloom fancies a meeting with Martha "one Sunday after the rosary," a devotion to the Virgin: "Then out she comes. Repentance skindeep . . . Hail Mary and Holy Mary. Flowers . . ." (p. 81). And Gerty MacDowell, the lustful rose who wears a "child of Mary badge," is compared throughout her chapter to the "mystical rose" of the evening service in a nearby church. Further, Miss Douce in the Sirens chapter, singing "Idolores" to the accompaniment of her "jumping rose," provokes associations with the Mater Dolorosa: "The voice of the mournful chanter called to dolorous prayer" (p. 282). At the same time she suggests Swinburne's "mystical

[12] *Ibid.*, pp. 87–89.

rose of the mire" and Marion Bloom herself: "Fate. Spanishy eyes. . . . Dolores shedolores. At me. Luring. Ah, alluring" (p. 271).[13] Finally, Mina Purefoy, the mother in the Oxen of the Sun, is related in Bloom's mind to Molly and in Stephen's to the rose and the Virgin. Identifying birth with divine as well as artistic creation, Stephen describes Mina as "a rose upon the rood of time," and again in Dante's words as *"vergine madre, figlia del tuo figlio"* (p. 385: "virgin mother, daughter of your son"—J. P. S.).

These continual analogies with Dante, Mary, and roses all reach their culmination in the final episode of *Ulysses*. For although Stephen does not ever literally see Molly, his indirect vision in Bloom's back yard presumably leads to an intuitive grasp of her all-embracing mystery. The very existence of the Penelope chapter in which Molly is directly presented testifies to the scope of Stephen's vision as it becomes apparent that Molly is the ultimate rose. Roses are frequently in her mind from her early recollection, "I had a splendid skin from the sun and the excitement like a rose" (p. 741), to her final reminiscence in relation to Bloom's proposal, "when I put the rose in my hair like the Andalusian girls used or shall I wear a red yes" (p. 768). Associated in her thoughts with love, sex, nature, and womanhood, roses come to signify to Molly the beauty and joy in created life. As she considers whether or not to wear a white rose for Stephen, she is led to a general affirmation: "I love flowers Id love to have the whole place swimming in roses God of heaven theres nothing like nature" (pp. 766–67). Beyond this, the roses, by recalling her thoughts to Bloom, reveal that despite her multiple suitors she too has been faithful at heart to the one suitor she truly loves. In fact, her monologue builds to a climax in a veritable deluge of blossoms as she recollects the day on which she first said yes

[13] In the Sirens chapter another hint of Molly as Dante's ultimate rose is found in the line, "The bright stars fade. O rose! . . . Castille. The morn is breaking" (p. 252). On the Homeric level there is possibly an analogy with Homer's rosy-fingered dawn.

to Bloom: "yes he said I was a flower of the mountain yes so we are flowers all a womans body yes that was one true thing he said in his life and the sun shines for you today yes" (p. 767).

Molly's rose does for the secular outlook what Dante's does for the religious. It expresses Joyce's ultimate affirmation of human life and its prime mover, human love. In doing so it embraces and harmonizes the seeming discords in human experience, as Dante's rose embraces and harmonizes the seeming discords in God's plan. For Molly Bloom, the eternal feminine principle in the human world, has been related by symbolic association to the various aspects of woman from Virgin to prostitute represented in the *Portrait* and *Ulysses*. She is simultaneously a mother, an object of desire and also of devotion, a creature of the flesh, a wife, an adulteress, and an embodiment of nature's eternal fruition. She is also a rose, traditional flower of birth, love, womanhood, sex, creativity, and female divinity, as well as particular flower of Bloom and Stephen's quests for these values. In her fundamental fidelity she remains for Bloom his one fertile rose, neutralizing all surface infidelities by her sublime transcendence of the moral and intellectual complexities of civilization. In her embodiment of qualities presumably the most basic in woman and humankind, she resolves for Stephen the conflict between white roses of religious asceticism and red roses of carnal lust.

But to Stephen, who is a more complicated character than Bloom, Molly's significance is more complex. The union of the white and red roses, to which her monologue shows her impartial, is certainly important. Representing nature and the natural in man, she transcends what had been for Stephen, as for his hero Blake, the antinatural moral dichotomies of the Church. But important as this is, it is not the whole of the story. For she is able to resolve Stephen's conflict between asceticism and lust, between Catholic and anti-Catholic extremes, between mother-love and resentment, by at last fulfilling the promise of the green rose of childhood. On one level that rose had been a symbol of Ireland—not the Ireland of the bigoted present but the ideal Ireland of international sympathies whose "uncreated conscience" it was Stephen's goal to forge in art. And surely in Molly Bloom, who is at once Irish, Spanish, Jewish, and universal, he has found a rose that can unite a nation with a world and resolve his conflict between love of his country and dislike of its narrow bonds.

On a more fundamental level, the green rose in the *Portrait* had been related to Stephen's quest for an "unsubstantial image" that would fill his emotional needs and so free him from "weakness and timidity and inexperience" (p. 71). In *Ulysses* this quest had been reexpressed in Aristotle's phrase, "an actuality of the possible as possible" (p. 26). But however expressed, it is clear that Stephen has long been seeking to realize an ideal once symbolized by a green rose and now brought to maturity in Molly. For Molly's rose turns out to be what all preceding roses were not: the wholly satisfactory embodiment in the external world of the fantasy image now substantial, the possible actual. His climactic vision of Molly thus gives Stephen a fertile subject for art in place of the watered-down, immature content of esthetic decadence.[14] And more important, it gives his art body because it gives him adult compassion essential not only to his writing but to his humanity. Stephen has finally found in mankind a genuine substitute for God, and has finally used Dante's rose to express not childish defiance but rather mature affirmation of the glory of human life.

Stephen has been able to follow Bloom to this affirmative vision of Molly because, in discovering his kinship with Bloom,

---

[14] Specifically Molly's comment, "theres real beauty and poetry for you" (p. 761), recalls Cranly's comment in the *Portrait*, "There's real poetry for you. There's real love" (p. 289). Since Stephen's inability to understand Cranly's comment was bound up with his inability to create real poetry, Molly's echo of that comment in her thoughts of Stephen acts as confirmation of his having learned what poetry is.

he has discovered his kinship with all mankind. No longer an egotistical being disdainfully apart, he has perceived that what is basic in Bloom is basic in himself and others, and that the beginning and end of Bloom-Everyman's travels is his own beginning and end. In other words, he has found Molly, the all-embracing mother of natural life, because with the aid of Bloom he has been able to find himself. In the Circe chapter Stephen had declared: "What went forth to the ends of the world to traverse not itself. God, the sun, Shakespeare, a commercial traveller [Bloom], having itself traversed in reality itself, becomes that self" (p. 494). And this dawning realization, which was to be fully confirmed in Molly, echoed his earlier comments on Shakespeare: "He found in the world without as actual what was in his world within as possible. . . . We walk through ourselves, meeting robbers, ghosts, giants, old men, young men, wives, widows, brothers-in-love. But always meeting ourselves. The playwright who wrote the folio of this world . . . is doubtless all in all of us" (p. 210). It is perhaps significant that Shakespeare has appeared more than once in *Ulysses* walking "in a rosery of Fetter Lane of Gerard, herbalist" (pp. 199, 276). For Shakespeare above all men had attained the final rose that Stephen was about to attain in Molly—an "actuality of the possible," a green rose matured, a realistic view of himself and therefore of the whole human scene.

Indeed, in the last analysis Joyce's work, like Shakespeare's, transcends such categories as classic and romantic. This does not mean that it is not in many ways romantic. Certainly his work includes the categories it transcends. And as one of the leading literary expressions of our age it is bound to be one of the leading expressions of our outlook. Deriving the substance of his art from the materials of his life, Joyce displays the romantic reliance on personal experience for incident or theme, and the romantic quest for freedom from external authorities in the discovery and expression of his own nature.

In addition, he has created to some extent in Bloom but most notably in Molly a highly romantic image of the natural in man uncorrupted by the complexities of intellect, civilization, or conventional social mores. More fundamental still, he has given his very real and ordinary people an almost transcendental import by elevating their natures and values to the level of ideals. These several characteristics are in part conveyed through symbols, such symbols as the rose, which, echoing Dante's, suggests the magnitude of Stephen's vision. But Joyce's symbols themselves are inextricable from his content since he, like all genuine artists, employs the symbolic method not for its own ingenious sake but for the sake of expressing an outlook that in our time is inevitably suffused with romanticism.

To begin with, the exploration of man's conscious and unconscious mind, which Joyce has developed more thoroughly than have his contemporaries, is a result of the nineteenth-century exploration of private emotions and the twentieth-century exploration of the hidden roots of those emotions. This exploration blossoms in symbols and frequently in roses because of the rose's markedly ancient emotional history and because of its equally ancient associations with unconscious as well as with conscious desires. The rose is not always, though often, romantic; it was the flower of the classics and of the nonromantic Catholic vision of things. But Joyce has used it, as have most other modern writers, not for purposes of expressing an objective or authoritarian vision but for purposes of expressing a subjective synthesis of experience. Moreover, in the development of his symbolic method he has fused medieval methods of polysemous correspondence with Blakean complexity, French innuendo, and modern psychology. In doing so, he has represented at least as successfully as any our present attempt to achieve harmony between inner values and the outer world through the union of private with public levels of symbolic meaning. He has therefore represented our correlative attempt to bring order out of seeming chaos, clarity out of seeming confoundment, and beauty or truth out of seeming crassness in an over-commercial world.

Yet Joyce's scope was broader than the term romantic can cover. He has used romantic methods to express romantic ends in a romantic age. But his ideals, while certainly lofty, are not unattainable, nor is he rent by the desolation that too frequently assails the modern pursuer of ideals. On the contrary, he condemns our vain pursuit of the "in vain" and our wasteful regret for the loss of things that can never be found. Certainly in Stephen, the artist as a young man, he has exposed the kind of idealism that can be only self-consuming and has condemned the arrogant sense of separate, exalted destiny that holds Stephen back from involvement in the common human destiny. What Stephen later discovers through communion with Bloom and Molly is the thing that Joyce is trying to reveal to the modern world: the ideal exists and is all-important but is to be found in everyday life. In Joyce's work the divided heart of two centuries is then healed. He has at last been able to unite the ideal with the real and so to make a peace with the present, possible world uncommon among romantic forerunners or contemporaries. This healing has been achieved through his vision of goodness, beauty, and love as discerned in a thoroughly average man and his thoroughly natural wife. It has been expressed in part through his embracing rose.

For Joyce's rose does not draw on wholly romantic sources or even on earlier sources in a wholly romantic way. His rose is pagan, medieval, and Renaissance as well, and does not, like many roses that draw on past tradition, tend towards nostalgia in its quality or towards disparagement of the present in its motivation. Rather, Joyce's flower alludes to past traditions in order to fully embrace his vision of modern life in its relation to man's life in any century. His use of Dante is marked, and through Dante he relates his rose of human charity to the established Christian rose of heavenly charity. At the same time, through Molly Bloom he embodies in his rose the primitive rose of "Gea-Tellus," mother of all natural life, who preceded and survived throughout the classical period from which the Homeric parallel for *Ulysses* was also drawn. And Molly's frank delight in earthly, sensual life, as well as Joyce's Chaucerian-Shakespearean delight in her, is Renaissance in its feeling, while his inverted, intricate ardor for the divine in man echoes the mortal-immortal rose of William Blake. More modern still are the explicit reference to Yeats's "rose upon the rood of time," the implicit debt to the French in the use of suggestion and indirection, and the existence of Freudian levels of unconscious sexual meaning. Encompassing so much, Joyce's rose goes beyond any other in its wealth of allusion to history.

All of these influences and roses ultimately combine in Molly's one affirmative flower that expresses the union of our time with all time, of the individual with the world, and of the ideal with the actual. At once including and transcending the limits of his romantic age, Joyce has chosen the rose that transcends all limits to express universal vision. The vision is simple in essence. Joyce's rose, like the roses before him, embraces the positive values in life brought about by love. But in Joyce, as in human life, love is simple only in essence and not in manifestation, as the roses of love have often shown. For the nature of love and so of roses has varied throughout the ages in accord with variations in social or religious views. From the classical flower of sexual love, through the medieval flower of God or romance, to the nineteenth-century flower of personal, transcendental vision, the blossoms of affirmation have been many and disparate. Combining these disparate blossoms into one climactic rose, Joyce has given human love the force of a religion and the breadth of an outlook that blends the present and the past. With the rose of untold centuries underlying his present flower, he has formed an affirmative symbol to express an affirmative vision most urgently required in this late age of the rose's bloom.

There will surely be flowers after us as there have been before us. The forms that they will take are not predictable. Yet in the times to come, it can safely be assumed, their meanings will remain entangled with our many loves. For the roses that embrace all man can wish or fear to lose have embraced his heights of rapture and the depths of his despair. They had already embraced these meanings long before the Christian era, but not until the rose of Dante did a single flower run the gamut of the love that leads from man to God. And not until our present in the flower of James Joyce did it run the other gamut that leads from God to man. Joyce has done for things terrestrial in an age that stresses man's survival what Dante did for things supernal in an age that stressed man's soul. Together they have mounted the two peaks of man's desire, while all between their summits lie lesser peaks and valleys in which the rose has blossomed for man's multitudinous wants. There will be no more roses only when there is no future, for out of our emotions, hope, like fear, is bottommost. But though the unknown future may hold countless unknown roses, those of the past and present enclose the span of all our love.

ACKNOWLEDGMENTS

For permission to quote from the works of authors discussed in this study, grateful acknowledgment is made to the following:

Basil Blackwell, for lines from *Italian Poets Chiefly Before Dante,* edited and translated by Dante Gabriel Rossetti (The Shakespeare Head Press, 1908)

Chatto & Windus Ltd., for lines from *The Motionless Dancer,* by Peter Yates (1943)

Constable and Company Limited, for lines from *Medieval Latin Lyrics,* translated by Helen Waddell (5th ed., 1951)

Criterion Books, Inc., for lines from *Collected Poems 1930–1955,* by George Barker (copyright 1957 by George Granville Barker)

Crown Publishers, Inc., for lines from *Remy de Gourmont: Selections from All His Works,* chosen and translated by Richard Aldington (copyright 1928 by Pascal Covici, Inc.)

J. M. Dent & Sons Ltd., for lines from *The Romance of the Rose,* translated by H. F. Ellis (1900)

E. P. Dutton & Co. Inc., for passages from *The History of Magic,* by Eliphas Lévi (Alphonse Louis Constant), translated by A. E. Waite (1930)

T. S. Eliot, for lines from *Complete Poems and Plays,* by T. S. Eliot (1952)

Faber and Faber Ltd., for lines from *Calamiterror,* by George Barker (1937); *Lament and Triumph,* by George Barker (1940); *A Private Country,* by Lawrence Durrell (1943); and *Complete Poems and Plays,* by T. S. Eliot (1952)

Farrar, Straus and Cudahy, Inc., for passages from *All Hallows' Eve,* by Charles Williams (copyright 1948 by Pellegrini and Cudahy)

Robert Graves, for "The Florist Rose," from *Collected Poems,* by Robert Graves (Doubleday & Co., Inc. and Cassell & Co., Ltd., 1948)

Grove Press, Inc., for lines from *Illuminations,* by Arthur Rimbaud, translated by Wallace Fowlie (1953)

Harcourt, Brace and Company, Inc., for lines from *Complete Poems and Plays,* by T. S. Eliot (*Collected Poems, 1909–1935,* copyright 1936 by Harcourt, Brace and Company, Inc.; *The Family Reunion,* copyright 1939 by T. S. Eliot; *Four Quartets,* copyright 1943 by T. S. Eliot); and for passages from *Mrs. Dalloway,* by Virginia Woolf (copyright 1925 by Harcourt, Brace and Company, Inc., renewed 1953 by Leonard Woolf)

Harvill Press Ltd., for lines from *Illuminations,* by Arthur Rimbaud, translated by Wallace Fowlie (1953)

David Higham Associates, Ltd., for passages from *All Hallows' Eve,* by Charles Williams (copyright 1948 by Pellegrini and Cudahy); and *The Figure of Beatrice,* by Charles Williams (1943)

The Hutchinson Group, for passages from *The History of Magic,* by Eliphas Lévi (Alphonse Louis Constant), translated by A. E. Waite (1930)

Alfred A. Knopf, Inc., for lines from *Collected Poems,* by Henry Treece (1946); and passages from *The Man Who Died,* by D. H. Lawrence (1928)

The Macmillan Company, for passages from *Essays,* by W. B. Yeats (1924); *The Collected Poems,* by W. B. Yeats (2nd ed., 1951); *Early Poems and Stories,* by W. B. Yeats (1925); and *The Collected Plays,* by W. B. Yeats (2nd ed., 1952)

New Directions, for lines from *Poems,* by Stéphane Mallarmé, translated by Roger Fry (copyright 1951); and *Collected Poems,* by Dylan Thomas (copyright 1939, 1942, 1946 by New Directions; copyright 1952, 1953 by Dylan Thomas)

Random House, Inc., for passages from *Ulysses,* by James Joyce (1934; Modern Library ed., 1940)

Rinehart & Company, Inc., for lines from *The Divine Comedy,* by Dante, translated by H. R. Huse (copyright 1954 by H. R. Huse)

University of California Press, for lines from *Poems,* by Jules Laforgue, translated by Patricia Terry (1958); *Selected Poems,* by Stéphane Mallarmé, translated by C. F. MacIntyre (1957); and *Selected Poems,* by Paul Verlaine, translated by C. F. MacIntyre (1948)

Vanguard Press, Inc., for lines from "Romance," "Poor Young

Simpleton," "Harvest," "The Two Loves," "The Canticle of the Rose," "A Hymn to Venus," and "The Shadow of Cain," from *The Collected Poems of Edith Sitwell* (copyright 1949, 1954 by Edith Sitwell)

The Viking Press Inc., for passages from *Back*, by Henry Green (1950); and *A Portrait of the Artist as a Young Man*, by James Joyce (1928); and for lines from *Collected Poems*, by D. H. Lawrence (1932)

Yale University Press, for lines from *Odes of Anacreon*, translated by E. Richardson (1928)

Mrs. W. B. Yeats, for passages from "The Crucifixion of the Outcast," "Out of the Rose," "The Tables of the Law," "Adoration of the Magi," and "Rosa Alchemica," from *Early Poems and Stories*, by W. B. Yeats (1948); and "The Shadowy Waters," from *Collected Plays*, by W. B. Yeats (2nd ed., 1952)

A portion of Chapter 2 first appeared under the title of "Dante's Mystic Rose" in *Studies in Philology*, October, 1955, and a portion of Chapter 7 first appeared under the title of "The Artist and the Rose" in *University of Toronto Quarterly*, January, 1957.

The author's parents acknowledge the aid of Nora Magid, whose offer to read the galley proofs was gratefully accepted.

INDEX

with the Elemental Powers," 109, quoted, 109; "Meditations in Time of Civil War," 115; "The Mountain Tomb," 115, quoted, 115; "Out of the Rose," 102, quoted, 102; "Rosa Alchemica," 104–6, quoted, 105–6; *The Rose,* 94, (note), quoted, 116; "The Rose of Battle," 97–98, quoted, 97–98; "The Rose of Peace," 96–97, quoted, 97; "The Rose of the World," 95–96, 200, quoted, 96; "The Rose Tree," 115; *The Secret Rose,* 101–7, cover design, 101, quoted, 93n; "The Secret

Rose," 110–12, quoted, 110, 111; *The Shadowy Waters,* 112–14, quoted, 112, 113; "The Symbolism of Poetry" (*Essays*), quoted, 107; "The Tables of the Law," 104, quoted, 104; "Three Bushes," 115; "To Ireland in the Coming Times," 98, 99, quoted, 99; "To the Rose upon the Rood of Time," 94–95, quoted, 95; *A Vision,* 115 and n; "The White Birds," quoted, 96; *The Wind Among the Reeds,* 106–11, quoted, 92, 98n

York, white rose of, 56 and n